Justice and
the Critique of
Pure Psychology

CRITICAL ISSUES IN SOCIAL JUSTICE

Series Editor: **MELVIN J. LERNER**
University of Waterloo
Waterloo, Ontario, Canada

THE JUSTICE MOTIVE IN SOCIAL BEHAVIOR
Adapting to Times of Scarcity and Change
Edited by Melvin J. Lerner and Sally C. Lerner

CHILDREN'S COMPETENCE TO CONSENT
Edited by Gary B. Melton, Gerald P. Koocher,
and Michael J. Saks

JUSTICE AND THE CRITIQUE OF PURE PSYCHOLOGY
Edward E. Sampson

In preparation

DEVELOPMENT AND MAINTENANCE OF PROSOCIAL BEHAVIOR
International Perspectives on Positive Morality
Edited by Ervin Staub, Daniel Bar-Tal, Jerzy Karylowski,
and Janus Reykowski

A Continuation Order Plan is available for this series. A continuation order will bring delivery of each new volume immediately upon publication. Volumes are billed only upon actual shipment. For further information please contact the publisher.

Justice and the Critique of Pure Psychology

Edward E. Sampson

Wright Institute
Berkeley, California

Plenum Press • New York and London

Library of Congress Cataloging in Publication Data

Sampson, Edward E.
    Justice and the critique of pure psychology.

    (Critical issues in social justice)
    Bibliography: p.
    Includes index.
    1. Social psychology. 2. Justice. 3. Psychology. I. Title. II. Series.
HM251.S2616 1983   302   83-9453
ISBN 0-306-41226-8

© 1983 Plenum Press, New York
A Division of Plenum Publishing Corporation
233 Spring Street, New York, N.Y. 10013

Printed in the United States of America

Foreword

Empiricist philosophy of science of the kind that promised truth through method and a unification of science now lies in disarray. Arguments over the indeterminancy of theoretical language, the inadequacy of induction, the empirical incommensurability of competing theories, the possibility or impossibility of scientific progress, and the applicability of natural science metatheory and methods to problems of human action have all led to a loss in confidence. As it is commonly said, the philosophy of science is now in a "postempiricist" phase. It is a phase marked by heated disagreement over the possibility of empirically grounded scientific knowledge. Because the orienting assumptions of traditional psychology had been largely derived from the early logical empiricist program for science, the general deterioration in confidence at the philosophic level was inevitably to have repercussions within psychology. The extensive ferment that has occurred within social psychology over the past decade, often termed "the crisis in social psychology," must properly be viewed within this context. And, in cases where criticisms of the traditional craft have been initiated on other than philosophical grounds, traditional logical empiricist answers have no longer been found sustaining. In effect, the science of psychology no longer rests on a firm metatheoretical base, and the future remains very much in the balance.

Within this critical period of search and reappraisal, there are few voices that equal in significance that of Edward Sampson. In particular, his assessments of the valuational bases for much social psychological theory will surely be considered pivotal by future chroniclers of the age. Not only have his writings stirred heated controversy within the establishment of social psychology, but Sampson's writings have served as a beacon of hope for many of those in the early stages of the professional development. As is clear, the present volume will demand keen interest. It essentially represents the first extended attempt by Sampson to elaborate the grounds for his critique of traditional psychology and to negotiate more fully the horizon of competing alternatives.

v

The selection of justice as a topical vehicle for his more extended exploration is auspicious. Nowhere else is there a better exemplification of the social psychologist's traditional attempt to disembed a critical topic from its social and historical context, naively to treat research as if it were a neutral reading of nature, and to assume that the results would offer a route to social betterment. As Sampson effectively argues, even the traditional research approach itself ensures that, at least from certain points of view, justice will be obfuscated. And too, this journey through the annals of justice research reveals the contours of Sampson's own intellectual trajectory. One gains an acute sense of a scholar finding that an otherwise "normal and sensible" institution of science, one in which he has long labored, is ultimately inimical in its consequences. Sampson's reaction constitutes "transformative psychology" at its best.

However, the topic of justice is, after all, a vehicle and not the culminating interest of the volume. Sampson's chief concern, and that which most of his audience will eagerly anticipate, is his move toward a positive solution to contemporary dilemmas. As with most of the "crisis" writers, Sampson has been far more agile in underscoring the problematics of traditional social psychology than in furnishing clear alternatives. It is this struggle toward new scientific forms that will, if satisfactorily achieved, be considered one of the major intellectual accomplishments of the century. It is toward this end that the present volume valiantly struggles. With appreciative sensitivity, Sampson considers seminal writings in the realist, critical, Marxist, hermeneutic-constructivist, wholistic, and poststructuralist schools—all significant enterprises for anyone seriously concerned with the future of psychology. Prospects and pitfalls are examined in each case, and the reader begins to grasp what must be entailed as the "new science" gradually emerges.

Sampson does not furnish the final blueprint in this volume. He is well aware that to do so at this point would be egregiously premature and that new scholarly institutions do not spring from the writings of a single individual. Further negotiation, adjustment, assessment, and reassessment are required both within and without social psychology. With his concept of transformative psychology, reference frame, and societal reproduction, however, Sampson makes a vital contribution to future colloquy. With his equilibristic attempt to synthesize new voices, while avoiding myriad pitfalls, Sampson begins to open the door to an exciting future.

KENNETH J. GERGEN

Preface

Contributing to the series Critical Issues in Social Justice provides me with both an opportunity and a challenge. The opportunity is clear: to gather into a single work, with the wisdom of hindsight, my previous contributions to the justice literature in social psychology. It is not my intention in doing this to provide an in-depth summary of my own or others' contributions. The material is all available in the original publications, where its vivid details can be studied. My intent, rather, is to reflect back on this material in order to reveal a development in my own work toward my concern with the ideological implications of psychology's understanding of justice.

The challenge is something I realized only as I appreciated the task of writing this book. I am aware of two key directions in my writings to date. The one involves my work in the social psychology of justice; the other, my several contributions to the analysis and critique of the discipline of psychology. For some, these might appear to be substantially distinct directions with little or no overlap. I do not believe that these are parallel pathways; they are amply crisscrossed routes that blend together to mutually develop and reinforce each other.

The challenge, then, is to demonstrate the enrichment that the critical stance provides for the study and understanding of justice, even as that critical stance itself emerged from and built upon this study. Whether or not I have been successful in meeting this challenge is something about which others will surely have much to say.

Another challenge emerged only after the work was completed in draft form and submitted for preliminary review. This represents, for me, a far more difficult, even troublesome matter. There have been many debates about where we are going or should be going and a sense of anguish, even despair, that many in the business of psychology experience. Some are searching for that certain someone or idea that will magically capture their imaginations and lead them from despair back into the sun. My own fantasies at times even see myself as that one with the light who can lead the way out.

I suspect that the reality, however, is somewhat different. Sadly, I must report that it is a long journey out, as we have collectively settled somewhere very deep within the dark tunnel. And the way out is not only up a steep grade but carries us very near to some politically dangerous turf. This particular guide also tends to use a very broad sword to sweep away the dangers that lurk along the path: I sometimes strike out at friends, thinking of them as dangers to be overcome.

This second challenge, therefore, involves somehow managing to communicate in a convincing manner to those who want a change and hope that this work will be useful to them, but who remain properly cautious about my guidance in this endeavor. I would like to thank those who, on reading the preliminary draft, urged more moderation and some sheathing of that sword. I know that I have valiantly tried to whisper rather than to shout that the emperor has no clothes. Yet, however I say it, he still stands before us stark naked, undoubtedly turning away those who recoil at such displays. While I may not be equipped by temperament or passion to meet this second challenge, at least I have tried hard to manage.

Contents

PART ONE

Introduction

I have organized this work into six parts reflecting different aspects of the overall project. In this opening part, my intention is to provide an introduction to the project itself, to outline in advance where the search has taken me, and to suggest some of the conclusions that will be developed more fully in the other sections and chapters.

Much of this first section is autobiographical, at least in a professional sense. I am concerned with detailing the unfolding nature of my own understanding, where I began and where I am; my present thoughts and understandings about the issues of justice; and my evaluation of psychology's contribution to its study and its attainment.

CHAPTER ONE

The Task

A peculiar feature of introductory chapters is that they tend to be written at the conclusion of a project. Thus, they contain insights in their beginning that could not have been present at the actual beginning. Such is the case with this opening chapter. I am now able to write an account that would not have been possible some 15 or so years earlier, when my own program of research and thinking on justice-related topics began. I see more clearly now than I did at that time the central thematic concerns that have guided my efforts.

I have spent the better part of my professional life examining the underlying framework that governs most psychological investigations of justice and other topics. I find that I have moved from merely puzzling about the ways that social psychologists have understood justice to a disquieting conclusion about the relation between psychology's analyses and society's existing social practices and institutions. To borrow from linguistic analysis, I am persuaded that the deep structures of the society inhabit the deep structures of the discipline. With a few notable exceptions, therefore, it is difficult to disentangle a genuine understanding of human behavior from accounts that are essentially ideological in their functions. In no area of inquiry is this difficulty more significant than in the study of justice: an area said to be at the root of the legitimacy of society (e.g., McCarthy, 1978) and of fundamental concern to all human endeavors (e.g., Lerner, 1975, 1981). My concern is that what passes for psychology's understanding of justice may primarily reflect ongoing social arrangements that in themselves are best described by its absence.

This has been neither an easy position in which to find myself nor one that has been without difficulty to communicate persuasively to others who share with me an interest in seeing their profession used to benefit humanity. And yet, it is a conclusion that I find inescapable. My task, therefore, is to share the route that I have taken to reach that conclusion and the several bases for my position. To this end, it will be helpful at the outset to outline some of the key perspectives that ground social psychology's concern with

3

the topic of justice. As my intent here is simply to highlight social psychology's contribution, those who are generally unfamiliar with the details of each approach will find it helpful to review the original work.

SOCIAL PSYCHOLOGY AND JUSTICE: BRIEFLY NOTED

Contributions to an area of study within a discipline do not develop in a social or historical vacuum. The importance of a given area of inquiry, the questions asked about it, the approaches employed in its investigation and, indeed, even the acceptability of the answers uncovered all reflect something more extensive than purely scientific curiosity and disinterested neutrality. This is not to say that investigators are invariably aware of the contexts within which their works emerge and to which they refer; it is simply to note that extrascientific contexts for the work we do always exist.

Relative Deprivation

Concern with questions of justice and fairness has existed throughout much of recorded human history. Aristotle takes credit for an early discussion about the fairness of exchanges among people; this marks the beginnings of the concern with distributive justice. Psychology's focus on justice, however, has been relatively more recent. The pioneering investigations of Stouffer, (Stouffer, Suchman, De Vinney, Star, & Williams, 1949; Stouffer, Lumsdaine, Williams, Smith, Janis, Star, & Cottrell, 1949) and his numerous associates, reported in two volumes at the conclusion of World War II, introduced one aspect of this concern with justice through the concept of *relative deprivation*. The empirical findings revealed differences in the perceived fairness of one's circumstances as a function of comparisons made between self and others in an apparently comparable situation. A member of the Air Corps, for example, felt himself to be relatively poorly off when not promoted, while Military Police who were similarly not promoted did not feel themselves to have been treated unfairly. In probing the bases for this difference in the evaluation of fairness, Stouffer and his colleagues observed that there were higher promotional opportunities in the Air Corps than in the Military Police; thus not being promoted in a high-opportunity situation was relatively more dissatisfying than not being promoted in a relatively low-opportunity situation. Justice appeared to be a matter of evaluations made on a socially comparative basis rather than existing in terms of some absolute scale.

Homans and Adams

A second and related aspect of psychology's concern with justice appeared in the 1961 publication by Homans in which the concept of distributive justice played a central role in his analysis of social behavior. The socially comparative quality of justice was retained; people were said to experience their situation as fair or as unfair as a result of comparing themselves with others in similar circumstances. However, Homans added a somewhat different slant by focusing more directly on the manner by which resources were distributed within a direct exchange relationship between people.

Homans had adopted an exchange model derived from the economic market place and applied it to what he viewed as the interpersonal exchanges taking place between individuals. A person would experience her or his exchange relationship with another as fair if their profits were distributed proportionally to their investments. A disproportionality was unjust and produced dissatisfaction.

It was up to J. Stacy Adams in 1965 to formalize this analysis and develop the distinct theory of "inequity in social exchange." Adams defined inequity in a social exchange as existing when the proportionality between one person's outcomes and investments relative to a comparison other's was not equal: that is, if person A received less (the outcome) than person B for doing comparable work (the investment), then inequity and hence injustice were said to be present. Adams developed the implications of this felt inequity, arguing that such a situation was both dissatisfying and motivated change toward equity.

Equity

Although my intent is not to develop the full history of the psychological treatment of justice, a crucial next step appeared in the 1973 publication by Walster, Berscheid, and Walster that expanded the scope and sophistication of the equity formulation of justice. The Walster group developed a series of propositions concerning the nature of humanity and the essential nature of the social order required to contain this human nature. Humanity was understood in a Hobbesian sense: it meant being out to maximize self-interest. Equity was posited as a basic principle designed to ensure that the potential war of all against all would be tempered by rules that allocated outcomes according to "investments."

Exploitation—that is, behaving in accordance with untempered self-interest—was controlled either by a kind of conditioned distress reaction (e.g., guilt or fear of retaliation) or a dissonance reaction over having behaved in a manner inconsistent with a socialized self-image. In updated versions (e.g., Walster & Walster, 1975; Walster, Walster, & Berscheid, 1978), this never-ending war for self-interest appears in the form of power moves designed to control the social definition of what are considered valuable investments that warrant highly deserved outcomes.

What I find especially intriguing about the equity work, in addition to its Hobbesian framework, is its view that justice as equity is applicable to almost all human activity ranging from the workplace, where the theories first gained their prominence, into the bedroom—to situations involving friendships, altruism, and so forth. In other words, an idea about justice in the workplace has been generalized to become a fundamental principle of human psychological functioning in nearly all facets of social life.

The Just World

Approaching the study of justice with the intention of uncovering a fundamental principle of psychological functioning, Lerner provided a series of experiments and theoretical treatises on what he termed the just-world hypothesis (see Lerner & Miller, 1978, for a good summary). It was Lerner's contention that people developed a fundamental belief that there was a rough correspondence between giving and getting: people generally got what they deserved. Rather than focusing on the distribution of resources in an exchange relationship or on the generalization of an equity principle to all human activity, Lerner's primary concern was with exploring the consequences that followed as people functioned in terms of this belief in a just world: for example, the tendency to blame or derogate the victim—"they got what they deserved"—in order to sustain the belief that the world is just and fair.

Lerner's work differs from most of the preceding in that it does not build upon an economic-exchange principle. Lerner does not define justice in a relationship in terms of the comparative proportionality of investments and outcomes; rather he sees justice as the fulfillment of a learned *personal contract*. The growing child learns that immediate gratification is not possible, that delay is necessary, and that the returns for waiting will generally be proportional to the frustrations experienced. The world is a just place, in this view, if it proves sufficiently trustworthy to provide the satisfactions later for pleasures withheld now.

The economic-exchange perspective on justice can be said to build upon a selfish motivation. People behave in just ways as an instrument or vehicle to accomplish their own ends. By contrast, Lerner differentiates justice from pure self-interest. He argues that "for the most part people *do not act* in obviously self-serving ways" (Lerner & Meindl, 1981, p. 220); that the motive for justice is founded on the notion of a personal contract, not on more instrumental and self-interested grounds; and that his view fits both the phenomenological experience of people in their everyday lives and has substantial empirical support.

Parallel to the position that I am developing, Lerner also observed that one reason why self-interest and economic-exchange principles have been so dominant in social psychology's inquiries is simply that most of the work has developed within employment contexts: "And, of course, it is in those contexts that we have institutionalized *the norms which dictate that we can and should do whatever is legitimate to serve our own ends*" (Lerner & Meindl, 1981, p. 230).

The Commons

A somewhat different emphasis has more recently appeared in the mainstream of psychological literature; it is represented by Hardin's (1968) discussion of the tragedy of the commons, Platt's (1973) notion of social traps, and Edney's (1980, 1981) recent attempt to examine several alternative psychological approaches to the problem of justice in a resource-scarce world. Fundamental political and social questions have emerged within this approach to the study of justice. The questions have been significantly extended from the microfocus of Homans and Adams to macrolevel issues of allocation when there is little to be allocated (also see Lerner & Lerner, 1981, on the same theme of justice and scarcity).

Who gets *what* when that *what* is a scarce resource takes the questions of fairness from the workplace to the arena of international politics and conflict. Which psychological concepts are applicable at this international level and what lessons psychology can teach us about fairness in the era ahead appear to the uncritical observer to be the key issues addressed in this recent approach to the study of justice.

Edney (1980), for example, argues that the issue of resource scarcity—the overgrazing of the commons—requires that social psychological insights be used both to reduce the kind of competitivness and collective overconsumption that is destructive of essential scarce resources and to increase individuals' trust in one another and in the common good. Edney's

analysis comes closer to Lerner's approach to justice than it does to the equity notions that have dominated the field's initial inquiries. The kind of
trusting personal contract and sense of shared fate that Lerner (1981) describes in terms of identity or unit relations mark these points of comparability.

Edney (1981) also recognizes the important role of political, social, economic, and historical factors in producing scarcity, inequality, and injustice.
He observes that scarcity is never "really necessary" (p. 7); it emerges from
social policies that, if exposed, would "create a profound social disruption"
(p. 7). To avoid this social disaster, "certain strategies are used for disguise.
Most of these are part of the complex allocation process" (p. 7). On the other
hand, having made this observation, Edney also concludes that "inequality
and injustice [are] in the nature of things *and that there are functional reasons for this*" (p. 19). Given this inevitability, he argues that "The obvious
functional issue is how to deal with inequality so that it combines the material necessities of preserving the commons with the social–ethical values of a
free society, in a way that does least damage to both" (p. 23). His approxi-
mate solution builds on the metaphor of the symphony orchestra, in which
high levels of coordination with inequality and yet harmonious productivity
are achieved.

Overview

Justice theory and research in social psychology has continued more or
less unabated since its rather recent beginnings. It has taken several directions but for the most part has built upon one or more of the previous foundations and has involved some of the following: (1) expanding on and developing equitylike formulations, including efforts to refine the formula and the
mathematics of the presumed cognitive calculus that is involved (e.g.,
Farkas & Anderson, 1979; Harris, 1976); (2) expanding the range of applicability of equity formulations and testing the validity of this extension (e.g.,
Walster *et al.*, 1973; Walster *et al.*, 1978; Walster & Walster, 1975); (3)
developing critiques that introduce principles or rules of distributive justice
that are based on nonequity formulations, including the contrasting principle of equality (everyone gets the same regardless of inputs) and the principle of need (people get what they need, not what they contribute; e.g.,
Sampson, 1975; Deutsch, 1975); (4) examining personality and situational
factors that moderate the experience and consequences of justice (e.g., Rubin & Peplau, 1975; Sampson, 1980); (5) exploring the socialization and development of justice understandings (e.g., Berg & Mussen, 1975; Damon,

1977); (6) seeking a cross-cultural examination of justice principles (e.g., Nader, 1975); (7) extending the just-world thesis and probing its centrality as a governing principle of human behavior (e.g., Lerner & Miller, 1978); (8) extending the range of concern with justice from the microsystem to the macrosystem (e.g., Edney, 1980, 1981).

This list is not intended to be exhaustive, but it will serve as a useful point of departure to be called on again later, as I develop my critique of social psychology's analysis of justice more fully. At this early point, I want to direct our attention to two themes that I believe permeate the preceding contributions of psychology to the study of justice. The first involves the extent to which a considerable amount of the work on justice, especially the founding efforts of Homans and of Adams, emerged within a definite sociohistorical context: the context of work defined in a particular socioeconomic structure and designed to serve certain key social and personal functions. This is the point also suggested by Lerner (Lerner & Meindl, 1981). The second theme involves the extent to which justice has been understood psychologically and individualistically, that is, as an outcome of individual psychological, especially cognitive dynamics (also see Mikula, 1982, on this theme).

JUSTICE AND THE WORKPLACE

There are two points worth noting. First, the early social psychological study of justice-related behaviors developed within the context of the workplace. Second, the workplace was beginning to come under the sway of the human relations approach to organizational psychology. The first point tells us that we might well expect justice principles to focus around work-relevant, especially quantifiable economic and other similar indicators. If we follow the growing cadre of critics of the human relations perspective, particularly the founding Hawthorne work, this second point would lead us to cast a very suspicious gaze on the ideology and manipulation that runs rampant throughout the human relations movement (e.g., see Roethlisberger & Dickson, 1939, for the original work; see Bramel & Friend, 1981; Carey, 1967, 1977; or Franke & Kaul, 1978, for several pointed critiques).

Workplace Factors

Both Homans and Adams built many of their analyses around observations either made at the Hawthorne plant or derived from that early work. Adams observed, for example, that many of the workers' complaints in the early Hawthorne studies focused on factors of justice rather than on physical features of their work environment. Some complained that their seniority was not duly considered in promotions; others that their abilities were not rewarded with pay raises. From Adams's perspective, these revealed issues of fairness, as indeed they did. These and related observations led Adams to formulate the equity principle. Homans was likewise concerned with distributive justice in work contexts, including the original Hawthorne setting, which served as a never-ending source of data for his theories of justice.

It would seem natural, within such settings, to formulate ideas about justice that focused upon and emphasized factors clearly relevant to the workplace, such as pay, promotions, seniority, skill level. It is not surprising, therefore, to read in Adams's formulation of equity that the relevant inputs involved such work-related factors as seniority and effort, while outcomes focus especially on pay, promotion, and fringe benefits.

Human Relations and Ideology

Locating these early psychological concerns with justice within the human relations approach to industrial relations is enlightening in other ways as well. The critics of the human relations approach have led us to question the sincerity of the psychological investigators' concern with worker interest rather than with managerial techniques of manipulation. Might this workplace-motivated concern with justice likewise be less a matter of a genuine concern with fairness than a concern with the managerial manipulation of fairness? There are really two aspects to this question. The first suggests that by undertaking their research within the already defined context of the corporate workplace, psychologists would implicitly assume its structural constraints as givens and so come to an understanding of justice that was already predefined and prelimited to those forms fitting corporate interests. The second suggests that this circumstance might thereby participate in the ideology of manipulation rather than in the study of justice in human affairs.

Bramel and Friend's (1981) reexamination of the Hawthorne studies develops a rather clear and convincing case for both of these concerns. They systematically document both the *realities* of worker behavior within the Hawthorne plant and the *fictions* that have become part of the folklore of social psychology's understanding of the so-called Hawthorne effect. The Hawthorne effect, as any reader of introductory texts knows, is the apparently astounding "fact" that whatever management did to the workers' physical environment or work schedules, it could, merely by demonstrating its caring concern for the workers, increase productivity and retain morale at a high level.

The reality, known long before Bramel and Friend's recent publication and even prior to Carey's much earlier critical analysis (published in 1967), portrays a rather different picture. Rather than being docile and merely interested in managerial concern, workers, as Bramel and Friend observe, were very actively engaged in looking out for their economic and job-security interests. This produced resistance, confrontation, work slow-downs, firings, and other "unseemly" happenings—unseemly, that is, if one is seeking to portray a harmonious management–worker relation.

I have focused on the "class bias" (to use Bramel and Friend's terminology) within the human relations approach so that we might entertain some suspicions about the programs of research and accompanying theories that emerged from this context and within this "movement." After all, if management, including the psychological and sociological investigators of the Hawthorne effect and related phenomena, conveniently failed to observe the real disharmonies and conflicts of interest that described the workplace, then might not their theories of justice derived from that setting likewise paint a distorted picture of the realities of justice and fairness in the work situation? And if those theories and principles have been handed down from Homans and Adams to subsequent generations of justice scholars, might we not find the same distortions that exist within the Hawthorne myth itself? That is, we might find scholars conceptualizing justice in ways that fail to get to its core, even as the Hawthorne effect was a basic failure to understand the realities of justice for the workers.

I am suggesting that some of the founding work on the psychology of justice begin within an assumptive framework that was never critically examined and yet was carried forward in most of the further work on justice. It will be a continuing and recurring theme of this book to bring into focus the assumptive frameworks that guide psychological inquiry.

JUSTICE AND PSYCHOLOGY'S ASSUMPTIVE FRAMEWORK

There are other elements of psychology's assumptive framework that I believe to be equally relevant in setting the stage for psychology's contributions to the understanding of justice. This then brings me to my second point. Unlike the preceding, which involves assumptions secreted within the social and institutional context of the inquiry, the latter refers to the very foundations of psychological inquiry itself. Let me briefly mention two basic attributes of psychological inquiry that constitute what I believe to be a serious dilemma for the field's analysis and understanding of justice:

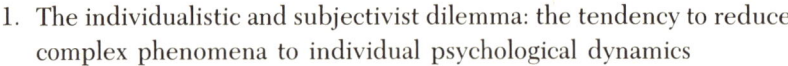

1. The individualistic and subjectivist dilemma: the tendency to reduce complex phenomena to individual psychological dynamics
2. The natural science dilemma: the tendency to search for basic principles that are universal and context-independent

Psychologizing Human Life

On the one hand, it is not surprising that people in the business of doing psychology should psychologize human life, viewing it primarily in terms of individual psychological factors and determinants. Justice in the workplace was thereby understood in terms of principles of individual psychological functioning. The subjective states and experiences of the individual became the standard against which to evaluate whether or not a work situation was just.

The terms by which the concept of equity was defined, for example, were subjectively determined. The evaluation of investments, outcomes, and even the degree of their comparative proportionality were all *as perceived by the individual*. Even the reactions to injustice were psychologized: a worker facing a perceived injustice might psychologically distort perceptions and thereby maintain the illusion of justice in the face of a reality that would not yield (see Mikula's parallel critique on this point, 1982).

On the other hand, this tendency to psychologize social behaviors such as justice serves to deflect attention away from any nonpsychological features of the situation. Effort is expended in developing precise ways to measure and assess individual psychological states and perceptions and to evaluate individual behavioral outcomes. The social context within which these individual perceptions and activities take place is put off to the side, occasionally alluded to, but rarely if ever systematically addressed. The individual's psychology dominates: if we can understand the psychological factors that are involved, then we can understand the nature of justice—in this case, justice in the workplace. Those following in the footsteps of the initiators merely apply the same framework and proceed systematically to test derivations that remain entirely within the realm of the psychological.

As Mikula (1982), a major and important contributor to the understanding of justice, has observed,

the research on justice has been mainly concerned with the role played by the notions of justice in the actions and judgments of single individuals, following in this way the individualistic assumptions dominating much of contemporary social psychology. As a result, the significance of the concepts of justice in the control and dynamics of interpersonal relations, the formation of interpersonal consensus about what should be conceived as being just, and the consequences of the corresponding disagreements, have all been seriously neglected. (p. 1)

A Wider Arena. One might suppose, however, that when justice is taken from the workplace and into the international arena, a change in this psychological overemphasis will take place (see Tajfel, 1982). A review of Edney's (1980, 1981) efforts to examine alternatives to the commons tragedy, however, fares little better in this regard than the approaches initiated by Homans, Adams, Walster, and others. The commons tragedy as Edney sees it involves an exhaustion of resources "because of overconsumption" (1980, p. 131). Solutions typically turn on changes in public morality. Failures occur because people resist changing their habits and beliefs. Solutions must somehow override these psychological resistances. Although Edney does not favor more totalitarian solutions, he observes that some persons in positions of political leadership may even require nondemocratic approaches to compel compliance from these resistant, overcomsuming hordes of selfish individuals.

To his credit, Edney (1981) also recognizes the social and historical roots of scarcity and therefore unnecessary inequality. Yet he simultaneously returns to a kind of individualistic analysis that undoes the very social analysis that he initially proposed. Resource scarcity is not reducible to selfish acts of individuals but rather results from the policies of particular nation-states. Although the individual may be the consumer, that individual does not act in a vacuum, nor is self-interest a kind of mysterious quality inherent in human nature. One of the problems with many "commons analyses" is that they build on an individualistic model. They fail to envision another scenario in which scarcity appears as a complex outcome of politics and practices that both require an ever-expanding market and the production of occasional scarcity in order to maintain price levels and profit margins. The individual is implicated in this process, but to reduce the process to individual psychology, I believe, seriously distorts both the nature of the problem and the recommended solutions.

Even Lerner's nonwork-centered analysis of justice is rooted in individual psychology. Let me quote:

It seems much more plausible that the transformations of raw self-interest into more effectively organized rules of conduct requires the kind of intelligence, symbolic processes, memory, and problem solving capability that could only be located in the individual "psyche." No social device contains the processes required for the "collective wisdom" needed to invent or shape the "social contract." (Lerner & Meindl, 1981, p. 215)

That other analytic possibilities exist seems to have escaped the majority of social psychological analysts who have simply adopted the individualistic assumptive framework of psychology without doubt or question. The contrasting model of systems theory, for example (e.g., see Bateson, 1972; Maruyama, 1979, 1980), which envisions a more complex and nonindividualistic framework for its anlysis of human systems, is omitted, as is the structuralist frame (e.g., Mayhew, 1980, 1981), with its clearly nonreductionist, nonindividualistic possibilities.

Context-Independent Principles

The second element governing psychology's implicit frame derives from the model of proper science that has thus far successfully dominated the field. In his opening remarks on the television show *Cosmos*, Carl Sagan most directly stated this model. Let me paraphrase: The laws of physics that we discover today, here on earth, are the same laws that applied some two thousand years ago, will be the same laws that will apply some two thousand years hence, are the same laws that apply on the distant planets of our solar system, and will be the same laws that we expect to obtain when we someday contact galaxies far out in space. In other words, the laws that govern the natural world are timeless and context-independent; they function in much the same manner wherever and whenever they are applied because nature itself functions by a set of timeless principles or rules. Our scientific task is to uncover and reveal those rules, so that we may use them to accomplish our own ends.

This model of both science and nature has a long and distinguished history. It emphasizes an empirical approach to discovering the laws that presumably govern nature. We cannot change those laws but can work with them to gain whatever human goals and ends we establish for ourselves. Thus, airplanes fly not in defiance of the laws of gravity but because of and in knowledge of those laws. Even the creation of new life forms based on gene splicing occurs because we have come to understand the laws by which nature recreates itself. In light of this knowledge, people can intervene and participate in nature's process.

Psychology developed as a scientific discipline squarely within this tradition. There were alternate pathways that it could have followed at different moments in its own history, but the pull of adopting the natural scientific model was too substantial. Thus, psychology dedicated itself to discovering the fundamental laws of human behavior; the expectation was that once these basic principles were discovered, they too would be timeless, general, and applicable to all persons everywhere.

It almost goes without saying that psychology was eager to discover the laws of human behavior so that it too could engage their use in behalf of achieving societal goals. The use of gravity in order to create flying machines, the use of nature's reproductive principles to create new life forms, and the use of psychological principles to predict and control human behavior were all cut from the same cloth.

When psychological inquiry was directed toward the study of justice, it was only "natural" to seek timeless principles. An equity principle thereby became one of those timeless basics of human psychological functioning. From the earlier work of Adams and of Homans to the more recent statements of Walster and others, we see this development sustained and even validated.

Although not subscribing to an equity principle, Lerner's analysis of the just-world hypothesis adopts a similar stance: he asserts that all people have a basic and fundamental need to believe that their world is a just place. He is not willing to locate this "need" in a "just-world gene," but he grants it such early primacy in socialization that it takes on a nearly genetic—that is, natural—base.

Even the cadre of critics of certain justice formulations have not fundamentally challenged either the psychologizing or timeless sense of the principle. Their primary attack, rather, has hinged on whether one justice principle is sufficient or if other principles must be added as well. Justice, however, remains for the most part a psychological matter, subjectively defined in terms of individual experience; the search continues for the timeless principles of justice behavior.

SUMMARY

To this point, I have suggested that the present state of our psychological understanding of justice is itself understandable as an outcome of both the context and assumptive framework within which the initial efforts were undertaken (i.e., human relations in the workplace) and the context and assumptive framework within which the science of psychology itself is practiced (i.e., the natural science model's search for timeless, context-independent laws). When psychology turned its attention to the study of justice, it adopted the frameworks that were the common currency at the time, without even giving this adoption a second thought. The very commonness of the currency is such that few were even aware of using it. Our understandings are thereby built upon assumptions that form a part of the seen but unnoticed background to our work. It is my intention, however, to cast some light upon that background, to bring it from the shadows into the foreground where we can better examine it and evaluate its impact and consequences both to our understanding of justice and to the people to whom we convey this understanding. This is what sets the task for this book.

MY OWN ASSUMPTIVE FRAMEWORK

To answer a question that quite legitimately should be asked of me, I too come with an assumptive framework that now guides my work and understanding. One key element of the framework I employ is its understanding both of the role of assumptive frameworks in guiding scientific investigation and an analysis that sees the frameworks within which the social sciences operate to be intimately related to the requirements of societal reproduction. This intimate relationship between social science and society requires that we seek a critical stance vis-à-vis whatever happens to be the common currency and orthodoxy of the time.

I have found that the writers of the Frankfurt Institute provide one of the foundations for my own ideas about psychology and society (e.g., Adorno, 1973; Buck-Morss, 1977; Fromm, 1955, 1941; Horkheimer, 1972; Horkheimer & Adorno, 1972; Jay, 1973; Marcuse, 1964, 1968). To be brief at this point, since the matter is considered further in a later chapter (Chapter 6), I am referring here to that long, heterogeneous, and complex literature that derived in large part from the Frankfurt Institute of Social Research and that set as one of its tasks the integration of Marx and Freud. Its larger task, however, involved critically reexamining the basic assumptions on which Western civilization has been founded, so that a more adequate theory and a more emancipating practice could emerge. Critical theorists waged an extensive and somewhat inconclusive war against the positivist and empiricist view of science, especially within the social and human sciences.

Let me briefly suggest critical theory's position with respect to the two issues noted previously. In addressing itself to the tendency to psychologize and individualize human life and to emphasize subjective over objective factors, critical theory argues for a dialectical analysis. It rejects either the extreme of basing our understanding within the subject or within the object. Given the tendency of much of the Western world to ground knowledge and understanding within the subject, the thrust of the critique makes critical theory appear initially to be entirely objectivist in its analysis, a kind of vulgar materialism. A more accurate portrayal of its views, however, would observe the emphasis on both subject and object. As Adorno (1973) has noted, the focus on the object keeps us aware of the limitations that a purely subjectivist science offers, even as the focus on the subject keeps us sensitive to the pitfalls of a purely objectivist position.

Needless to say, the tendency of psychologists of justice to base their ideas entirely on the perceptual world of the subject is, in this view, likely to be distorting. How, if we base our entire understanding on subjective appraisals, can we differentiate between the manipulation of subjects' perceptions by heavy-handed Machiavellians, who benefit from the perception of unjust allocations as just, and the reality of just allocations? The problem is that we carry along in our understanding of justice potentially distorted and ideological views without, however, being able to recognize or deal in any systematic manner with this possibility.

There is another facet to this rejection of a purely individualized analysis. In the view of critical theory, we can grasp the individual only as part of the larger whole, as part of society and of history. The individual—or, for that matter, interpersonal processes—is a part within which are revealed the operations of the larger sociohistorical totality. To begin and end our analysis with the part is seriously to distort our understanding. Insofar as the part reveals some larger processes operating within it, only by bringing those larger processes into our central focus can we better grasp the meaning of that part.

This criticism can be observed in the existing psychological inquiry into justice. The very concept of equity as a psychological principle, for example, ignores the extent to which investments and outcomes and their proportionality are elements of a larger sociohistorical process. Equity is not simply a principle that defines the way the individual mind works; it is a principle expressing exchange relationships within a market economy. We make timeless and natural what is a sociohistorical product; a market economy is neither timeless nor natural but a piece of the fabric of our own contemporary form of social organization.

A second example of this "bias" is apparent in the idea that justice involves resource allocation. Justice is said to exist whenever either the outcomes of this allocation complete some equation or when the procedures employed to make the allocation are fair. The emphasis on the allocation of resources, isolated from the process whereby resources are produced, re-

stricts the understanding of justice to distribution, not production. We delete from our analysis the very economic system that produces the resources
in the first place. The production system becomes the given, taken for
granted as part of the background; our concern focuses only on the manner
by which resources, once produced, are allocated. This too is a point to
which I will return in later chapters.

What I am noting at this introductory moment is that the critical perspective calls into question the assumptions that, in rarely being noted, are
covertly affirmed in our inquiries about justice. In this latter instance, by
defining justice in terms of resource allocation, we carry along unnoticed by
our interest the system whereby resources are both produced and allocated:
by implication, that total system presumably is just. We attend closely to the
way by which two people negotiate over the allocation that they confront; we
pay little attention to the justice that exists or fails to exist within that allocation itself. The latter requires that we view the larger processs involving production and distribution and not simply allocation in isolation from the totality.

The timelessness that characterizes our scientific approach has also
been soundly critiqued by the Frankfurt group. History is seen as an active
force: not merely a backdrop for actions but a shaping influence in its own
right. There are no timeless laws or principles of human behavior; laws are
historically located and constituted even as they constitute the moving flow
of human history.

The critical perspective is concerned with the way in which, by ignoring
history, human activity appears to be timeless. Ahistorical approaches grant
a kind of permanence and naturalness to the existing framework of society,
including the existing base of power and interest, rather than opening these
to more critical analysis and understanding. By positing equity, for example,
as a timeless principle, we assume the existing shape and form of society that
produces this principle; in this way we contribute to reproducing the society
as though it were natural and beyond human intervention or modification.

Timeless principles in the area of human life thereby take on more of an
ideological function than perhaps even those who advocate such principles
intended. Regardless of their intent, the elevation of "today" into an "eternal
forever" fails to challenge the interests that benefit from today's existing arrangements.

CONCLUSION

As I noted in the opening part of this chapter, I have the advantage of
writing now, at the conclusion of a substantial number of years of work con-

ducted without that conclusion yet in mind and hence without its guidance. I have tried, however, to introduce some of the central themes that will be addressed within the remainder of this book. The task as I see it is to consider the psychological understanding of justice within the framework of a more critical perspective—to combine our understanding of justice with our understanding of society and history. To accomplish this task, we will necessarily have to participate in a critique of what I call "pure psychology" and probe the potentially ideological functions that psychology may implicitly serve.

I hasten to add and even to repeat that I have not always stood where I now stand. As I entered the business of examining the psychology of justice, I did so within the frameworks that I am now holding open to critical analysis. It will prove helpful, therefore, if in the next several chapters I review the program of research in which I was engaged during these last fifteen years and which led me away from that uncritical starting point and toward the position that I have briefly summarized in this opening chapter.

These next several chapters, written today, have a vision that they could never have had at the time the work was undertaken. They will seem, therefore, more polished and sensible now than when I first undertook the work, because they are guided now by the sensitivity of hindsight. I hope, however, to capture some of the flavor of the original stumbling hesitancy, self-evident discovery, and growing transformation over the years of this research program.

PART TWO

From Mastery to Justice to Critique

I could not have known clearly at the time, in the early 1960s, that my theoretical paper on status congruence (Sampson, 1963) would motivate a series of research projects that would eventually lead me to the study of justice. Nor could I easily have known that in reflecting back on that work, a clear search for a theme would emerge. That search and that theme, seen with the excellent perception of today, describes the content and approach of the several chapters within this section.

My intention in this section is to provide a brief, focused review of a progression in research and in thinking. Those who are not familiar with the specific details of the research program or of the initial theoretical article will not be significantly enlightened as to those details by reading these chapters. It would be far better for those so concerned to refer back to the original studies. My main attempt in this part is to detect biases and uncover themes in my work that helped me reach a more critical perspective on the psychological analysis of justice. I believe this examination provides a useful document of the way in which our research and thinking are trapped within certain frameworks of which we usually remain oblivious. It is also a document that reveals some of the clues in our everyday scientific work that permit a breakout from the orthodoxy that binds us.

CHAPTER TWO

Status Congruence and Cognitive Consistency

A hypothesis proposed by several sociologists (e.g., Benoit-Smullyan, 1944; Lenski, 1954; Parsons, 1949; Weber, 1946) established the basis for an initial theoretical paper that motivated a later series of empirical investigations. This hypothesis did not impress me at the time (1963) as involving a question of justice. We know that people in a given society or group typically have a variety of status attributes that can be and often are ranked. For example, one's occupation may be ranked in terms of its perceived prestige; likewise, one's income can be ranked, as can one's education and so forth. The sociological hypothesis of interest was the idea that these multiple systems of ranking tend toward an equilibrium or balance. The concept of status congruence, crystallization, or equilibration was developed to describe this tendency—a tendency for all the status rankings for an individual to be roughly at or about the same rank position.

Status congruence could be used to describe the individual or the social system itself. For example, we can describe social systems as varying in their degree of status congruence. By this we would mean that some societies have a better fit among the several ways they rank people than do other societies. On the other hand, we can also describe a given individual as being congruent or incongruent. In this latter case, the person's several status ranks are either in line with one another (e.g., all high or all low) or are incongruent (e.g., the person ranks high on one dimension but low on others).

In either the individual or the societal case, the assumption is made that incongruence is an undesirable state and will motivate action directed to changing it toward a greater congruence among status ranks. A society with low congruence is expected to be in turmoil by comparison with one characterized by high congruence; an individual with low congruence is likewise expected to experience and express symptons of dissatisfaction by comparison with an individual whose status ranks are congruent. Several early research studies (see below) suggested general support for this point of view, even though subsequent research raised questions about whether congruence–incongruence or simply one or another of the status ranks by itself constituted the problem.

Lenski (1954, 1956, 1967) purportedly demonstrated that political attitudes were more liberal and hence presumably change-oriented when status congruence was low. Exline and Ziller (1959) report that incongruent small groups experienced greater tension and dissatisfaction than status-congruent groups. Adams (1953) found more friendship, trust, and intimacy among groups with congruent status ranks than among incongruent groups. Kleiner, Parker, and Taylor (see Sampson, 1963) reported greater frustration and stress that led to a higher incidence of mental illness when there was incongruence between an individual's educational and occupational ranks than when the match was congruent.

What I believed that I had discovered in 1963 was a potential merger between the theories of status congruence, deriving primarily from sociology and the small-group literature, and the then dominant theories of cognitive consistency that marked a great amount of social psychological research and thinking (e.g., Festinger's theory of cognitive dissonance, 1957; Heider's analysis of balance, 1958; Newcomb's view of symmetry, 1953). It seemed to me that incongruence in status ranks, the tendency to prefer and move toward congruity, and the distress and dissatisfaction that were otherwise created all reflected the operation of a *basic psychological principle:* the need, drive, or motive for cognitive consistency. In order to make this jump between the study of status congruence and the psychological state of cognitive consistency, I first had to argue that the essential reason why status incongruence was troublesome was that the inconsistent status ranks created inconsistent behavioral expectations. In other words, the connection between status factors and cognitive consistency was accomplished through a translation of status into behavioral expectancies and status congruence into a consistency among these expectancies. I referred to this "new" theory as a theory of *expectancy congruence*.

EXPECTANCY CONGRUENCE

The expectancy congruence model of 1963 argued that each position along a status dimension—whether the dimension involves education, occupation, income, or whatever—had a corresponding set of behavioral expectations for the person occupying that position. Incongruency among status ranks thereby implied an inconsistency among expectations for the individual's behavior. The troubles, distress, and dissatisfaction that incongruent status positions entail, however, is not merely an internal distress, as we suppose something like cognitive dissonance to be; rather, it is also an interpersonally stressful event.

My thinking at this point leaned more in the direction of Mead (1934) and Newcomb than Heider or Festinger. The former tend to emphasize the interpersonal side of seemingly psychological principles while the latter, especially Festinger, locate the prime determinant of consistency within the individual's mind as a kind of gestalt principle of closure. My preferences were to view the inconsistent expectations of differing status positions not simply to be intrapsychically disturbing but, in addition, to constitute an interpersonal problem. After all, how does one interact with someone about whom one has inconsistent expectations?

In terms somewhat like those of Goffman (1959), I envisioned people as presenting pictures of themselves, or *faces*, to one another, and there was an interpersonal demand for the many faces to be more or less consistent. This consistency, in turn, facilitated coordination and social mastery. It is far easier to interact with another person who presents one face or whose several faces provide a consistent set of expectancies than it is to interact with someone whose multiple faces make it difficult to know who one is or where one stands. The female boss in a traditional (and sexist) society is one such example, raising the question of whether subordinates are to relate to her as a traditional woman or as a boss (e.g., see Riger & Galligan, 1980, for an interesting discussion of this issue). The young manager offers another example; people wonder whether to relate to this person as someone who is quite young or as a manager.

In this theoretical view, therefore, status congruence translated into expectancy congruence. The distress was not simply an internal demand for cognitive consistency but also an interpersonal demand. This reflected a deeply seated bias in my own understanding of social behavior. Psychological theories of cognitive consistency were best seen in terms of an interpersonal model; in other words, there were social pressures towards "balance" and not merely intrapsychic demands.

TWO CENTRAL THEMES

As I look back on this theoretical paper, but especially on my theoretical predeliction to understand psychological principles as social and interpersonal principles as well, I observe two central themes:

The 1963 paper sought to explain status congruence in terms of a conflict of expectations that thwarted the smooth coordination between interacting people. My emphasis was on the *mastery and control* over interpersonal relations as a basic social psychological principle. Justice was never even mentioned or, for that matter, even considered as I recall. Discrepant status ranks did not suggest injustice, as they might well have; rather, in the view I then emphasized, status incongruence was a problem because of the obstacles to mastery (to predictability and control) that were involved. As we will soon see, only later and somewhat surprisingly did the theme of justice intrude itself and open to question my initial overemphasis on mastery.

In a sense, the 1963 paper was a mixture of excessive psychologizing with a bit of social psychologizing thrown in. I turned my explanatory attention to a psychological principle of cognitive consistency, which I treated as though it were a universal quality of the human mind: minds abhor inconsistency. Admittedly, however, I waffled a bit by suggesting that this quality of the mind was learned in the course of socialization and was sustained by an interpersonal process.

However, it was apparent that underlying the phenomena I was about to study was what I assumed to be a fundamental psychological process—one of those timeless principles that avoids inquiring about the particular society within which such principles may operate or the broader social goals which it helps sustain. In this case, the process that I then saw at the root of *all* human behavior involved a concern with mastery, in particular, mastery over the social world. Mastery was best achieved, in my view, if people behaved in consistent ways and presented consistent images of themselves to others. Those who failed to do so not only suffered interpersonal tension but were also subjected to interpersonal pressures to "return to consistency."

This emphasis of several decades ago is not an event of past history now dormant and forgotten in the field but remains to this day a central perspective governing a considerable range of psychological theory and research (e.g., see Rothbaum, Weisz, & Snyder, 1982, for a good example of what I mean). Themes of mastery and control appear today in psychology's concern with such seemingly diverse topics as "learned helplessness" (Seligman, 1975), locus of control (Lefcourt, 1976; Rotter, 1966), stress management (Averill, 1973), and even psychoanalytic formulations of the therapy process (Weiss, Sampson, Caston & Silberschatz, 1977). The personal history of my search thereby reflects something that is truly neither personal nor dead history.

CHAPTER THREE

Research on Status Congruence

The Emergence of Justice

The preceding theoretical analysis led me to believe that the attributes of a person's different status ranks were basically attributes of interpersonal mastery, and that, therefore, status incongruence—existing when the several rank positions a person holds fail to recommend consistent behavioral expectancies—was dissatisfying and troublesome because of the challenge to mastery that it posed. With these thoughts in mind and a good NIMH grant in hand, the natural next step was to devise a series of laboratory experiments that could systematically examine several derivations from this mini-theory (see Sampson, 1969, for a summary of much of this work).

One hypothesis became central to my analysis and separated it from other approaches to status congruence. In my view, psychological expectancies were the important element mediating status variables. Therefore, the mere presence of status incongruence—for example, high ranking on one dimension and low on another—would not be sufficient to create the challenge to mastery unless the two rankings were expected to covary. Not every set of status rankings would produce the negative effects of a loss of mastery; rank inconsistency in this case should not matter. A test of this hypothesis became the centerpiece of Brandon's (1965) doctoral dissertation, conducted as part of the research program on status congruence.

THE KEY EXPERIMENT

The study was rather ingenious, combining the usual laboratory procedures and controls with real rather than momentarily created status factors. To this end, subjects were recruited and assigned to a three-person group on the basis of the particular status qualities they brought with them. In order to establish one dimension based on what we termed *personal status*, we recruited graduate student males, upper-division males, and freshman females. We reasoned that within the context of the university world, this provided a "natural" status hierarchy, with the high-to-low order being apparent to all. Needless to say, we employed the proper techniques to validate this impression, discovering that students did feel that an actual status hierarchy was reflected by these imported status characteristics.

The laboratory task required the three-person team to make certain products that could ostensibly be "sold" to the experimenter. Teams were informed that the experimenter would purchase good products for $100 each but would levy fines of $150 for each faulty product. Teams were informed that no actual money was involved—that this was merely a device for keeping score.

Three specific jobs in this mock factory were created; each varied in its difficulty and responsibility. This comprised the second status dimension. The cutter's job was rated as highest in overall responsibility; it required following a pattern and cutting out six basic product forms at once. Any slip of the cutter's hand would ruin six products at the same time. The job of draftsperson was second in this status hierarchy. This person's task was to use carbon paper and a ruler to produce sets of squares that would then be given to the cutter to prepare for the final product assembly. The third and final job in this assembly line—that of the folder—had the least responsibility and difficulty. The only task the folder faced was to fold one piece of paper at a time into quarters.

As the third status dimension, Brandon selected what she called the "representative leader" position. All subjects had been recruited for this work through the student placement center. They were given a real hourly wage for their work regardless of their actual performance. Whether or not future employment was possible was left an open issue; however, it was tied to this third status dimension. Based on the stories they gave to three TAT cards, which the experimenter presumably scored for the students' leadership skills, one subject was chosen as a liaison representative who would meet with the experimenter and be involved in possible future productive activity for pay. A second subject was chosen to serve as the understudy, just in case the first one chosen could not meet again. The final subject was given no future role.

Therefore, three status dimensions were created in this laboratory environment: (1) personal status based on year in school and gender, (2) job status based on the overall difficulty and responsibility of the task assigned, and (3) representative leadership status based on whether or not the person had the qualities needed for possible future work. We reasoned that dimensions 1 and 2 and dimensions 1 and 3 would be expected to covary, while dimensions 2 and 3 were either not linked or only weakly linked by an expectancy of correlation.

If two dimensions were joined by an expected positive relationship, we assumed that people anticipated congruity between status positions on these two dimensions. Thus, for example, when we say that personal status and job status are expected to covary, we mean that someone who ranks high on one dimension is *expected* to rank high in the other. Whenever this expectancy is violated, therefore, psychological tension should occur and pressures to restore congruity should be apparent. This is what we anticipate will occur with respect to those rankings that are expected to covary (i.e., 1 and 2; 1 and 3).

On the other hand, if status dimensions are not expected to covary, any inconsistency in ranks on these dimensions should not evoke psychological tension and therefore should not reveal any disruptive pressures or, at best, only weaker pressures. Insofar as someone was ranked high in terms of job role in this study and low in terms of representative leadership position (e.g., "cutter" and "no future position"), we anticipated that this would not prove disturbing because there was little expectation for these two dimensions to be positively related.

The basic design of Brandon's study provided us with an opportunity to evaluate this one central hypothesis derived from the expectancy congruence theory. By manipulating the status positions of our subjects according to the kinds of jobs they were assigned and the kinds of representative leadership positions they were given, we could evaluate the effects on group performance and attitude both when incongruity undercut mastery and when it did not. Brandon established five types of experimental conditions, running a total of six groups under each:

1. *Completely Consistent.* In this condition, status positions on all three dimensions were consistent. Thus, for example, the male graduate student was the cutter and was selected to be the representative; the male undergrad was the draftsperson and the understudy; the female freshman was the folder and had no representative position.
2. *No Consistency.* The effort was to create a maximally incongruent group. To this end, the graduate male was the folder and the understudy; the younger male was the cutter and had no leadership position; the female was the draftsperson and the group representative.
3. *Expected Consistency.* There were actually two conditions involving a consistency between rankings that were expected to covary. We examined each of these separately. In the first case (condition 3), personal status and job status were central. The older male was the

cutter but had no representative position; the younger male was the draftsperson and the representative; the female was the folder and the understudy.

4. *Expected Consistency.* In this second case, the dimensions of personal status and representative leadership position were joined. Thus, the older male was the folder and the representative; the younger male was the cutter and the understudy; the female was the draftsperson and had no representative position.

5. *Unexpected Consistency.* This final treatment condition joined the two rankings that were not expected to covary: job status and representative leadership position. In this, the older male was the folder and had no leadership position; the younger male was the cutter and the group representative; the female was the draftsperson and the understudy.

With three status dimensions, it would have been possible to create other combinations for examination. These five were chosen, however, to reflect the major theses that were being examined in the present context. Measures were obtained on such variables as "experienced tension within the group," "hostility within the group," "pleasantness of the group atmosphere," "concern with doing good work." These were paper-and-pencil, postexperimental self-reports. A total score was computed on the basis of these subjective states.

Confirming the hypotheses, Brandon found that the two expected consistency conditions (3 and 4) showed a pattern of less tension and difficulty than either the unexpectedly consistent condition (5) or the maximally inconsistent condition (2). In other words, it appeared that an inconsistency of status ranks by itself did not produce psychological distress unless these ranks were expected to covary.

FROM MASTERY TO JUSTICE

None of this, however, proved to be the key turning point for our thinking about status congruence. That point emerged from a consideration of the then embarassing standing of the completely consistent condition (1).

In the completely consistent condition, status ranks on all three dimensions, including both those expected and those not expected to covary, were consistent. Rather than discovering this to be the most psychologically pleasant and tension-free condition, Brandon's research suggested that it lay halfway between the two most pleasant and the two least pleasant conditions.

We puzzled over this treatment's location on the pleasantness scale. Thinking back now, we might have answered this puzzle by arguing that the unexpectedly consistent ranks somehow detracted from the otherwise positive quality produced by expected consistency and so placed this condition at its halfway point. We took a somewhat different tack, however, that moved us directly into the literature and conceptualization of justice.

One of the key characteristics of the completely consistent conditon is that *all* the rewarding elements within the experimental situation went to one person, namely the graduate student male; in turn, *all* the nonrewarding elements were given to another person, the freshman female. It seemed that, in our passion to create mastery via cognitive consistency, we had violated some principle of fairness or justice. The status elements that we had assumed were simply attributes of mastery might also be seen to involve attributes of justice. In creating a condition in which status attributes were entirely consistent, we had inadvertently created a condition in which the just and fair allocation of rewards was violated.

Recall that the major theoretical analysis that motivated this research revolved entirely around the idea of mastery. The argument was that it was troublesome to coordinate interactions with people whose inconsistent status ranks implied conflicting expectations for their behavior. A question of fairness in the allocation of benefits within the experimental situation was the farthest thing from our minds at that time.

The perfect vision of hindsight in this case provides a fascinating documentation of the meaning of paradigmatic blindness. Once the experimental variables were defined in terms of mastery, they literally could not be seen in terms of another possibility, in this instance, justice. And so we thought of the individual's personal status not as an attribute of deserving—which justice researchers would clearly employ in their framework—but rather as a matter of role expectations. Similarly, when we assigned jobs and representative positions, we likewise thought of these in terms of role expectations rather than the equally likely possibility, unavailable to our awareness at that time, of the allocation of rewards.

JUSTICE AS EQUITY OR AS EQUALITY

As we reviewed these findings, it appeared that justice had been sacrificed in order to achieve mastery. In creating a condition in which interpersonal mastery and predictability were substantial, we had created a condition in which one person got all the benefits and another none of them. This analysis of the completely congruent condition, however, was not quite that simple, as became apparent when we reviewed the available justice literature. Much of that literature stressed the definition of justice as equity, as based on a contribution principle. From this perspective, it would presumably be fair for the person with the greatest investments, as measured by personal status and job responsibility, to receive the best of everything in the situation while the low-standing person got what was remaining. Thus, justice as equity did not seem to be violated by the experimental treatment we had created. Yet, the unpleasantness ratings of the completely congruent condition suggest that this form of justice was not entirely satisfying. Perhaps justice required an equality of allocation and not simply the matching of investments with outcomes.

CONCLUSION

Two important issues emerged from this investigation. The first suggested to us that mastery alone was not a sufficient basis for understanding and explaining our research findings. The second suggested that justice itself had two separate meanings, one emphasizing equity, the other, equality.

We next reasoned that both mastery and justice were significant factors in all interpersonal behavior. This clearly moved our thinking well beyond its focus on mastery alone as the sole factor of prime importance in interpersonal relationships. However, we had not only suddenly discovered two factors but had also discovered two meanings for justice: equity and equality. This would prove to be an important interpretation with far-reaching consequences to the development of a critical perspective on both justice and on the field of psychology.

The entire framework that had guided the research program had not only emphasized one factor, mastery, but had located the entire explanatory force within a psychological process: the need for consistency. People preferred consistency so that they could better coordinate their behavior with that of others and so feel more comfortable. That justice was an important explanatory concept implied not only that an additional psychological factor had to be considered but also that something beyond the merely psychological might be operating. This latter thought was then only a vague and disquieting notion to be nurtured as I began to probe further the several meanings of justice as equity and as equality. The critical seed was beginning to grow, however, and to cast some doubt about the primarily psychological framework within which my work on status congruence to that time had been conducted.

The possibility of defining justice in different ways, including both equity and equality, shifted the emphasis from the purely psychological to the social, the structural and even the historical. The normative framework within which fairness judgments are made began to loom as a significant factor to be considered.

This entire enterprise brought the social dimension into focus in yet another way. I had to reflect on the reasons why I and so many others had placed the theme of mastery into so central a position. Did this concern with mastery reveal a broad cultural bias operating in the background of the work? If I were thinking then in the terms of today, I might well have phrased this question in the language of Habermas (1971), whose ideas we examine in later chapters: that is, I would have been able to view the concept of mastery within the context of the cognitive interest in technically useful knowledge suitable to any civilization but especially central to advanced, industrialized settings. At minimum, these questions and doubts led me to wonder about the timelessness and universality of psychological principles and hence about their immutability.

CHAPTER FOUR

Equity and Equality as
Sociohistorical Principles of Justice

To understand a psychological principle as a sociohistorical principle is to en-gage in a striking transformation of that understanding. The bases for this change in perspective were beginning to emerge from the empirical investi-gation examined in the preceding chapter.

Two conclusions from that research pressed toward a reformulation of the nature of psychological principles. The first was the realization not only that the concentration on mastery had blinded me to an alternative possibil-ity but also that a similar blindness might be implicit in much if not all psy-chological work. What would be revealed if one sought to examine these im-plicit frameworks that governed our thinking in psychology? The second involved the emerging distinction between the two justice principles and the nagging questions about why one, equity, had taken such initial disciplinary precedence over the other.

This second lesson forced my thinking further toward the transforma-tion of the psychological into the sociohistorical. The equity version of justice seemed ill suited to dealing with some of the empirical findings of our work on status congruence. The alternative, justice as equality, was more appro-priate to our findings, yet the main thrust of justice work in social psychology—beginning with Homans and Adams in the early 1960s and carried forward most vigorously in the 1973 paper by Walster, Berscheid, and Walster—enshrined equity as a fundamental psychological principle of justice.

By the time of my 1975 paper, the focus of my dissatisfaction with the prevalent work on justice in psychology was taking shape. In that paper, I had moved from my initial concern (Sampson, 1969) with the failure of eq-uity to account for justice behavior in my own work and that of others, to a concern with why equity itself had become so dominant a theory of justice. In this, I was no longer concerned simply to offer an alternative conception of justice; rather, I sought to examine some of the ways in which the different formulations of justice themselves reflected and, indeed, might even reinforce a particular sociohistorical configuration.

The point is an important one. Whereas my earlier work had basically argued that equity was incorrect as a principle of justice, my 1975 paper began to argue that these so-called psychological principles, whether of equity or equality, were neither incorrect nor correct in any simple sense of the terms. They were derivatives of a particular sociohistorical context and so were better understood as historical principles that could vary by time and place rather than being timeless psychological principles of human behavior. I no longer argued that equity was wrong but that the more important issue was to discover the larger contexts within which it was a correct assessment of what people came to accept as just and fair. I did not yet know at that time (1975) the true force or extent of this argument or its broader implications; however, in the final paragraphs of the paper, I alluded to the possible ideological consequences of a psychology of justice that implicitly adopted a given social form without examining the social values and interests that underlay that form.

EQUITY AND THE MARKETPLACE

What most impressed me in this period of my work was the apparent match between a marketplace economic system and a marketplace psychological principle. The equity formulation introduced as a psychological principle an idea that in almost every respect was a copy of the marketplace principle. For example, the psychological theory of equity spoke of human relationships in terms of the exchanges of valuable goods; it emphasized the investments and outcomes of such exchanges; it introduced a dynamic principle that viewed people as calculating their own ratios and comparing them with the ratios they calculated from comparison others. The economic person, a character suited to early marketplace economies, had entered as a fundamental principle of psychological functioning.

A further parallel developed as I later reflected back on the equity and exchange formulations of justice. One of the important properties of a marketplace system such as that found in early capitalism is the requirement that all items for exchange be reduced to quantitatively comparable and measurable values. The lack of comparability between apples and oranges is resolved by making them equivalent units in some exchange formula. To achieve this, the items must be abstracted from their context and lose their own particularity. As goods assume this abstracted and equivalent characteristic, labor is measured in the same terms. You give me ten hours of your labor and I give you a set amount of money in exchange.

The Fetishism of Commodities

The reduction of all unique qualitative differences and distinctions to the same quantitative measuring scale permits qualitatively different items to be made equivalent and hence more readily exchangeable. This aspect of the marketplace had been described many years before equity theory as the "fetishism of commodities" (e.g., Buck-Morss, 1975; Lukacs, 1971; Marx, 1961, 1962, 1965; Ollman, 1971). This "refers to people's misconception of the products of labor once they enter exchange" (Ollman, 1971, p. 198). Specifically the fetish conceals the values that are part of the human activities of production and conveys these values as though they involved relations between abstracted products. This is said to be a process especially characteristic of capitalism.

The fetishism of commodities describes a process in which the actual relations between people are disguised and so appear as though they were merely relations between things. Furthermore, once they take on this quality, the entire process appears to be "natural" and "inevitable." That is, items of exchange appear *in themselves* to possess certain amounts of exchange value, and the sociohistorical process involved in this achievement is lost; people thereby relate to reifications of their world without being aware of the processes by which such reifications developed.

Equity theory seems to have adopted this particular view of human life as its understanding of the universal quality of human psychology and social relationships. All "psychological goods" are simply made equivalent; their unique qualities are erased as they become simple "investments" or "outcomes." For example, the amount of work put into a job is made equivalent to one's gender or race as an item of investment, even as money received and respect received become equivalent terms of "outcome."

The apples and oranges problem is neatly resolved. There is no problem in computing equity when "being female" grants one x investment points even as does y amount of work, or when receiving n amount of pay as an outcome becomes equivalent to receiving z amount of respect. The unique, qualitative distinction between the kinds of investment and kinds of outcome is eliminated in the pursuit of the most abstract common denominator. This is a characteristic of the particular economic system that the equity formulation in psychology adopted uncritically as a universal psychological description.

TESTING SOME DERIVATIONS

If I am correct in arguing that the equity formulation reflects the underlying economic system of society, it would seem reasonable to expect that people who are differently located in that system would reveal different tendencies to follow the equity formulation. This possibility led me (in my 1975 paper) to examine the effects of other variables on the applicability of equity as a general psychological principle. I was especially keen to examine the role of gender, concluding, after reviewing several studies, that "females tend towards equality and males towards equity in their social relationships with others" (Sampson, 1975, p. 55).

It is important to understand the basis for this prediction, for it is a key to the emerging critique of pure psychology. We seem to have two possibilities. In the one, we argue that we have discovered something fundamental about the way the human mind functions and proceed to examine both the consequences of this invariant principle for human behavior and the conditions under which it operates. This is the direction that the formulation of justice on the basis of equity has adopted.

The other possibility, however, is to view human psychology as revealing something about the underlying social system and therefore as being historically and socially situated, not timeless or placeless. Following this direction would lead one to formulate hypotheses linking one's differential location within the social system to the kind of psychological experiences one has. This view is similar to the Miller and Swanson (1958) thesis, which argued that the individual's family setting, whether bureaucratic or entrepreneurial, would influence the extent to which a reciprocity principle of exchange were followed. Both Berkowitz and Friedman's (1967) experimental evidence and the work of Muir and Weinstein (1962) provide support for this kind of analysis.

The usual way that psychology deals with these "external" variables is to argue that the principle (e.g., equity) is fundamental but operates differently as a function of certain personality or situational factors. In this manner, all people are presumed to be equity theorists; however, some people in some situations are expected to act differently. In adopting this approach, psychology retains its demand for an invariant law and attaches conditions to its applicability. I adopted a contrasting view, however, by suggesting that these very conditions, when carefully examined, are not external to the law but *internal* to its very operation and status as law: that the law itself is not invariant in the usual sense of that term but is better seen as being sociohistorically situated.

This is not merely a difference in emphasis but a very different view of the status of psychological principles and laws. I will have more to say about this in Part 4 and so will delay further discussion until that time. For the present, however, it is important to note that I was employing an analysis of the underlying social system as a central factor in shaping and limiting the kinds of psychological law that are uncovered; further, I employed this model of analysis to see whether people differently located in that underlying social system operated in terms of different laws.

Definitions of Persons and Principles of Justice: Gender

At this point, it made sense to suggest that people who were socialized to play central roles within the society's economic system would be more likely to conform to the equity principle in their relationships with others than would those socialized primarily into noneconomic or less economically central roles. This translated into the expectation that males would be more inclined to follow equity formulations than would females. As the 1975 review suggested, this possibility had some important empirical support. That review also suggested that women were not alone in their "refusal" to be equity theorists in their human relationships; people who were close friends or whose concerns were more oriented toward maintaining a harmonious relationship with others likewise declined to follow the equity principle. In other words, the equity formulation was a good copy of a highly competitive marketplace economy in which getting ahead and winning were more important than establishing a harmonious relationship with others.

As I would later discover, several others had reached a very similar position in their critique of the pure equity formulation. Deutsch (1975), for example, wrote of different principles of justice, including equity as only one—it emphasized economic values—and including equality and need as justice themes governed by noneconomic values. In a similar manner, Lerner (1975, 1981) suggested that justice principles varied as a function of the nature of the relationship between people. Lerner defined three possible relationships: identity (we are the same), unit (we are similar), and nonunit (we are different). Equity is more likely to hold under nonunit than under either identity or unit relationships.

Kidder, Fagan, and Cohn (1981) add further to this emerging picture of differences in justice principles as a function of the nature of the relationship experienced between the actors involved. Their addition is the suggestion, paralleling my own 1975 conclusion, that women tend to operate on somewhat different principles because they tend to define more unit and identity relationships with others by comparison with the nonunit preferences of most men.

Class Differences in Preferences of Justice

I have also recently come across several other studies suggesting social-class and cultural differences in the preference for a particular solution to the distributive issue. Robinson and Bell (1978), for example, examined several hypotheses involving people's perceptions, as a function of the respondents' location within the social system, of whether equality or equity is just. They hypothesized that people who benefited from a stratification system would be more likely than those who did not to see its allocations as fair, even though it was unequal in its reward distribution.

In other words, if you are well off within a given system, you are more likely than those who are less well off to believe that the prevailing equity, giving you more and others less, is reasonable and fair. Robinson and Bell report general support for this expectation in both the United States and Great Britain. For example, nonwhites, especially in the United States, judge equality as fair; on the other hand, those who feel themselves to be in an equitable situation—they are already getting what they feel they deserve—judge equality to be unfair.

CONCLUSION

These several empirical findings not only set limits to the operation of an equity formulation of justice but, more importantly, force us to reconsider the very meaning and understanding of what had heretofore been taken simply as a psychological thesis. In the 1975 paper, I observed the following:

Equity is a solution to the distributive problem with more sociological and historical significance than many of its psychological proponents seem to recognize: i.e., equity is not as much a psychological law about human nature as it is a psychological outcome of a culture's economic socialization practices. (p.58)

The point I was attempting to make at that time is that the empirical work on gender and class (among other factors) should not simply be taken as setting limits on the operation of a fundamental psychological principle of justice as equity. More importantly, this work has taught us something about the limits of invariant psychological principles themselves. The emerging critique on the very nature of our so-called invariant psychological laws—which constitute one aspect of what I have come to call "pure psychology," was now taking shape.

A further issue also emerged from the preceding perspective. It is one thing to call into question the invariant quality of psychological principles and to cast them, as Gergen (1973) suggested, as historical principles. It is another matter, however, to ask questions about why such psychological work has emerged—what values and interests it serves. I had observed a connection between equity theory in psychology and a particular economic system. This observation led me to begin to question the role that psychology might play in reproducing a particular economic system through its theoretical contributions to human understanding.

PART THREE

Expanding the Critique

When my work first gave rise to the idea that a basic psychological principle can better be understood as a sociohistorical, socioeconomic, and sociopolitical principle, I was still not clear as to its broad implications for psychology, the human sciences in general, or society. Nor had I then developed a coherent argument—of the sort that had characterized Gergen's (1973) work, for example—on which to ground my assertions, beliefs, and conclusions.

In this Part, I follow up those initial ideas and preliminary thoughts in more detail. This will require that the critique of justice be enlarged to a critique of psychology itself. Chapter 5 introduces my initial probe into psychology's values and ideals (Sampson, 1977, 1978). This took me in the direction of critical theory without, however, the awareness at the time that this indeed was where I was headed. I remained generally ignorant of the extensive literature that had marked this pathway long before my own initial efforts and that had laid a foundation for the very route I was following.

Chapter 6 examines this literature of critical theory which I belatedly discovered and to which I continue to turn in order to enrich and deepen my own grasp of my field and its role in social history. The detail and complexity of critical theory prohibits me from doing more than introducing some of its key notions in Chapter 6. The missing detail appears in the original sources, which I cite and which form the basis of my own interpretation and use of this decidedly European analytic mode.

CHAPTER FIVE

Psychology's Ideals

Examining the Examiners

At this point in my work on justice, it became apparent that my concerns were not like those underlying most of my colleagues' contributions to the justice literature. I was not so much concerned with understanding the psychological dynamics of justice *per se* as I was with comprehending the field of psychology that had produced the existing understanding of justice. I believed that we could never understand justice in itself without first understanding more about the way we went about understanding justice. This belief would soon broaden, and I would argue that before we could understand whatever specific content areas we examined through our psychological inquiry, we would have to examine the field conducting the inquiry. Mine became a metapsychological concern, an examination of the discipline and its ideals. Two key papers emerged from this metapsychological analysis. The first (Sampson, 1977) examined what I termed a "self-contained individualistic ideal" permeating psychology; the second (Sampson, 1978) sought to locate that ideal within the paradigm of science that governed the field.

Two things immediately become apparent to anyone who tries to develop a critique of psychology or of the human sciences in general. First, the shoulders on which one must stand are very tall and have a substantial history. Second, in spite of this lengthy history of criticism, very little has changed over the last several decades. Much of what one hopes to present by way of critique has previously been noted somewhere, even in the relatively near past; yet the field plods on relentlessly in spite of these often biting and, in my view, insightful critical analyses. It seemed, then, that I would simply be adding one further footnote to a history that, in some thirty years, would be cited by the next critical analyst who, in turn, would confront the same story and the same fate.

Although this awareness might fuel despair, it also fuels the very thesis on which the critique itself is founded. The forces for retaining psychology and the human sciences in their existing form run deeply to the roots of the society, making critiques appear to be little more than worthless tokens in the economy that governs the field.

READING PSYCHOLOGY

My initial foray into the critical dimension sought to uncover what I termed psychology's "ideal American social character." I hoped that this analysis would reveal the extent to which psychology affirmed and so helped to sustain a given ideal. Looking backward, I think I can better frame the intent of that work now than I did in the 1977 paper. The search for an ideal social character was not based on a lengthy historical study of the American character; I attempted to fathom the American character by giving psychological theory and research a deep, interpretative reading. This has become an important and recurring point.

One might have proceeded in the study of social ideals in at least two ways. The first, clearly not the path that I followed in the 1977 paper, would have been to undertake a careful examination of the American character, perhaps along the lines of a Riesman (1950), Fromm (1964), Lasch (1978), or Toffler (1980). This would have entailed a lengthy analysis of American culture and sociopolitical institutions. The American ideal character or the ethos of the culture would presumably emerge at the end of this complex examination.

The path that I followed, by contrast, required assuming that the theories and research findings of psychology, when critically read, would reveal the product of this complex sociopolitical environment. That is, one could grasp the cultural ethos and its ideals through the study of those who studied the people of the culture.

Although I was not fully aware of the broad implications of adopting this second pathway, I believe it to be a rather important insight. The basic idea is that psychology studies a social product, the individual. The field usually fails to be aware either of this feature of its work or of its implications. The individual that is psychology's research subject is the creation of a given sociohistorical system. What psychology thereby discovers—at least if it is done well—provides us with an entry into the cultural ethos and ideals. To repeat, psychology is usually unaware of this feature of its work. Psychology tends to behave as if it were studying something basic and fundamental about "human behavior," the "human mind," or "human nature." However, by viewing psychology's research as the study of a social product, one can use its insights to ascertain the ideals and ethos of the culture that creates those products.

We are accustomed to this kind of reasoning in our analysis of the products of another culture, such as its media, architecture, art, music, and so forth. We use these products of culture as vehicles for fathoming something about the ethos, practices, and life experiences of the culture. In much this same manner, one can use psychology's understandings of the research subject as the product that is our guide to the culture.

The next step involves using these insights as the basis for a critique both of the discipline and perhaps of the underlying culture. This step must seem as controversial and perhaps as unfair as is the first step in this process. After all, the product of the culture is used both to fathom the ethos of the culture and to critique those who study the product uncritically.

The theory and research of psychology—especially of social, personality and developmental psychology—enter this analysis in two ways. First, they become a way of grasping the underlying cultural ethos through their descriptions of particular human qualities and traits; second, we probe the unfolding understanding in order to make a critical examination of the discipline that has provided such revelations. This second step is not as unfair as it may first appear. It sounds as though I were killing the messenger for having delivered some bad news. In my view, however, psychology is not simply a messenger, nor is it a passive vehicle; instead, it is a means of shaping and constituting properties. Psychology's messages participate in sustaining the very culture from which those messages emerge. Psychology's reflections help reproduce the reality it studies and reflects. This theme is more fully developed in Part 5.

Psychology and the other human sciences both reflect social reality through their theories and research findings and help sustain the very reality they reflect. It seems reasonable, therefore, to use these disciplines both as a vehicle for understanding the nature of social and cultural process and pursuing a critical examination of the disciplines for their role in sustaining this sociocultural process.

SELF-CONTAINED INDIVIDUALISM AND ANDROGYNY

By employing some recent psychological theory and research in the manner just noted, I suggested (Sampson, 1977) that an ethos of self-contained individualism pervaded both U.S. society and psychology's understandings:

Our culture emphasizes individuality, in particular a kind of individual self-sufficiency that describes an extreme of the individualistic dimension [p. 769] . . . . The self-contained person is one who does not require or desire others for his or her completion or life; self-contained persons either are or hope to be entire unto themselves. Self-containment is the extreme of independence: needing or wanting no one. (p. 770)

This same theme, but with a somewhat more complex understanding, will appear again later (Part 4), where the individualistic thesis becomes one of the centerpieces of my critique of pure psychology. At the time of the 1977 paper, however, I saw the self-contained ethos as a kind of narcissistic withdrawal into one's own being and argued that this ideal could be seen in three key areas of psychological investigation: androgyny, moral reasoning, and conceptions of mental health.

I argued that the very concept of androgyny, which ostensibly opposed destructive gender stereotypes, also represented an ideal with its own destructive qualities. Androgyny described the condition of persons who contained within them both male and female qualities: in a sense, such people were complete, as they contained within themselves the total package of desired human qualities. I suggested that this appeared to represent the opposite of real interdependence and to reflect a possibly tragic, not a desired, state of human relations under contemporary social conditions.

The contrast was between the apparent atomistic independence that the androgynous ideal represented and an alternative model of interdependence. The latter, for example, would not insist that one and the same person contain both male and female qualities. Rather, the desired ideals could be located within the interdependently acting community in much the way that Bales (1955, 1958) viewed leadership dynamics within small groups: that is, no single person represented all the functions requisite for group survival; these were distributed more widely throughout the group. Another possibility involved persons who reflected one ideal cluster at one point in life and another at some later time (e.g., see Carlson, 1972; Riegel, 1976). It seemed to me that by defining the ideal as being present in persons who, in themselves, held all that was essential to the culture—and at the same time in their lives—psychology was emphasizing but one among several possible distributions or arrangements of culturally esteemed and essential qualities: the one, indeed, that seemed to be the most atomistic and least demanding form of interdependent functioning.

It was clear that in my argument the facticity of androgyny was not at issue: I did not dispute the empirical research findings showing androgynous individuals to be better adjusted than sex-typed persons. Also, I never argued in support of sex-typing. What I was saying, rather, is that the reality of androgyny as a desired social type could be understood only within the context of a social form in which self-containment and individualism rather than interdependence were desired ideals. I further questioned the type of social form in which this was ideal.

The structure of the 1977 analysis of androgyny was precisely as I noted earlier in this chapter. A psychological finding was taken as the vehicle for grasping the underlying cultural ideal or ethos of self-contained individualism. I then looked at the field of psychology that had both discovered this cultural ideal and, in discovering and presenting it as though it were an essential and positive quality of human nature, was participating in reproducing the very society that reflected the ideal in the first place. Finally, I raised some questions about the implications of a self-contained ideal for effective problem-solving in an era with high demands for interdependence.

THE SOCIETY OF INDIVIDUALS

Let me develop this idea further by calling on the equity formulation of justice as another example. My questions about equity theory were not entirely about its facticity or accuracy in depicting how people made their individual decisions regarding justice. Many of my questions focused on the kind of society in which that formulation of justice was prevalent and about the impact of the discipline's presentation of equity as though it were a timeless rather than sociohistorical principle. I asked questions about the kind of society and the kind of political, economic, and organizational arrangements in which it made sense for people to believe that justice prevailed in all matters, including business and friendships, only when there was a comparative proportionality of investments and outcomes. I suggested the answer: these judgments rested on a socioeconomic form, capitalism, where everything is reduced to an exchangeable commodity.

In 1977 I made this same point with respect to androgyny, moral development, and mental health. The argument parallels the case of equity theory. My questions about androgyny inquired about the kind of society in which having both male and female qualities was the cultural ideal. I suggested that this self-contained, individualistic perspective might, as with equity, reflect a property of capitalism. The individualism and the privatism that self-containment implies are qualities that others (e.g., Habermas, 1975) have observed to be important to the maintenance of capitalism.

One paradox in the preceding speculations is that those advocating androgyny had framed some of their concerns about the extremes of sex typing within the very same socioeconomic analysis that I was viewing as being equally troublesome for the androgynous solution they had recommended. In other words, it seems that capitalism was being accused both of leading to excessive sex typing, for which androgyny was an essential remedy, and of leading to the self-contained, individualistic ideal which I argued androgyny also reflected.

Although my thinking on the connection between many of psychology's concepts and the underlying capitalism of United States society was not well formulated or precise at that time, and although some might see the preceding paradox as demonstrating the nonimplication of society's socioeconomic form in psychology's concepts, the nagging suspicion of a linkage remained uppermost in my developing reflections. This entire matter is probed more extensively in later chapters, especially in Part 5.

MORAL REASONING

The next concept that I turned to in 1977, psychology's approach to moral reasoning, opened the door to a link between the roots of human reasoning and thinking and a particular social form. I did not fully explore this possible connection in the 1977 paper, in great measure because I was not fully cognizant then of the implications of the position I had adopted. In 1977, however, I viewed the Piaget–Kohlberg (see Kohlberg, 1968, 1969) approach to moral reasoning as yet another example of the societal ethos of self-contained individualism. I was specifically concerned with the extent to which the zenith of moral reasoning involved allegiance to abstract, general principles that required the indivdiual to "take distance and separate self from group" (Sampson, 1977, p. 776). In other words, moral reasoning at its best emphasized the individualistic thesis; it required disembedding self from group and communal contexts and stressing principles that transcended time and place.

In some later works, including my 1978 paradigms paper and my 1981 cognitivism paper (Sampson, 1981a) the broader implications of the ethos secreted within this cognitive-developmental view of moral reasoning were examined. I was especially concerned to connect this concept of reasoning with particular social interests. In the 1977 paper, I emphasized the gendercentricity of formal moral reasoning. Along with Gilligan (1977) and Haan (1978), I expressed a concern that the high point of moral reasoning had been defined in terms of a male-dominant world view, another illustration of both the cultural ethos and a value bias.

By 1978, I began to view this bias as inhering not only in specific concepts of psychology but in the very model of proper science that the field adopted. I argued that this paradigm emerged both within the male subculture and, simultaneously, along with the emergence and expansion of industrialized and technologically advanced society. While this analysis was not entirely restricted to the capitalistic economic system, it appeared that the forms of industrialism and of capitalism were intertwined and well synchronized.

I further developed and expanded this theme in the 1981 paper. I argued that the form of reasoning held in highest esteem by the Kohlberg–Piaget and other similar cognitivist positions in psychology reflected a major and totalizing cultural theme: the victory of instrumental rationality (see Horkheimer, 1974; Habermas, 1970, 1971; Marcuse, 1964). Because these ideas are more fully examined in later chapters, here I have only touched on them lightly in order to illustrate the irresistible press of my thinking in a direction that would send me headlong into the critical theory of the Frankfurt scholars.

CHAPTER SIX

The Critical Theory of Society
Discovering the Roots

How often do we stumble hesitantly and somewhat intuitively forward, only later to discover that the position we reached, however inexact or fuzzy it may be, stands fully within a tradition to which we had been oblivious? For me, this pattern seems normative. I had moved fully into developing both my critique of justice as equity and my critique of psychology's ideals and its scientific paradigm without once citing as references the work and the writings of the Frankfurt school. Somewhat like Molière's character, who discovered the existence of prose only after he had long been speaking it, I discovered critical theory after I had already begun to use it. That discovery, however, gave focus and greater precision to my halting, though hopefully persuasive, earlier contributions.

Most psychologists—and I say this in the absence of clear empirical confirmation—are not familiar with the critical theory of society that emerged in the 1920s and 1930s in Germany under the able guidance of Horkheimer, Adorno, Marcuse, and many others. It represents a tradition that American psychology neither followed nor gave much if any serious attention.

Some would argue that its tradition was not followed in the United States in part because most of the early publications were not translated from the German or because the ideas seemed more relevant to Germany, with its budding fascism, than to the democratic tradition of the United States. Others might argue that critical theory was not followed in the United States because of its clearly political stance, derived in great measure from Marx's ideas. Some would say that it was not followed here because our psychology is a science, while the Frankfurt group specialized in philosophy and speculation.

Of course, many in psychology would argue that a critical theory of society is surely not relevant to them as psychologists, though it might well be relevant to people in the other social sciences. Psychology is somehow insulated from society and from social concerns, so it is exempt from requiring any social analysis, let alone any critical social analysis. Still others, and I think that I would place myself among this hypothetical group, would suggest that although the previous reasons are partly correct, the pathway of critical theory was not followed also precisely *because* of its relevance to the United States: that is, because American psychology was so deeply embedded in its culture that it was unable critically to examine that very embeddedness.

The history of any field is written primarily from the standpoint and in the service of the present. It is rare to find a history written in which the pathways chosen are sharply marked off from those not chosen; yet, in some ways, understanding why a given tradition was *not* followed is as instructive as understanding the background to the tradition that *was* followed. It is understandable, given the present positioning of psychology, that the historical precursors to the Frankfurt group (Hegel, Marx, Heidegger, Husserl, and so forth) play such a minor role, whereas another set of historical figures (e.g., Locke, Hume, and Mills) take up more space in the historical accounts of modern psychology.

Given the centrality of the Frankfurt tradition to my own thinking and given what I see to be a movement in certain segments of psychology toward that tradition, it will be helpful if I devote this chapter to a brief review of some of the key themes of the critical theory of society. These themes and ideas, though dated in some respects, remain viable tools for psychological analysis even today. I believe that they provide us with an alternative view of our discipline. As we consider these themes, I suspect that the reasons why this path was not taken will become apparent.

Strictly speaking, this chapter is not about critical theory *per se*, nor is it an attempt to provide an in-depth analysis of its basic arguments. My intention is to outline what its thoughts have contributed to my analysis and understanding. Besides the original materials, there are several useful secondary sources which those interested in an in-depth review of critical theory can read, especially Jay (1973).

Four Threads of the Critical Perspective

The threads that, when joined, constitute the diverse view commonly called critical theory comprise several interdependent themes and emphases: the theory is historical and holistic; it introduces a materialistic base to an idealist superstructure; it is concerned with rationality and ideology, with domination, and with the use of reason to achieve emancipation. Any one of these by itself offers a somewhat distorted and truncated view. Together, however, they provide what I believe to be a useful glimpse into the critical perspective, whether one considers it to be a coherent theory as such (it really is not) or a way of understanding and intervening in the world (which it attempts to achieve).

HISTORICAL AND HOLISTIC

In a brief paper ostensibly summarizing "Institute activities," the Frankfurt Institute's director, Max Horkheimer (1941), offers us a useful view of both the historical and holistic emphasis of the critical perspective. He outlines several key thoughts, two of which are central to this first theme.

1. Concepts are said to be formed historically. By this Horkheimer means that the categories we employ in our analysis of human life "must take account of the historical character of the subject matter to which they pertain . . . in such a way that the categories are made to include the actual genesis of that subject matter" (p. 121). The contention is that the genesis of a phenomenon must be included as part of our understanding of that phenomenon and hence a part of the very conceptual tools we use in this understanding. Basically, in order to understand how things are, we must understand how they came to be. The meaning of an item of culture or social practice changes historically; this must be reflected in the way we understand that item or practice.

2. Parts of the social field contain and reflect the whole of that social field. In this connection, Horkheimer speaks of *induction* as a tool of analysis. He contrasts the kind of inductive process that is typically used from the kind he sees as essential to a critical social analysis. Typical inductive processes gather a set of individual events and from them seek to abstract to a general principle or law; the move is from the particular to the general. By contrast,

Induction in social theory . . . should seek the universal within the particular . . . and instead of moving from one particular to another and then to the heights of abstraction, should delve deeper and deeper into the particular and discover the universal law therein. (p. 123)

In order not to be misled, the reader should note that the term *universal* as used here does not refer to transhistorical principles but rather to the search within each particular event for fragments and reflections of the total system in which it is embedded. There is an intriguing affinity between Horkheimer and Anaxagorian logic (see Ogilvy, 1979) that also appears at the roots of relational rather than identity-based thinking. The parallel appears in the assertion that the parts that compose any totality represent that totality within them. One must thereby begin the search for understanding by grasping the totality and from there inducing, in Horkheimer's special sense, the qualities of the parts comprised by it.

This kind of analysis is interesting and important. Horkheimer proposes that we employ the particular event as a device for uncovering the universal that is concealed within it. For example, the relationship between father and child within the family is used to expose the long arm of societal authority:

A single human relation, for example, that between a father and his child, is constituted by the fundamental relations that govern the social system . . . . The privacy of the family relation . . . opens and leads into the prevailing social realtions . . . . Owing to its intrinsic relation to every other particular moment of the whole, the content and function of every given aspect changes with every change of the whole. To isolate and fix the particular moments is therefore impossible. (Marcuse, 1960, p. 160)

Societal relationships of authority are reproduced in the particular context of the family. The social form of authority is the unviersal in this case; it appears in each and every part of the society that we may examine. Our aim is to grasp this essential relation rather than to build up a universal principle by merely collecting bits and pieces of particular events.

And Justice

Both of Horkheimer's ideas can be seen within the critical analyses that I have been proposing. Equity theory, for example, is taken as a historically formed concept and not as a timeless, ahistorical principle. It therefore becomes important to understand the historical location of that concept and how it came into being as a social concept in order truly to understand equity and its view of justice. Note, it is the historical genesis of the concept, not its genesis within the individual's life history, that is at issue here. Socialization studies, while important in their own right, primarily inform us about the ways in which people acquire their culture's concepts, not about how those concepts were developed or what they mean.

Horkheimer's second point can be observed in my view of equity as the particular element that contains within itself the underlying universal, namely, a marketplace economy. In other words, the particular view of justice as equity is probed until it reveals the operation within it of the universal structure of the socioeconomic system in which it is embedded. It is the part whose meaning is derived from examining the whole.

Rationale

Several reasons are proposed for adopting this historical and holistic point of view. For one, it is argued that the present moments we live in and examine through psychology are products of a social history. In failing to understand this relationship between the past and the present, by emphasizing only the present, we distort our understanding: we tend to ascribe a timeless quality to the phenomena we uncover today and so attribute to nature what is actually the product of human endeavor and history.

Writing in a different context about the works of Darwin and evolution, a zoologist (Wake, 1981) noted that Darwin's ideas sent biology in two directions: one examining "how things work"; the other, "how things come to work." In commenting further, Wake noted that "Now scientists are realizing that if they want to understand how things work, they must also understand how they came to be. Likewise, scientists who want to understand how life has evolved, must have an appreciation for how life is" (p. 3). This insight from the biological sciences captures the point developed in the Frankfurt group many years ago with respect to the social sciences. It suggests that in all disciplines that examine phenomena embedded in history, it is essential to connect the *is* with the *was* in order more fully to understand both.

In 1973, Gergen brought this point of view clearly into the mainstream of social psychological inquiry in a provocative paper arguing that

In essence, the study of social psychology is primarily an historical undertaking. We are essentially engaged in a systematic account of contemporary affairs . . . . In this light, it is a mistake to consider the processes in social psychology as basic in the natural science sense. Rather, they may largely be considered the psychological counterpart of cultural norms. (pp. 316; 318)

Needless to say, Gergen's paper inspired several debates (e.g., Hendrick, 1976) and several counterarguments (e.g., Schlenker, 1974), which for the most part adopted the ahistorical emphasis of the natural science paradigm. As Wake's position suggests, however, those natural sciences that deal with living systems must be concerned with history. To argue in opposition to a historical perspective because it is nonscientific is surely to miss the point of the historical position with regard to the analysis of all living systems.

History and Contextualism

One of the key elements in the historical-holistic thread of critical theory has appeared in certain streams of psychological work in a variety of *contextualisms*: approaches that likewise insist that the meaning of elements in systems be grasped in terms of the contexts in which they appear. The cohort analyses that Baltes and Nesselroade (1972) and Woodruff and Birren (1972) have introduced mark two such efforts within psychology. They link individual development with cohort development and thus emphasize cultural moments rather than purely individual events.

Baltes and Nesselroade's data have suggested, for example, that people of the same chronological age are often less alike than people of different ages who are evaluated within the same historical context. That is, two subjects, both assessed at age 15 but born respectively in 1960 and 1940 might reveal greater differences than two subjects assessed in 1980 at ages 15 and 20, respectively. This historical series and hence cultural context proves more relevant than their individualized developmental stage.

Without reviewing the entire list of comparable efforts to contextualize psychological analysis and understanding, let me briefly note a few. Sarbin's (1977) recent works have attempted to introduce what he called "contextualism" as an alternative worldview for psychology, but especially for the analysis of personality. Addressing his work to the meaning of meaning, Mishler (1979) insisted that it was meaningless to speak about meaning in a literal, that is, noncontextual sense. His argument can be seen to emerge from within the hermeneutic approach which shares a certain affinity with critical theory (e.g., compare Gadamer, 1975, 1976; and Habermas, 1971. Also see McCarthy, 1978; and Ricoeur, 1972). This perspective is often posited in opposition to natural science understanding (e.g., Winch, 1958).

The ethnomethodological movement within microsociology (e.g., Garfinkel, 1967; also Wilson, 1970) and the ethogenic approach coming primarily out of the work in England on situated actions (e.g., Harre, 1977; Harre & Secord, 1972) likewise emphasize the importance of context in the analysis of human behavior. Finally, the approach of systems theory (e.g., Bateson, 1972; Bertalanffy, 1968; Dewey & Bentley, 1949; Maruyama, 1979, 1980; Miller, 1965; Wilden, 1980), including its several derivatives (e.g., family systems work: Ackerman, 1966; Kantor & Lehr, 1975; also see Handel, 1967), also emphasizes the importance of the whole in determining the nature and function of the parts that compose it. Even Sperry's (1969, 1977) neurophysiological analysis of consciousness adopts a very similar explanation of the relationship between parts and wholes. Several of these analyses will be examined more thoroughly in later chapters.

It is not my intent to discriminate sharply between these several points of view and the historical-holistic thrust of critical theory. Let me simply note, however, a few key distinctions. In most cases, the whole or totality which is of special interest to the critical theorists refers to the underlying social structure said to permeate all parts of the social field. This emphasis gives a somewhat distinct accent and political focus to their work that some (but not all) of the other contextualizers seem to lack.

In addition, although many systems theories appear to share much with this totalizing aspect of critical theory, there have been several important disagreements between critical analysis and systems approaches (e.g., Habermas vs. Lhumann). Some systems analysts adopt a mechanized conception of purpose and intention and a mechanized view of the process of change, as compared with the critical theorists' emphasis on the agent's potential for self-reflective, informed control over the movement and direction of "the system" (see Wilden, 1980, and my discussions in Part 4). Writers in the critical tradition—such as Habermas (see McCarthy, 1978) and Giddens (1979)—have observed the extent to which systems theory, in particular its understanding of the self-regulation of society, could be seen as "the highest expression of the technocratic consciousness" (McCarthy, p. 10) of our contemporary era. Giddens is especially sensitive to the ideological implications of the systems perspective. He sees it as being one of the most far-reaching and significant applications of a directly manipulative and controlling ideology in existence today (Giddens, 1979, p. 196; also Wilden, 1980).

Another point of discrepancy between the major thrust of the critical perspective and this plethora of apparently holistic and even historical approaches that have entered the mainstream of psychology concerns the failure on the part of the majority of contextualizers to depart from an idealist root and adopt the kind of materialist philosophy that provides the critical cutting edge of the Frankfurt group's analysis. Sarbin's contextualism, for example, seems unable to move far from the world of the subject's mental processes and so loses the edge that the materialist emphasis of critical theory sustains.

THE MATERIALIST WEAPON

In its usual sense, materialism reduces all phenomena to their material, objective base. Crude materialism argues that everything that exists is material; from the material issues the world of the phenomenal or mental. A misunderstanding of Marx as simply a crude materialist, for example, would lead one to emphasize the economic substructure as the base from which all other forms of the social world, including the mental, mechanically issue.

As employed in critical theory, materialism does not refer simply or directly to the reduction of human life to physical matter and its movements. To be materialist, rather, is to refer to the practical activities and tasks of particular people living and working in a particular society at a particular moment in its history. In effect, the Frankfurt group sought an antidote to the overwhelming press of idealism within Western philosophical and social thought. Idealism had made the subject and the mind the supreme master and grounding for the world. In so doing, it had failed to provide a weapon against the potential deceit of the mind. This weapon came in the form of a materialist analysis, with its emphasis on the ongoing social practices of a group and not simply on matters of the pure mind.

There are several interrelated aspects of this materialist position. For one, the insistency is always in locating the actual social world and its practices, within which people live and work, rather than soaring into the abstract reaches of pure thought. For another, the materialist emphasis preserves a point of tension between mind and matter, between concept and object. This tension helps to sustain "a critical weapon of defense against belief in the infinity of the mind" (Horkheimer, 1972, p. 28). Still further, this emphasis calls attention to the transformation of concrete events in the world and not simply to changing the outlooks or mental pictures that people maintain about their lives and conditions.

The common error is to assume that critical theory sought to replace idealism with materialism; its real aim, however, was to retain each in tension, so that each could serve as the watchdog of the other. This latter sense is captured in the following passage from Adorno (1973):

The duality of subject and object must be critically maintained against the thought's inherent claim to be total [p. 175] . . . . But it is not the purpose of critical thought to place the object on the orphaned royal throne once occupied by the subject . . . . The purpose of critical thought is to abolish the hierarchy. (p. 181)

Thus, the materialism that marks critical theory argues that the concept, idea, or thought does not exhaust all that is reality; the remainder, the material world of human practices, including work and labor, have an existence in reality beyond the conceptions that seek to contain, capture, and describe them. It is important to realize that this brand of materialism is not intended to do away with thinking and mental activity but rather to guard against the latter's becoming the totality and against the establishment of a simple identity between subject and object.

Jay's (1973) review of the Frankfurt group stresses this key theme, especially central to Adorno's writings, of *nonidentity:* the subject does not overwhelm the object and so define it entirely within its terms (as in pure idealism), nor does the object overwhelm the subject and so define it entirely within its terms (as in crude materialism).

This use of the materialist position marks my own critical analyses of the dominance of cognitivism in contemporary psychology (see Sampson, 1981a). I examine this theme in more detail in Part 4. The basic critical point, however, is the fresh vision of psychological work that a materialist refocusing brings about. One really does not clearly see the extensity of the subjectivism that marks much of contemporary psychology—its reduction of phenomena to the mental activities of the processing subject—until one has an alternative, materialist stance from which to view the field. The implications of this critical cutting edge for the analysis of justice, in particular for viewing its ideological functions, is likewise examined in more detail later. What should be clear at this point, however, is the degree to which the Frankfurt group employed materialism as a tool and as a weapon of critique.

IDEOLOGY CRITIQUE

If knowledge will make people free, then why aren't they? In one form or another the dilemma posed in this inquiry has been of never-ending concern to the critical perspective. The Enlightenment and the centuries that followed brought with them an exponential explosion in human knowledge and a parallel increase in the possibilities of extending the range of human control over nature and over life itself. Yet with this rapid growth in knowledge and control have come wars, genocidal destruction, poverty, and hunger: not enlightenment but the continuation and escalation of human misery and barbarism. There remains a deep core of unfreedom, domination, and exploitation. The early Greek union of knowledge, reason, and liberation has not worked out quite as anticipated:

If by enlightenment and intellectual progress we mean the freeing of man from sueprstitious belief in evil forces, in demons and fairies, in blind fate—in short, the emancipation from fear—then denunciation of what is currently called reason is the greatest service reason can render. (Horkheimer, 1974, p. 187)

This passage from Horkheimer is echoed in many ways throughout the literature of critical theory. It represents their concern with the *depth* to which the distortion and oppression of human potential has penetrated in the modern era: to the very deceit of the mind's power to reason; to the very core of real human subjectivity and agency. The theme in this passage also marks a somewhat different emphasis than one finds in the original Marxian answer to the opening inquiry. Both, however, open the door to a consideration of the essentially subjective and ideological side of the human enterprise. Ideology critique, where critique requires the reflection on systems that distort and constrain human experience in the name of human growth and development, becomes a central element in the analyses of critical theory.

For Marx

For Marx, the capitalist substructure created a superstructure consisting of the ideas and consciousness that masked the real relations between people; such ideas were ideological and thereby a false consciousness. History under capitalism was unfolding "behind the backs of the people." The real forces of production in which the contradictions and distortions of capitalism existed were concealed from awareness. In at least some interpretations of the Marxian outlook (e.g., Wellmer, 1971), history would undergo dramatic changes as the inexorable press of economic forces and the contradictions inherent in capitalism led to its historically necessary demise.

Although ideology was a prominent and necessary feature of capitalist existence in this view, ideology critique was only ambiguously related to eventual human emancipation. That is, if the economic forces were *inevitably* to be transformed as the contradictions inherent in capitalism built up to their breaking point, then the role that "knowledge" would play in this entire endeavor is not clear. For Wellmer, at least, Marx is ambiguous on this point: Is there an inherent logic to the historical process that will carry on to its conclusion or is consciousness of the process required to be its motive force?

If it is the former, then people and their consciousness are an "epiphenomenon of 'objective' conflicts between productive forces and conditions of production" (Wellmer, p. 97). If it is the latter, then an ideology critique designed to advance human knowledge and enlightenment is a key element in the transformative process.

Toward Freud

Among the major critical theorists (e.g., Adorno, Horkheimer, Marcuse, and, recently, Habermas), there was a major shift away from the mechanistic determinism of the economic substructure and toward the detailed examination of the superstructure of human consciousness itself. This is the essential turn toward Freud that the critical theorists added to the purely economic base of traditional Marxian understanding. In this endeavor, ideology critique was an essential step in the move towards liberation: knowledge and reason, not the sheer mechanics of history, were vital to societal transformation. This shift in emphasis, however, brought despair rather than joy to many of the founding theorists. Initially, it appeared that they could develop the kinds of understandings essential to human liberation; it soon became clear that the distortions of ideology ran deeply into the fabric of the culture and that of the individual's very being.

Some saw the person as constituted through language and thus profoundly shaped by social practice (e.g., Coward & Ellis, 1977). Thereby, the task of change was more akin to the psychoanalytic process of "working through" (e.g., Habermas, 1971) than to anything more direct or superficial. More knowledge would not be freeing, for the very forms in which that knowledge appeared were part and parcel of the prevailing systems of distortion.

This sense of despair over the possibility that knowledge could be liberating, and hence that the critique of ideology was an essential step in the process of societal transformation, emerges very clearly in the works of Adorno and Horkheimer. In one of their major joint efforts, the *Dialectic of Enlightenment*, they probe the depth to which the Enlightenment and its advocacy on behalf of human reason had been transmuted into a kind of instrumental rationality that eventually produced precisely the opposite: the domination rather than the freedom of humanity.

The Inversion of Mastery

The central theme of the Horkheimer and Adorno critique of the Enlightenment is their argument that in the pursuit of technical and instrumental control over the forces of nature, humanity has paid the price of domination and social control over its own nature. Horkheimer and Adorno employ the story of Odysseus's encounter with the Sirens as metaphor for the depth of distortion and sacrifice required of people: self-domination becomes the inevitable outcome of the human effort to control Nature. This is the inversion of mastery.

In Homer's account, the voyages of Odysseus take him into the regions of the tempting and dangerous Sirens. He has been warned that whoever hears their song, with its promise of happiness, will perish; yet he has no choice but to pass within their reach. So as to honor his contract and yet survive, Odysseus develops a strategy. He has his oarsmen's ears filled with wax so that they can row on without ever hearing the song. He has himself lashed tightly to the ship's mast, so that even as he hears, he will not be able to act. For Horkheimer and Adorno, this story represents the penetration of self-sacrifice and self-distortion—the transformation of second nature—that has emerged within the Western world as it has pursued the taming of first, or external nature. People are not simply dominated by the external world in which they live but have engaged in a self-domination so as to manage their lives.

A central point they derive from the story is the deceit of the human mind that results as people seek to conquer nature by first conquering what is nature in themselves: this is the dialectic of enlightenment. The forces marshaled to master nature turn about and become the forces that master those in whose name the mastery of nature was itself sought.

Horkheimer and Adorno see the subject seeking to govern the object (nature) and in this very process being swallowed up and destroyed. The identity between subject and object eventually destroys the subject itself. The dialectic represents the process whereby what begins affirmatively as the conquest, administration, and technical control of nature ends up creating just its opposite—namely, self-understandings from the viewpoint of technical control (see Schroyer, 1973, p. 218). The result is a technocratic consciousness or instrumentalized rationality in which the core of domination is both contained and concealed.

Odysseus's ploy is either not to hear (the fate of his men) or to hear impotently (his own fate): "temptation is neutralized and becomes a mere object of contemplation" (Horkheimer & Adorno, 1972, p. 34). The world of the mental (contemplation without action) takes precedence as the device with which to conquer nature and, in turn oneself. Thinking and reasoning become the measure of domination; but it is an administered thinking restricted to enslavement, not freedom.

Horkheimer and Adorno developed a treatise in which instrumental reason and the *Schein* of rationality (Schroyer, 1973, p. 211) respresent the core of human domination today and hence the target for an ideology critique designed to permit knowledge and reason to achieve their liberating effects. In answer to the opening question regarding the disjunction between knowledge and freedom today, the critical theorists would point to the form in which contemporary knowledge appears and the manner by which reasoning develops: the very forms of instrumental reason thwart the use of knowledge for anything other than further technical control and enslavement.

Marcuse's (1964) analysis of one-dimensionality and Habermas's (1971) analysis of the technical interest of knowledge (aspects of which I consider later) further develop this thesis in which "the unleashing of technical rationality is perceived to be the most decisive of all forms of domination of men by men" (Wellmer, 1971, p. 133). This same argument has pitted the critical perspective against the positivist version of science, especially in the realm of the human sciences (e.g., Habermas, 1971).

Instrumental Reason. Central to instrumental or technical rationality is the refusal to deal with ends or goals, instead focusing only on means. As Horkheimer (1974) comments, such reasoning is concerned primarily "with the adequacy of procedures for purposes more or less taken for granted" (p. 3), and ultimately "proves to be the ability to calculate probabilities and thereby to co-ordinate the right means with a given end" (p. 5). The ends themselves, however, are not included as part of such reasoning. According to positivism, ends or purposes are not considered to be a proper part of science because a decision among ends involves nonscientific issues of value.

Technical matters of control, rather than the purposes for which such control may be warranted, become central. "Practical questions, or questions about societal goals, are reduced in public discussion to technical questions: problems which can only be solved according to the objective standards of science and technology" (Schroyer, 1973, p. 218). Technical knowledge increases while knowledge about purposes, goals, or ends retreats; the latter fail to be developed as part of public examination and debate. Eventually, our core thinking processes turn to issues of technique, not ends.

Needless to say, once ends become covertly adopted as givens and remain unquestioned in the background, the existing structures of domination and privilege remain unchallenged in public discourse. Public concern focuses primarily on the manipulation of technique and the administration of means to achieve pregiven ends (see Cole, 1979, for some especially interesting examples of this approach in American as contrasted with Japanese industry).

The political domination of one group by another is thereby encouraged but carefully disguised by reformulating all matters in terms of technical or instrumental rationality. Social problems are defined as matters of technical control and management rather than as issues demanding a critical examination of the existing pattern of goals and interests. Those who benefit from the prevailing arrangements of society accomplish a political domination through the unquestioned acceptance of these arrangements and the understanding that rationality is restricted to instrumental themes.

Within and beyond Capitalism

I have been describing a shift in emphasis in critical theory from a version of Marx to a version of Freud. The former focuses on the almost mechanical way in which the economic substructure of capitalism, as its inner contradictions unfold, creates the conditions of its demise and its eventual replacement by a more humane form of social and economic organization. The intervention of human consciousness or knowledge is ambiguously related to this transformation; thus ideology critique tends to be relegated to a lesser standing. The shift from Marx toward Freud, however, introduces two themes.

The first examines the distortions in consciousness that have occurred as Western civilization abandoned a concern with questions of value and turned toward the primacy of questions of technique. Although the seeds of this mode appear early in human history, as Horkheimer and Adorno's use of Homer suggests, its nurturance and full growth required the development of highly technological and industrial societies: where mastery has become both means and end; where nature is no longer the alien-other to be tamed but the technical and political products of the human effort to tame nature have, instead, become the new problems (see Ogivly, 1979). This emphasizes the near totalizing role of instrumental reason in human affairs and the definition of intellect and reason in terms of primarily technical concerns.

The second theme examines the degree to which this form of reason has been impressed upon the human psyche. The distortions lie well beyond the grasp of reason itself: the very tools for reasoning are themselves part of the error to be eliminated. Thus the critique of ideology becomes central to the attempts to restore people to their rightful place as conscious actors who are able collectively to make their own history. This critical process demands a profound working through, akin to that of analytic therapy.

One consequence of this shift is that it encompasses more than capitalism in its indictment of forms of social organization that are unfreeing. The Soviet and fascist forms of clearly totalitarian domination are unequivocally included as part of the problem, not the solution. An error of understanding has gripped many of those, especially in the United States, who have either pursued or rejected the implications of the critical perspective. Some of its followers have foolishly assumed that their only enemy is capitalism; unlike Horkheimer and Adorno, among others, they have failed to observe the enemies of human freedom that abound in totalitarian social forms that are noncapitalist.

On the other hand, many of those who have automatically rejected the critical view have likewise been foolish in their assumption that to embrace its tenets is to embrace the Soviet or Chinese forms of organization. The main message of the critical perspective is its opposition to all forms that dominate and enslave humanity, including those that seem to be freeing while, in the critical view, they are actually grounded in exploitation and domination. Capitalism remains central to their indictment. It has the sure appearance of freedom and rationality, even as its domination necessitates a profoundly ideological distortion. This makes the task of an ideology critique more central even as that task faces its most formidable opponent.

EMANCIPATORY KNOWLEDGE

One of the premier contemporary critical theorists, Habermas (1971), observed that within the human sciences, only Freud's psychoanalytic theory and practice served what he termed an emancipatory rather than a purely technical interest because it is the only "tangible example of a science incorporating methodical self-reflection" (p. 214); the understanding that is eventually reached has causal and explanatory power:

Psychoanalysis does not grant us a power of technical control over the sick psyche comparable to that of biochemistry over a sick organism. And yet it achieves more than a mere treatment of symptoms, because it certainly does grasp causal connections, although not at the level of physical events . . . . The causal connection between the original scene, defense, and symptom is not anchored in the invariance of nature according to natural laws but only in the spontaneously generated invariance of life history . . . which can . . . be dissolved by the power of reflection. (p. 271)

In this formulation, Habermas has built upon the Hegelian distinction between a *causality of nature* and a *causality of fate*. The former describes causal connections that represent an invariant relation between nature's laws of the physical universe. The causal connections of the latter, by contrast, have emerged during the course of an individual's life history and refer to second or learned nature. These kinds of invariance can be dissolved through reflection and the powers of reason: for example, particular early-life traumas, such as the "laws" of the Oedipal triangle, can be dissolved through a certain kind of therapeutic discourse. Habermas's encounter with the peculiar causal properties of the psychoanalytic theory and practice expands on several themes that the founding critical theories viewed as essential.

Theory and Practice

Basic to understanding the nature of emancipatory knowledge is an understanding of human agency and the role of knowledge in human action. This theme is commonly seen in terms of the relation between theory and practice: that is, the way that the knowledge about the causal properties of personal and social pathologies (the theory) can affect and transform one's actual behavior (the practice). Thus emancipation is concerned with the connection between theory and practice, between the comprehension of distortions and their practical transformation in action.

Because people can use language and discourse to reflect upon their own actions, we require a different understanding of the role of causal laws in human affairs as compared with the laws of physical nature. People act in terms of their knowledge and their understanding of their circumstances. The knowledge that people obtain about the laws that govern their actions can operate to transform those very laws.

The boundary conditions involved with laws in the social sciences include as a basic element the knowledge that actors, in a given institutional context, have about the circumstances of their action . . . . Self-fulfilling or self-negating prophecies, in other words, are seen as predictions which, by the fact of their announcement or propagation, serve to create the conditions which render them valid, or alternatively produce the contrary consequence . . . . It becomes clear [therefore] that every generalization or form of study that is concerned with an existing society constitutes *a potential intervention within that society*. (Giddens, 1979, pp. 244–245)

People can and do reflect on the conditions of their life; the knowledge they obtain about those conditions becomes part of the base of resources which they employ to reproduce or transform those very conditions. The potential for knowledge that transforms practice is thus part of the very quality that constitutes humanity: language and discourse. Emancipatory knowledge, however—that is, theory that is ripe with practical consequences—does not invariably issue from all forms of knowledge. Ideology in particular serves to entrap action in routine and unfree ways. As Ricoeur (1972) observes,

ideology is a distortion stemming from violence and repression, comparable to the effects of censorship as described by Freudian psychoanalysis, with the result that ideology is an effect of meaning for which the subject lacks the key. In principle, an ideology is not aware of itself as an ideology. (p. 159)

If they are to be effectively dissolved and emancipated from their causal net, these systematically distorted meanings—or, as Habermas terms them, *sup-*

pressed dialogues—that characterize ideological or nonemancipatory knowledge demand the engagement of the same critical, self-reflective ability as is implicated in psychoanalytic working through.

The telos of analysis, therefore, is to return to the subject the lost or renounced powers of self-reflection and thus to restore real self-direction. Habermas interprets Freud's thinking on this matter—*Wo Es war, soll Ich werden*—as meaning a return of reflexive self-awareness and agency to replace the nonreflexivity or "itness" of the forces that propel from behind one's back. Thus, where "itness" was, "I-ness" will become.

In the emancipatory interest of knowledge we find the interweaving of theory with practice. Again, calling upon Freud's model, Habermas observes that it is one of the few in which the very test of the theory is to be found in transformative practice. The truth of the theoretical assertions is validated against a changed course of behavior and experience for the individual. In like manner, "The truth of critical social theory is a *vérité à faire;* in the last resort it can demonstrate its truthfulness only by successful liberation" (Wellmer, 1971, p. 72). The suitable testing ground for the validity of the propositions of critical theory lies in the erosion in reality and everyday practice of the structures that distort and constrain human freedom and self-determination. In this, the critical theorists echo Marx's thesis "that the meaning of history can be recognized theoretically to the degree that human beings undertake to make it true practically" (see Habermas, 1973, p. 248). The validity test for a theory is the successful transformation of the constraints to real human subjectivity and agency: the making of history with will and with consciousness. Only in its realization in a new form of life that is free from domination and open to the formation of a public will can a theory of the good life be validated: a practical change, not a pure theoretical enlightenment.

And Traditional Psychological Theory

It is important to observe that the emancipatory interest that is the telos of critical theory is by no means represented in what Horkheimer (1972) has described as traditional scientific theories. It is a recurrent theme of my own writings that most psychological theories, including those dealing with matters of justice, have overly represented a nonemancipatory focus. I will shortly develop the thesis that psychological theories, for the most part, have tended to serve ideological functions: to stifle rather than advance human agency and subjectivity by helping to reproduce the very social arrangements that sustain systematically distorted understanding.

The very positivist thrust of much psychological work, especially its concern with a technical control over human processes that parallels the control achieved over nature, reflects a counter emancipatory possibility (see Bandura, 1982, for one example). I develop this thesis in later chapters and so wish only to connect it at this time with the impact of the critical perspective on my own thinking about psychology.

CONCLUSION

Let me repeat the point with which I opened this chapter. My intent was not to provide an in-depth analysis, overview, or even carefully reasoned critical commentary on the body of materials issuing from critical theory. My intent has been to outline the key messages that I gleaned from a reading and a reflection on these works. This has provided me with the basis of many of my own insights and analyses regarding psychology today. It is my contention that all those who submit themselves to this same body of literature are likely to have an enlightening experience and thus to emerge somewhat transformed by this immersion.

This sometimes puzzling body of work is not a logically tight, cogently argued, irrefutable theory. Rather, as even Adorno was wont to acknowledge, it is a somewhat loosely connected, variously argued, mixed bag with a set of dominant messages which emerge clearly through the bits, pieces, and fragments that pass for the critical perspectives. It is somewhat like a complex mosaic: when you see it up close, it is only a series of colored bits; from a distance, however, some patterns emerge, some dominant figures and themes. It is an inviting mosaic, however viewed; a challenging perspective especially for those closely trained in traditional psychological science.

The Critique of Pure Psychology

We are now at a point at which it is possible to pull together the bits and pieces of the critical perspective and apply them both to the general study of psychology and its application to understanding justice. My intent is to build a firm basis for challenging the deep structures of the existing approach to psychological analysis.

This concern is metapsychological. I am not seeking to develop just another theory within the existing framework of psychology but rather to open that framework to question and, by implication, to recommend a different form for the field. It is my contention that additional theories within the present frame will only serve to perpetuate the very distortions that have guided our psychological science to date. We do not need simply more theories of the same sort; we need a new base from which to derive those kinds of theory that will make a practical difference in human affairs.

So that I may develop the main outlines of this critique, I must be permitted a few liberties. Perhaps the one major liberty, however, is to be able to speak of psychology as though it were somehow a monolith without differentiated parts. In one sense this is not an inappropriate image. There is a recognizable mainstream in the diversity that is psychology, represented by the major journals, figureheads, papers, theories, studies, and so forth with which every graduate student is expected to have some familiarity. Furthermore, there is a common historical heritage.

In addition, the liberty I seek is one that I had others have routinely taken in generating the previous critiques of the discipline (e.g., Buss, 1979; Cronbach, 1975; Gergen, 1973; Riegel, 1979). Finally, there is the common Western heritage of scientific psychology, a version of both the methodology and the underlying philosophy that emerged during the 16th and 17th centuries, that was refined over the following several hundred years and that so significantly advanced the natural sciences.

We have become accustomed to thinking about the *three* psychologies: psychoanalysis, behaviorism, and humanism. As though this division were not sufficient to challenge the monolithic assumption guiding this section, we are also familiar with the great diversity that lies within each of these so-called movements within psychology. There are many varieties of analysis, behaviorism, and humanism.

Let me quickly dispense with more of this review. It is sufficient for me to note that I am well aware of the great and apparent diversity that describes our discipline of psychology; yet I believe it meaningful to speak of a psychology in general. The deep structures made up of the shared premises and assumptive framework that underly this apparent diversity is the primary focus of my analysis and critique.

When I write about "pure psychology," I refer to a field that is built upon three major foundations, whatever particular diversity it may take as we move away from that base: (1) a positivist–empiricist approach to knowledge; (2) a truncated understanding of human subjectivity; (3) a romance with abstracted individualism. These three building blocks describe what I term pure psychology; each provides the focus for a chapter in this section.

CHAPTER SEVEN

Positivist Empiricism versus Alternatives to the Objectivist Illusion

Many works have been written describing the history of positivism, the challenges of traditional positivism, its rebuttal, and so forth: for example, Adorno, Albert, Dahrendorf, Habermas, Pilot, and Popper (1976), Husserl (1965), Giorgi (1976), and Harre and Secord (1972), to name only a few in this vast literature. So many treatises have been forthcoming over the years that it is somewhat surprising to see the central tenets of positivism still prevailing in the discipline. I believe that its perseverance is less a testimony either to the absence of any significant challenges or its great success as such than it is a matter of its societal suitability. It will not serve my present purposes, however, to dredge up this material and restate the details of the debates. Rather, let me simply address myself to what may be considered to be two central tenets of the positivist–empiricist approach to knowledge in psychology and the other human sciences: (1) the privileging of immediate experience and (2) the search for universal laws.

THE PRIVILEGING OF IMMEDIATE EXPERIENCE

Empirical observation (i.e., sensory experience) is the essential basis of our knowledge about reality and for determining the truth or falsity of our propositions about human activity. Objectivity in our science, therefore, demands that we validate our assertions about reality against our own and others' observations of that reality; intersubjective agreement is the key to determining what is and what is not an objectively verifiable or falsifiable assertion.

In this view, there is an essential dependency between the certainty of what is known and the experience of the subject as knower. The subject's experience provides a copy of reality; the accuracy of the copy or its correspondence with reality is assured through the methods of empirical inquiry and intersubjective agreement: checking my copy with yours. No interaction is assumed between the activities of the subject and the body of facts copied by the subject's sensory experience. The facts exist independently "out there" and are available to any competent observer.

A key assumption is that a language of observation exists that is based on the direct experience of reality and is thereby free from theoretical biases. This convenient fiction (i.e., the purity of an observational language) implies that there are statements about reality that are intelligible in the same way to all members of the community, thus assuring intersubjectivity. As discussed by Keat and Urry (1975), such statements are said to be *ontologically privileged* because they refer to genuinely real, existing things in the world. We already know them to be *epistemologically privileged* because only empirical observations can be known with a high degree of certainty, as contrasted with the lesser certainty of theoretical and nonobservational forms.

Critics have termed this preceding state of affairs the *objectivist illusion*. The belief that there is a self-subsistent world of facts "conceals the transcendental basis of the world of facts, the generation of meaning from structures of experience and action" (McCarthy, 1978, p. 41). A subject-free or subjectless epistemology conceals the collective and historical activities of human communities that generate the very world of facts that are taken to be independent of their formation in social life. As Wellmer (1971) has commented, "In the social sciences this leads to a misrepresentation of the object under scrutiny and to an accommodating conformism on the part of the scientists" (p. 14).

THE SEARCH FOR UNIVERSAL LAWS

Positivist science seeks to develop theories that reveal the recurring regularities among the observed relationships in reality. Universal laws are generated on the basis of these empirical regularities. Explanation involves demonstrating that a specific event is an instance of the universal law.

True to their Humean heritage, universal laws refer only to empirically observed regularities, not to logical or necessary connections between events. Laws express nonnecessary connections between events, the truth or falsity of which must be empirically determined. The purpose of theories is to provide the set of universal laws employed in explaining the phenomena of interest. Theories permit *explanation* as well as *prediction* and *control*. These three mark the understanding of proper science that most psychologists learn early in their training.

As some critics have observed (e.g., Bhaskar, 1979; Maruyama, 1979, 1980; Wilden, 1980), this formulation works well but only in *closed systems*:

that is, in systems of a primarily mechanical sort in which one can find a reasonably invariant relationship between the parts. Unless we incorrectly understand human life, society, and history to be a closed system, the feasibility of this positivist requirement is shattered.

The self-reflective quality of human agency—people reflect on their actions and so modify their behavior in light of their knowledge of it—introduces an open rather than a closed system as the necessary basis for analysis. Human affairs function nonmechanistically; there is an ongoing interchange between the system and whatever is taken to be its environment. Living systems are necessarily open in that their survival requires this interchange with their environment. The effects of self-reflection and this kind of interchange introduce possibilities for evolution and transformation (i.e., morphogenesis) of the structural relationships among the elements of the open system (e.g., see Maruyama, 1979, 1980). The term *morphogenesis* describes a changing pattern of relationships in response to information exchanges rather than the kind of static and mechanical closure that is useful only when dealing with closed systems.

The mechanical view required under the positivist form of analysis does not obtain in open sysems; the conjunction between explanation, prediction, and control likewise does not hold in any simple or direct way. In spite of this, the positivist thesis remains strong, perhaps because "It supplied the social engineers of the industrial system with the legitimation of measures in accordance with the dominant value system" (Wellmer, 1971, p. 21).

Several important alternatives to the positivist–empiricist world view are available for us to examine. What some refer to as the *realist* metatheory and others describe as *naturalism* introduces one kind of alternative to the objectivist illusion and mechanistic quality of positivism. Another alternative is represented by *hermeneutics*. Finally, certain *poststructuralist* perspectives seek both to offer an alternative and to bridge the gap between realism and hermeneutics.

REALISM

The realist metatheory (e.g., Bhaskar, 1979; Harre, 1970; Harre & Madden, 1975; Keat & Urry, 1975) builds much of its case against the positivist–empiricist view by challenging the Humean understanding of causality on which positivism is based. Several additional questions also emerge concerning the empiricist approach to knowledge. The Humean view argues that a cause–effect relationship exists whenever there is a constant, recurring conjunction between two events in which one temporally precedes the other. Our actual observations never reveal anything more than, for example, billiard ball A touching ball B which then moves from its otherwise stationary position. We say that A causes the movement in B. What we really mean, according to the Humean account, is that A temporally precedes B, and, on all the occasions on which we have made our observations, the touching of B by A is followed immediately by B's movement. There is nothing more to the matter: empirically observed, recurring regularities between events.

To the realist, on the other hand, this Humean regularity theory does not go far enough. A regularly recurring empirical relation between A and B gives us *reason to suppose* that there may be a causal connection; but when we speak of causality, we mean somthing more than that (see Ginsburg, undated). According to the realist perspective, we must, if we are to speak of causation, search for the *underlying mechanism* that links A and B together and that serves to generate B from A.

One example of a realist approach is found in Harre's (1970; also see Keat & Urry, 1975) challenge to Hume's analysis of a vibrating string that causes a particular sound. In the Humean account, all that is meant is that when string A vibrates, sound B regularly occurs. Harre observes that we are now able to describe the actual underlying mechanisms by which the vibrations in A produce the sounds of B; further, when we say that A causes B, we mean something more than their mere temporal contiguity. We intend all that the underlying mechanisms of sonics in physics and the neurophysiology of hearing imply.

As long as the Humean account is sustained, an empiricist perspective makes sense. In this view, our task is simply to record all the regularly recurring constant conjunctions of empirically observed events, evolve laws based on them and then explain and predict phenomena as instances of these laws. However, once a realist position is introduced, the task becomes more complex, especially in that the underlying mechanisms we seek are typically nonempirical structures whose presence must be inferred in order to explain the phenomena that are observable. We search for the underlying generative structures and cannot rest comfortably with the surface features that are observable. As we will later see, this point is especially relevant to considerations involving the concept of ideology and false consciousness when "what is real is not necessarily true": that is, the reality we empirically observe may be systematically distorted; all analyses that fail to probe beneath its appearances to the underlying generative structures and mechanisms are therefore potentially distorted and ideological.

HERMENEUTICS

A dilemma that confronts those who seek to grasp the essentials and the nuances of human life involves the apparent contrast between people and physical objects. People think, plan, delay, anticipate. People respond in terms of the meanings that events have for them and not simply in terms of the bare qualities of a presenting stimulus. Is there not therefore a difference between the pathways to knowledge that must be followed for those probing the complexities of a meaning-endowing-and-responding creature as opposed to those who probe the features of the physical world? Indeed, billiard balls in motion do not seem to intend their motion or to act in terms of wishes, aspirations, or goals. People do. And, although it was a significant advance for the physical sciences to rid themselves of "intending qualities" for their subject matter—the orbits of the planets are not intentionally chosen by them—perhaps the ready parallels to human behavior are neither proper nor accurate.

Questions of this sort have led to a distinction between those sciences that employ a positivist–empiricist approach to *explain* the behavior of the objects of the physical world and those sciences of human behavior that must employ a differently cast view—not in order to explain but rather to *understand* people and their lives. In these latter sciences, the aim must be to grapple with the meanings that are central to human activity; meanings can only be grasped by an approach that employs *Verstehen* on the part of the investigator.

To understand human life, one must gain access to the web of meanings that guide people's behavior. It is not sufficient to gaze from afar or from the outside. Rather, one must become a part of the subject's community of understanding in order to grasp the meanings and rules he or she employs in guiding actions. This demands a kind of anthropology for the social scientist, who must join the community under study in order to grasp the meanings involved in the actions of the community members. In this view, interpretative understanding or *verstehen* is the essential ingredient to understanding within the human sciences (see Rabinow & Sullivan, 1979).

It is clear that insofar as different cultures, communities, and historical moments create different webs of meanings and rules to govern their actions, there cannot be a single, universal standard by which human behavior can be grasped. In essence, there is no privileged language of *literal* observation to be applied to all human actions, no basic set of building blocks that constructs any and all realities regardless of their time and place: that is, no epistemologically or ontologically privileged outside position. The investigator must gain access to the only privileged knowledge that does exist, namely, the point of view of the participants in the situation under study. Therefore, only *indexical*, that is contextually bound, rather than literal analysis is possible (see Bar-Hillel, 1954; Garfinkel, 1967).

Commentary

I hasten to note at this point that the realist and hermeneutic alternatives to the positivist–empiricist metatheory differ between themselves. Furthermore, several analysts (e.g., Bhaskar, 1979; Giddens, 1979) have argued that the hermeneutic point of view has more in common with the positivist thesis than initially meets the eye. In this view, therefore, the realist position represents the only serious alternative to positivism.

It is not essential to my position to examine this latter argument, although parts of it will appear in my emerging critique of pure psychology. It is important to note, however, that of these two general alternatives to the positivist account, the one that has been gaining most substantially within some of the human sciences (e.g., especially the microsociological emphasis of ethnomethodology and the phenomenological and humanist perspectives within psychology) has taken off in the hermeneutic–interpretative direction. Although its emphasis on the meaning-dependent quality of human life is clearly a central and necessary aspect of any acceptable approach, by deleting the real underlying structural bases that generate "meanings," hermeneutics falls too readily into alignment with a purely subjectivist analysis akin to the subject-dependent position of positivism. More recently, a third alternative to challenge the dominance of the positivist–empiricist model has developed, one that appears to join the best of both the realist and the hermenuetic accounts.

A POSTSTRUCTURALIST SYNTHESIS

The third contender that has recently appeared on the international scene enlarges and, I believe, deepens the nature of the debate against positivism and introduces some serious possibilities for an alternative view. For want of a better term, I shall refer to this as the *poststructuralist* turn most generally represented by work coming out of France and centering on some of the ideas of Lacan (see Coward & Ellis, 1977; Lemaire, 1977; Turkle, 1978; Wilden, 1980) and Derrida (1974, 1978, 1981) among others. Aspects of this view are appearing in the U.S. tradition, especially in the emerging focus on metaphor (e.g., Lakoff & Johnson, 1980; Winter, 1981).

I see this alternative as attempting a synthesis of the realist and hermeneutic perspectives: it uses the properties of language (the hermeneutic moment) and the fixing of meanings in language by social structural and historical practices (the realist moment) in order to develop a model for understanding and transforming human life. As the prefix *post* implies, this movement both builds upon and goes beyond the historical precedessors of structuralism, especially as represented in the linguistic analyses of Saussure (1959) and the probings of myth and kinship revealed in Lévi-Strauss's contributions (1968a, 1968b; also see Kurzweil, 1980).

Although I am not interested in unfolding the full scope of poststructuralism, it will be helpful to our understanding of its status as a kind of synthesizing alternative to positivism to review some of its central thoughts. Language and symbolic practices are key components of the poststructuralist movement: "Because all the practices that make up a social totality take place in language it becomes possible to consider language as the place in which the social individual is constructed" (Coward & Ellis, 1977, p. 1).

The language system that so intrigued the structuralists was a rather rigid and formal system; the language practices that inform poststructuralism are rather more like the unconscious and thus appear fluid and artistic, not formal. As Wilden (1980) has observed, the shift is from a kind of digital view, with its precise binary categories of either/or and its logic of identity, to a kind of analogue view, where the precision of binarism and the logic of identity yield to the more fluid transitions of the nonidentity logic of both/ and: a world of difference, not neat opposition.

Given the centrality of language to all human endeavors, the basic tenet of the poststructuralist analysis is to employ language as the key to unlock the riddles of human existence. Saussure originally argued that the elements of language are not substances or entities but relations of difference. Once we enter the world of linguistic practices, we enter a world in which relations rather than entities are central.

For example, the sound elements (what Saussure referred to as "signifiers") of a language have no intrinsic or inherent meaning but are discernible only in terms of their differences from other elements within the system. The sound "a" is what it is only by virtue of its being different from all other sound elements, such as "b," "c," and so forth. Context and location within a system thereby become the critical aspects of language analysis and the analysis of all human practices: the focus is on relations, not entities. This insistence on context and on the irreducibility of elements to something inherent in them as substances already stands in defiance of the positivist demand for literal meanings or context-independent terms.

There is more to language, however, than this systemic quality. A further characteristic that is central to the poststructuralist frame involves the extent to which language processes share a fundamental similarity with the kinds of dynamics that Freud uncovered to describe the unconscious: processes of metaphor are said to parallel condensation and metonymy is said to parallel displacement. In other words, processes that are seen to be basic to language parallel processes that were described as characterizing the unconscious.

Metaphorical usage involves condensation in that whole scences and complex distinctions are represented by a single substitution: for example, an argument is metaphorically described as being like a war (see Lakoff & Johnson, 1980). Metonymy and displacement are said to be parallel in that one element is used to refer to another: for example, "The *ham sandwich* is waiting for his check" (Lakoff & Johnson, p. 35) is used to describe the person who had ordered the ham sandwich who is now waiting for the check.

These properties of language and of signifying practice suggest the inevitable need for a kind of hermeneutics of deciphering in order to grasp meanings. In addition, these linguistic qualities suggest the inevitable slippage of meanings within everyday life and discourse. This view, therefore, informs us of the inadequacy of any purely objectivist approach to understanding. In other words, if meanings are constituted through a process akin to metaphor, then not only must there be a deciphering in order to gain access to such meaning (and hence an interpretative base for the human sciences, including psychology), but, in addition, it is meaningless to expect to find a single, objective frame within which to grasp meaning, truth, reality, and so forth.

This position has recently been developed by two American linguistic scholars, Lakoff and Johnson (1980), who argue persuasively that all meaning in language is metaphorical in nature and thus "the way we think, what we experience, and what we do every day is very much a matter of metaphor" (p. 3). Therefore, there can never be a purely objectivist base or ground for meaning; as they observe, "Truth is therefore not absolute or objective but is based on understanding" (p. 197). Their challenge to the objectivist illusion of positivism derives both from their analysis of metaphor as the base of human experience and from the properties of metaphor.

The Realist Moment

The realist or materialist moment of this seemingly subjectivist analysis appears at two key places: first, in the social nature of language; second, in the role that social practices play in fixing certain meanings or metaphorical linkages over others. People are formed in and constituted by their language; they are subjected to it rather than being entirely its masters:

> The lesson of this . . . was that man is to be understood as constructed by the symbol and not as the point of origin of symbolism. The individual, even prior to his or her birth, is always already subject-ed to the structure into which he or she is born. The structure is what sets in place an experience for the subject which it includes. This demands a radical re-estimation of the position of the individual; it should no longer be possible to adhere to the notion of the individual as embodying some ideal pre-given essence. Being always subject-ed, the subject can never be the transcendental . . . source. (Coward & Ellis, 1977, pp. 3–4)

The systems of signifying practice are aspects of the underlying material culture: the distinctions that are linguistically drawn and the kinds of metaphorical connections that are made—a culture's root metaphors (Pepper, 1961; Winter, 1981)—arise within, reflect, and reproduce a particular sociohistorical arrangement. The signifying practices that cast our very being in one form rather than another, that direct our conceptual system, that shape our understanding and our experience of self, others, and life are part and parcel of particular sociohistorical practices.

Illustrative Metaphors

Let us briefly examine three metaphors that I believe illustrate the way in which social practices fix the otherwise variable and fluid flow of metaphorical usage, producing one particular world view rather than another: (1) the metaphor "Argument is war"; (2) the "conduit" metaphor; (3) the "mechanism" metaphor. The first two derive from the account developed by Lakoff and Johnson (1980); the third stems from the writings of Pepper (1961) and especially Winter (1981).

1. Lakoff and Johnson suggest how metaphorical usage structures our conceptualzation and experience. They observe that in defining an argument as if it were a war, we speak about "indefensible claims," "attacking the opponents weakest point," "shooting down the opponents argument," and so forth. In other words, we fix the otherwise potentially wide range of meta-

phorical meanings by connecting one concept (argument) with another (war) and thereby experiencing all arguments as though they were like wars, to be won and lost. They note a different cultural possibility

> where arguments are not viewed in terms of war, where no one wins or loses, where there is no sense of attacking or defending . . . a culture where an argument is viewed as a dance, the participants . . . performers, and the goal . . . to perform in a balanced an aesthetically pleasing way. (pp. 4–5)

2. Lakoff and Johnson offer the "conduit" metaphor as similarly expressing a particular cultural preference, in this case, for viewing "ideas and meanings as objects," "linguistic expressions as containers," and "communication as sending" (see Lakoff & Johnson, 1980, p. 10). In this example, we see the objectivist illusion which their notion of metaphorical conceptualization attacks: the view of ideas and meanings as though they were objects that could be placed in linguistic containers and sent merrily on their way from a sender to a receiver, who simply opens up the container and removes them. This metaphor fixes our experience of thoughts (sentences, ideas, meanings, and so on) as though they had "meanings in themselves, independent of any context or speaker" (p. 11).

This cultural metaphor makes it seem as though meanings were intrinsic to the words used, as though words were simply some kind of objective marker of reality. To illustrate the failure of this conduit world view, Lakoff and Johnson introduce the following sentence: "Please sit in the apple-juice seat" (p. 12). They observe how the meaning does not inhere in the words but demands a context for its proper rendering. In this case, the overnight guests are arriving for breakfast, and all but one place at the table has orange juice. The remaining place or seat is the apple-juice seat. The statement directs the guest to take it. Yet, our culture fixes the conduit meaning and thus highlights one world view while suppressing or hiding other possibilities.

3. Winter (1981; also see Pepper, 1961; Sarbin, 1977) describes the root metaphor of contemporary Western civilization as being like a mechanism. The world is seen as if it were a great machine, organized technically and around the mechanical press of forces. He observes how "we operate on a linear, mathematical time line that often has little to do with personal or biological rhythms. We measure on linear scales what can only be measured in terms of a space-time that grows and unfolds" (pp. 1–2). In other words, our industrialized modern culture fixes the root metaphor in terms of a mechanistic image rather than in terms of the rhythms of "life and nature."

Each of these three examples reveals how what is otherwise freely moving within signifying practice becomes fixed in a certain position by the ongoing practices and institutions of a particular society and civilization. A fourth example, one I believe to be central both to our civilization and to psychology's deep structure, the fixing of the concept of personhood, will be examined in more depth in Chapter 9. As we will see, it too reflects a highlighting and a hiding (to borrow Lakoff & Johnson's terminology), focusing our experience around one set of meanings while supressing other possibilities.

Derrida's Challenge to Empiricism

Before moving on from the poststructuralist challenge to the positivist–empiricist domination of modern psychology to other aspects of my critique of pure psychology, one further element should be put into place: Derrida's challenge to the empiricist notion of an immediate rather than a mediated present. Jacques Derrida (1974, 1978, 1981) is a contemporary French philosopher who has built his analysis around language but has challenged what he calls the *phonocentrism* (that is, speech primacy) of most linguistic analyses.

Derrida locates himself within the tradition of Freud, Nietzsche, and Heidegger (and *we* might add, Marx), all of whom have introduced a radical challenge to the immediacy of self-consciousness within the Western philosophical frame. It is Derrida's thesis that the apparent immediacy of consciousness to itself is incorrect: what appears immediate is always already mediated by a memory trace. In other words, what appears to be an unmediated present, a pure and direct experience, is always already inhabited by an absent trace. He refers to this trace in various ways, using writing rather than speaking to illustrate what he means: writing substitutes an inscription for the otherwise present standing of speech.

Derrida's complex argument is that writing (broadly understood as anything that is akin to a nonpresent trace) is prior to speaking: what we take to be immediate and present builds upon the nonpresent inscription that informs it. Derrida's analysis parallels Freud's challenge to the certainty of self-consciousness. Both challenge any purely empiricist position that builds certainty upon what we presume to be immediately sensed in our present awareness.

Ricoeur (1970, 1979) captures this challenge in the following passage describing the fundamental illusion of Western civilization as that illusion which bears the hallowed name of self-consciousness. This illusion is the fruit of a preceding victory, which conquered the previous illusion of the *thing*. The philosopher trained in the school of Descartes knows that things are doubtful, that they are not what they appear to be. But he never doubts that consciousness is as it appears to itself. In consciousness, meaning and the consciousness of meaning coincide. Since Marx, Nietzsche, and Freud, however, we doubt even this. After doubting the thing, we have begun to doubt consciousness. (Ricoeur, 1979, p. 328)

Insofar as the empiricist position builds upon the ground of certainty provided by the immediacy of self-consciousness, the Derridian challenge to the immediacy of self-consciousness poses serious questions about the very grounds of empiricist certainty. Derrida's analysis suggests that the inscriptions that inhabit the apparent immediacy of presence are cultural products akin to the positioning of metaphorical usages that we previously noted. What we thereby take to be immediate and the ground for the certainty of our observations is mediated by traces; these are culturally produced forms for experiencing. As Ricoeur has observed, this analysis provides a profound challenge to the very house of mastery which we have built and in which we reside.

Although I have not attempted to develop the full scope or intricate base of argumentation for his position, Derrida's contribution to the poststructuralist movement casts further doubt upon the positivist–empiricist base which still dominates our psychological world view. His analysis leads us to be doubtful about the purity of our observations and the language that we use to convey what we believe we see immediately and without mediation.

For the most part, metatheoretical discussions of this sort within psychology only slowly seep into the mainstream and somewhat influence the approaches that are employed. Journals continue to abound with research that is primarily within the purview of the positivist–empiricist view, stressing refined statistical and computer-based methodologies or ingenious experimental manipulation rather than exploring the base structures and mechanisms of the very science that is thereby practiced.

CHAPTER EIGHT

Psychology and Subjectivity
A Truncated Analysis

Two general approaches to knowledge have varied in their dominance throughout Western history. The first, associated with idealism, adopts a skepticism about matter and so locates the ground for whatever certainty of knowledge is possible within human reason and mental events. The second, associated with materialism, adopts a skepticism toward reason and emphasizes the difference between the objects of mentation and the objects of reality; it grounds certainty in the material reality from which mental processes are said to develop. The idealist position sees "the notion" to be first and reality second; the materialist position reverses this ordering, seeing reality to have dominance over the notion (see Colletti, 1979). Where idealism emphasizes the spontaneity of human thought, materialism emphasizes its receptivity to external determination.

Kant sought a resolution of those two opposing points of domination. He argued that even as thinking required something other than itself in order to be thought, thinking was nevertheless a process with principles of its own: we have both sensibiilty (the materialist moment) and understanding (the idealist moment). Thought is not the totality, because the world of objects in themselves must exist for there to be something of which thought is a representation. Yet, neither is sensuous or material reality the totality, for the processes of the understanding are transcendent and give the manifold of sense impressions their form of organization.

Kant, however, let thinking appear to prevail in stressing the essential unknowability of things in themselves. This easily led to a primacy of the transcendent and presumably universal principles of human understanding as the real ground for all knowledge. In addition, the universalization of things mental and the correlative emphasis on individual acts of knowing reduced both history and society to mere backdrops for the main event. It required a more dialectical approach, partly initiated by Hegel and further developed by Marx, among others, to pull together the strands otherwise missing in the Kantian attempt.

For Hegel and Marx, the synthesis suggested in the Kantian view was not entirely a matter of individual mental activity; it was generated on the basis of social and historical activity, in particular, work. In agreement with Kant and in opposition to the copy theories of pure empiricism (see Chapter 7), Marx argued that the world of objects was not simply given but was a synthetic construction. The issue, however, is to pinpoint the locus of that constructive process. Is it within the mind of the individual, as the idealists and Kant maintained? Or does it lie in the social sphere of human work? For Marx, it is within the latter that we see the significant bases of knowledge construction: *there is an essential form-giving quality to human productive activity.*

It is important to grasp this essenial distinction. Kant stressed the spontaneity of the human mind in constituting the phenomenal world. Synthesis was a result of the operations of the mind. Although for Marx there was a similar spontaneity to human understanding, the synthesis was not given in mind but in material production. Kant therefore introduces an idealist synthesis while Marx introduces a material synthesis. Whereas for Kant the categories of the mind constitute the world, for Marx there is a form-giving quality to the practical endeavors of human work and production. One central implication of this distinction pertains to the absolute and universal quality of the mental synthesis in the Kantian system as contrasted with the historical quality of the Marxian material synthesis: work and production change historically; thus their form-giving qualities result in a consciousness that has a historical dimension.

This dialectical effort, while separating the two processes, granted neither primacy nor totality to either one but emphasized their essential interpenetration within any actual moment of human history. It was not adequate to understand the dynamics of thought as somehow transcending the ongoing life and history of people. Nor was it adequate to understand the processes of human life in full independence from the notions and ideas that people formed about themselves and their world. Either pole—that is, either a purely mechanistic materialism, reducing the individual's mental processes to a mere copy of the underlying social order, or a truncated subjectivism, granting ontological primacy to the mental processes of the individual—was seen as an adequate representation of the actual dialectical processes involved. The structures and mechanisms of the objective social process that fashions individuals are also fashioned in and through the activities of those individuals.

Furthermore, both objects in reality and objects in thought do not retain an eternal identity in themselves but rather reveal at any one moment a particular stage of social development. The dialectical process thereby is not grasped by reifying the two elements (i.e., subject and object), but only by seeing how their interpenetration itself varies historically.

AND PSYCHOLOGY

Over the years, psychology has had its romance with one or the other perspective or, in some cases, has aligned itself with one side by denying the relevance of the other: radical behaviorism, for example, has eschewed any references to consciousness and subjectvity. Psychological ecology (e.g., Barker, 1965, 1968; Wicker, 1979) represents one of the clearest statements in which mental events derive from the structure of the environment. On the other side, the more cognitively oriented psychologies portray an active, somewhat Kantian subject whose internal mental processes hold the key to understanding human behavior.

Although I have not undertaken any systematic body count, it is my impression, shared with others (e.g., Cartwright, 1979), that this cognitivist view has become increasingly dominant within the discipline. The basic thesis of cognitivism is its argument that structures and processes within the individual's mind play the major role in behavior. For cognitivism, it is more important to understand what is going on within the person's head as she or he confronts an objective stimulus situation than it is to understand the properties of the situation itself. Basically, people are said to behave in terms of their definitions of situations (see Sampson, 1981a).

In the cognitivist versions of psychology, the subject stands forth as primary: the actor is abstracted from the contexts of action; any substantial reality to the material world is reduced to subject-dominated categories. I refer to this as psychology's truncated subjectivism. Its truncation is revealed in its identity of subject and object.

Let me be more explicit about what I mean by a truncated subjectivism. Basically a psychology of the subject without a psychology of the object, or better still, of their dialectical interpenetration, yields only a partial and distorted psychology. The thoughts of Viktor Frankl (1959) on his concentration camp experiences offer one useful illustrative example. In his efforts to make the insanity of daily life in the camps intelligible, Frankl developed a theory that emphasized the importance of meaning to the human subject.

The problem that I believe Frankl did not satisfactorily address is the extent to which, having endowed the subject with a search for meaning, he failed to endow the reality of prison life with its own meaning independent of the experiencing victim's. For example, he speaks of human freedom in the camp, arguing that people were really free *in the most important sense of that term* because they could adopt whatever attitude they wanted toward their circumstances.

I am not taking exception to this human capacity to adopt an attitude, a subjective definition of the circumstances that surround them. What I take exception to, however, is the extent to which this adoption takes precedence over the harsh realities of being imprisoned. The freedom to have a mental representation, while important, fails to give due weight to the surrounding material conditions of deprivation, torture, and the absence of actual freedom. This is one example of the dilemma that psychology's truncated subjectivism encounters.

Psychology's subjectivism is truncated in that it places a main burden on the mentation of the individual; the material reality enters the equation, but only in terms already processed by the actor's meaning-endowing capacities. There is no room in such a formulation for systematically distorted perceptions. Because reality is entirely defined in subjective terms, it cannot itself be other than it is experienced as being. In other words, the incorrigible framework for grasping reality is the subjective state of the perceiver (checked against the states of other perceivers). There is no way thereby to accommodate the possibility that this incorrigible framework, even though shared widely within a given group or community, is itself corrigible.

INTERACTIONISM

The essential correction of this truncated theory of human subjectivity requires that we systematically introduce a theory of the subject–object dialectic. Some would argue that interactionism in psychology has accomplished this and thus my request has been met. Unfortunately, with few if any exceptions, interactionism falls back upon the same problem that it purports to remedy (see Sampson, 1981a). It does indeed include two terms, one of the subject, the other of the object; but the object is primarily defined in terms of the subject, thereby reducing the interactions once again to a truncated subjectivism.

Some might then argue that Piaget's interactionist formulations have adequately solved this problem. It is correct that on the surface, Piaget's dual concepts, assimilation and accommodation, appear to involve a true interaction between subject and object. With assimilation, the properties of the object are assimilated to and become a part of the transforming properties of the subject. It appears that with accommodation, the subject is transformed by accommodating to the qualities of the objects with which it interacts. If so, this could define one piece of the resolution required. A closer reading, however, reveals the nature of the problem that is involved.

In the first place, the actual reality of the object as such remains unchanged by the actions of the subject upon it. What is changed is not the object but the subject's apprehension of the object. In other words, mental events are modified, but the object itself remains relatively unscathed. In the second place, as cognitive development advances from its primitive to its more advanced stages, Piaget sees mentation increasingly substituting for real-world action. People manipulate thoughts in their heads rather than acting on actual material events. In this, therefore, Piaget is barely interactive in a dialectical sense, in which both subject and actual object are changed in and through their encounter, not simply the subject's conception of the object (also see Buck-Morss, 1977; Riegel, 1976; Wilden, 1980, for a further critique of Piaget).

Ahistorical Interactionism

An even more insightful critique of the deficiencies of interactionism as it has thus far appeared in psychology has been developed by Gadlin and Rubin (1979). Their critique returns us to the essentially social and historical quality of the terms that are said to interact. Gadlin and Rubin examine the interactionist position as a presumed resolution of the person–situation debate in psychology. Let us look briefly at this debate before we examine both the interactionist resolution and Gadlin and Rubin's critique.

In a sense, the person-centered position carries on with the subject-dominated or idealist tradition, whereas the situation-centered model represents the object-dominated or more materialist point of view. The former emphasizes the way in which personality traits render the person's behavior stable and consistent across various situations. The latter emphasizes the variability of individual behavior across situations, locating whatever consistency emerges in the attributes of the stimulus situation rather than the person. Interactionism presumably resolves the apparent differences in causal primacy (person vs. situation) by speaking of behavior as a multiplicative result of the two.

What Gadlin and Rubin suggest, however, is that interactionism has accomplished its resolution by adopting a nonsocial and ahistorical position: person and situation are seen to be entities defined separately both from their interaction and from the web of social history within which they exist. They call upon Riesman's (1950) historical analysis of changing social character to explain what they mean.

Riesman distinguished between an inner-directed and an other-directed social character to describe two types of national identities that emerged during the course of relatively recent Western social history. The inner-directed character describes the person, representing an earlier historical epoch, who reflects the person-centered position. The other-directed character represents the situationist position of the more modern era. In other words, Riesman's inner-directed social character is the type described by person-centered theorists who emphasize the role that personality traits play in providing stability to individual behavior consistently across situations as though guided by an inner voice. In turn, Riesman's other-directed social character describes the personality type of the situation-centered theorists—the individual whose behavior shifts as the circumstances change. The actions of other-directed persons vary as a function of the situation-specific signals detected by their sensitive antennae.

By linking the dominant concept of personhood to the developments of social history, Gadlin and Rubin lead us to see that the emphases within psychology's understanding are less about persons in themselves or situations in themselves than about the changing nature of each over time. The shifting emphasis in psychological understanding, from person to situation, reflects the actual historical shift in the social definition of individuals from inner to other directedness.

What, then, about interactionism? For Gadlin and Rubin, this attempt to integrate conceptually what are basically two different historical types fails insofar as it treats the matter abstractly and separate from the social and historical context:

It is our position that the person–situation controversy reflects essential and conflicting features of sociopsychological reality; that the controversy cannot be resolved merely by clarifying conceptual confusions, because the confusions reflect persistent qualities of the person's situation in contemporary society. (p. 218)

What is both unique and significant about this analysis is the way in which it calls our attention to the social and historical embeddedness of the very terms we employ (i.e., *subject* and *object*, *person* and *situation*). We are not dealing with things in themselves that are transcendent and come together to interact but with items that vary as a function of their particular social and historical location. The dialectical interpenetration does not take place between two static items but rather between changing items whose relationship of interaction unfolds historically.

THE CONTRIBUTIONS OF HABERMAS

A more substantial and complex contribution to the analysis of the relationship between human subjectivity and the sociohistorical process, one that goes beyond the kind of truncated subjectivism that dominates much of modern psychology, emerges from Habermas's perspective (1971, 1973). In a sense, Habermas completed the movement initiated by Hegel's critique of Kant as modified and expanded by Marx. Habermas suggested three knowledge-constituting syntheses which he refers to as *interests:* (1) the technical, instrumental, or purposive-rational, issuing from the world of work; (2) the practical or communicative, issuing from the world of interaction and understanding; and (3) the emancipatory or critical, issuing from the world of self-reflectivity. As with the Kantian, Hegelian, and Marxian schemes, these knowledge-constitutive interests

are not regulators of cognition which have to be eliminated for the sake of objectivity of knowledge; instead, they themselves determine the aspect under which reality is objectified, and can thus be made accessible to experience to begin with. They are the conditions which are necessary in order that subjects capable of speech and action may have experiences which can lay claim to objectivity. (1973, p. 9)

In other words, these three form the basis within which experiences are organized and given their form. It is apparent that Habermas has attempted to describe an intimate link between knowledge and social practice in a manner congruent with a materialist thesis. The requirements of work and labor constitute one set of conditions under which knowledge of a particular form is constituted: this is knowledge oriented toward technical control over nature. Interaction and communication serve as the frame for another kind of interest in knowledge: this is knowledge oriented toward mutual understanding. Human self-reflectivity provides a third form giver for knowledge: this is knowledge oriented toward "emancipation from seemingly 'natural' constraint" (1971, p. 311). Habermas has thereby extended Marx's emphasis on work and labor as the material base of human knowledge to include additional, transcendental, knowledge-synthesizing conditions. It will be helpful to several of our later critiques briefly to examine some of these ideas in more detail.

The Technical Interest

Knowledge constituted within the purview of the technical interest is founded on social practices involving work—in particular, the achievement of a technical mastery and control over nature and people. The focus is on a form of knowledge that is or can become technically exploitable (i.e., predicted and controlled). This is the kind of knowledge that characterizes the empirical-analytic sciences.

Reality is disclosed "from the viewpoint of possible technical control over objectified processes of nature" (1971, p. 191). The language forms are "either formalized or at least formalizable" (1971, p. 191); they have been "separated out of [their] embeddedness in interactions" (p. 193) and refer to an abstracted, generalized and repeatable kind of experience. The reality that is disclosed is technically controllable "under specified conditions . . . everywhere and at all times" (p. 195).

The Practical Interest

Knowledge constituted within the interest in communication and social interaction is focused around intersubjective meaning and mutual understanding. The hermeneutic and interpretative sciences fall within the framework of this interest. The focus is not on the achievement of predictability or technically utilizable knowledge, but rather on the meanings involved in ordinary discourse and the goals that are normatively valued. In that the meanings involved always occur and are rendered intelligible within the particular context of their use, the reality disclosed in the practical interest is necessarily contextual and particularistic.

In contrasting the technical from the practical interest, Habermas observes the following key distinction:

Insofar as the employment of symbols is constitutive for the behavioral system of instrumental action, the use of language involved is monologic. But the communication of investigators requires the use of language that is not confined to the limits of technical control over objectified natural processes. It arises from symbolic interaction between societal subjects who reciprocally know and recognize each other as unmistakable individuals. This *communicative* action is a system of reference that cannot be reduced to the framework of *instrumental action*. (1971, p. 137)

The Emancipatory Interest

Habermas suggests that neither of the preceding two interests maintains a concern with understanding its own grounding in a knowledge-constitutive interest and in a given sphere of social practice. Only a third interest, the emancipatory, seeks to ground itself within the framework of a self-reflective or critical focus. The knowledge constituted within the purview of this interest is geared to grasping itself and the conditions—personal, social, and historical—within which it is formed. The emancipatory interest is focused around uncovering systematic distortions in the roots of human consciousness itself.

CONCLUDING COMMENTS

Although Habermas's analysis is not without its critics and accusations of being excessively idealist in its roots, it represents an attempted alternative to the otherwise truncated subjectivism that I suggest characterizes much of psychology's own understanding. At minimum, it seeks to locate the essential features of human subjectivity within society and history. It links the forms of our thinking to the changing forms of social life. In a real sense, Habermas urges us to press through the processes of the mind in order to uncover the roots in ongoing social life, including, but not restricted to, the world of work. And this latter point is not to be taken lightly.

Insofar as the world of work—that is, the pursuit of technical mastery over the unruly forces of nature (among which are the presumably unruly forces of "human nature")—has tended to dominate Western civilization (e.g., the root metaphors of mechanism to which I referred in Chapter 7), thinking and subjectivity that is not geared to its requirements is relegated to a secondary or lesser status. At least with Habermas's analysis we gain an understanding of essential alternatives that are themselves grounded in other spheres of human endeavor (mutual understanding and human emancipation from domination); these alternatives not only synthesize different forms of understanding but occupy equal stature with the now dominant technical forms.

For psychology, this suggests the need to go beyond examining the ways in which cognitive development proceeds in the area of purely technical control and mastery and also to examine the development of subjectivity and understanding in nontechnical, nonmastery-grounded directions. The latter for the most part, however, have not been a central feature of contemporary psychological analysis (see Sampson, 1981a). Thus, technical understanding, fitting a world obsessed with mastery and control, dominates without adequate sensitivity to its being but one of several possibilities. The other directions are a central feature of Habermas's contribution and suggest the profound meaning of truncation: not only has psychology emphasized the subjective over the material but, within the subjective, it has emphasized the technical over other groundings of human knowledge and understanding.

CHAPTER NINE

Psychology's Subject
The Abstracted Individual

Few could reasonably take exception to the idea that the discipline of psychology emerged to study the individual person: this is presumably the proper object of disciplinary inquiry or what I call "psychology's subject." The task of the field has been to develop the laws of individual functioning. Although a general consensus has emerged in regard to this matter, disagreements remain concerning just what it is about the individual person that should be studied: behavior, cognitive processes, neurophysiological processes, and so forth. And there continue to be disagreements about the methodologies that are required both to ground psychology's work in the scientific tradition and to capture the essence of the human subject. Finally, even though specific subspecialities within psychology—for example, social psychology—are presumably designed to examine something "more than" the individual person, they generally round down to the study of the effects of other individuals on the individual who comes under their scrutiny (e.g., Allport, 1968).

There are serious difficulties entailed in this uncritical adoption of the individual person as psychology's subject. The individual person is not a simple fact that can be immediately apprehended as such but a social, cultural, and historical creation, that is, a mediated object. Personhood is not a given, nor is it simply something earned as the final stage of successful individual socialization and development. Rather, it is a sociocultural and historical product, mediated by the underlying principles and structures of a particular social system that define what it means (the concept) and what it is (the actuality) to be a person.

Psychology has implicitly assumed that the person who is the object of its inquiry is a factual and self-evident entity with attributes that it studies empirically and about which it theorizes. This very assumption has itself rarely been addressed systematically or examined critically. Two recent exceptions, however, offer some suggestive clues. Both Sarason (1981) and

Pepitone (1981) have introduced a position that challenges this taken-for-granted character of psychology's subject.

Sarason, for example, argues that one of the central problems with American psychology, in particular what he terms the "misdirection" of clinical and health psychology, is its naive rootedness in the notion of the self-contained individual: "American psychology, invented in and by American society, went on to invent its subject matter: the self-contained individual. The necessity for reinvention is at hand" (Sarason, 1981, pp. 835–836).

Pepitone's reflections on the history of social psychology describe an *individuocentric* position that characterizes much if not all of social psychological inquiry: that is, adopting the individual as the only reality and the fundamental unit of analysis and individual dynamics as the source of all social and cultural dynamics. This describes the bias toward individualism and the opposition to relationism, which must be seen against the backgound of the society and history from which much of modern psychology has evolved (also see Mayhew, 1980, 1981, on this theme).

THE ABSTRACTED ENTITY

The subject psychology examines is an abstracted individual; the focus is on a character who has been fully extricated from the social and historical context in which she or he is embedded—the context that gives meaning to the concept and actuality of personhood and individuality. As both Sarason and Pepitone suggest, psychology's adoption of the abstracted individual was not its own invention. Psychology somewhat uncritically followed the long tradition of Western civilization, within which it was embedded and from which it clearly emerged. Descartes's famous formulation, "I think, therefore I am," crisply captures a central thesis of this world view. What certainty we can have about knowledge is a function of individual human thought (see Chapter 8). The only thing about which we can have no doubt is the person who is doing the doubting. Needless to say, Descartes and the tradition he initiated failed to ask any questions about this "I" who is doing the thinking.

In this Cartesian viewpoint, the individual was presumed to be a substance or *entity* (a thinking entity as distinct from a material body) rather than a *relation*. As several authors have observed (e.g., Wilden, 1980), this view provided a philosophical basis for the emerging physical and economic paradigms in which a kind of atomistic individualism was central. Wilden, for example, sees the Cartesian emphasis on "clear and distinct ideas" to have a parallel in the necessity for a "clear and distinct individual" who would function as a substitutable part of the machinery of the emerging industrial era. The *communitas* of the earlier era was reduced to an aggregate of individual atoms.

A society that is understood merely as an aggregate of separate individuals loses its own organizational or structural properties. Society becomes the sum total of its individual parts; the parts gain a privileged ontological status as entitles whose essences and behaviors shape the whole. Basically, by understanding the entitles as the essential substances out of which relationships are themselves constituted, one reverses the order of things in which relationships constitute entities. First comes the individual and from her or him issues the world.

Locating the causative agency within the atomistic individual leads us to psychologize and individualize away social issues and social action. Social ills are seen as the outcome of individual problems; social action becomes a series of individual actions. The individual becomes the enterprise to be probed and explored, while the societal remains relatively free from scrutiny or transformation (e.g., see Caplan & Nelson, 1973, on the way psychology understands the problems of black Americans).

As one commentator observed,

labor . . . is . . . mystified if it is seen primarily as individual *praxis*. Individuals carry it out, to be sure, but as social individuals carrying out aspects of a complex and highly organized social *praxis*. No step of the activity is not social . . . . My tools, my place of work, the materials I work on, my very patterns of work—all these dimensions of individual *praxis* develop only in and for a society at a certain point in history . . . . Strictly speaking there can no more be a purely individual *praxis* than there can be an individual reason. Social individuals work with social tools, using social skills on a social field, to accomplish socially-defined purposes. (Aronson, 1977, p. 223)

The problem is that psychology has uncritically adopted the atomistic individual as the world creator and has ignored the social forms that are essential in shaping the concept and the actual life of that individual. People do not simply exist in independence from one another and then recombine to form society. Nor is the very concept of personhood somewhat transcendent from society and history. Insofar as our psychology insistently extirpates the actor from the scene, we become incapable of learning that the scene is as important in shaping the actor's performance as the actor is in shaping the scene.

THE IDEOLOGICAL TURN

Wilden (1980) argues that this orientation toward entities rather than relations, which is at the core of Western epistemology, is not merely an accident in understanding but rather emerged along with the development of industrialization and capitalism. He describes the *ideology of the entity:*

necessarily the product of the sixteenth-century advance in physics engendered by technology, an ideology which sought to justify a program which would not concern itself with the "government of men" (theology) but with the "administration of things" (natural science) . . . the rationalization of the reduction of the "person" to the status of a cog in the social machinery. (pp. 91–92)

For Wilden, the view of the individual as an abstracted entity contains our understanding in ideological forms that help sustain the underlying socioeconomic structures which, in the short run, depend on this understanding for their reproduction. It is not for nothing that psychology has retained the abstracted individual as its subject. We will have more to say about this shortly. At this point, however, it will prove helpful to consolidate my argument that personhood is a mediated rather than immediately self-evident concept and actuality by turning to the excellent analysis developed by Geertz.

GEERTZ'S ANALYSIS OF PERSONHOOD

Based on his extensive fieldwork in Bali, Java, and Morocco, the cultural anthropologist Clifford Geertz (1973, 1979) presents perhaps one of the best single statements of the concept of personhood that has dominated the Western world. His work in Bali, for example, introduces the Western reader to the "cultural apparatus in terms of which the people of Bali define, perceive, and react to—that is, think about—individual persons" (1973, p. 360). As Smith (1978) noted in his use of Geertz's analysis, the complexity and subtlety of the work do not permit a simple, shorthand account. We must read the full text in order to deepen our appreciation of the multiple ways in which personhood can vary culturally.

What clearly emerges from Geertz's examination of the Balinese "cultural apparatus" is the distinctively different way in which cultures place their unique accent marks around what we have heretofore taken for granted as a unitary, self-evident phenomenon. Read Geertz's conclusion carefully:

The Western concept of the person as a bounded, unique, more or less integrated motivational and cognitive universe, a dynamic center of awareness, emotion, judgment, and action organized into a distinctive whole and set contrastively both against other such wholes and against a social and natural background is, however incorrigible it may seem to us, a rather peculiar idea within the context of the world's cultures. (1979, p. 229)

Geertz observes that the crux of the Balinese concept of personhood is their "social placement, their particular location within a persisting, indeed eternal, metaphysical order. The illuminating paradox of Balinese formulations of personhood is that they are—in our terms anyway—depersonalizing" (1973, p. 390). This depersonalized Balinese accent permits us to appreciate better what Geertz describes as their concern with ritual and their stage fright lest any individual spontaneity show through their standardized identity.

THE BOURGEOIS INDIVIDUAL

Geertz's description captures the essential qualities that the person of the Western world presumably possesses: (1) a bounded universe, (2) an integrated center of thought and action, and (3) an entity set contrastively against others and the world. This is the person that psychology has uncritically adopted as its subject, a mediated product of society and of history, grasped as though it were an immediately given reality "out there." This conception of personhood did not arise in a vacuum but emerged in the Western world along with industrialization and especially the socioeconomic system of capitalism. It will be helpful briefly to examine the thesis that joins this Western concept of personhood with a specific kind of social being, the bourgeois individual. This joins us again with the perspective of critical theory (see especially Adorno, 1967, 1974; Habermas, 1975; Horkheimer, 1972; Horkheimer & Adorno, 1972; Marcuse, 1964, 1966, 1968).

Basically, Geertz's description is the critical theorists' description of the bourgeois individual, the creation of liberal capitalism. One must approach this definition with the touch of irony it warrants, however, in order to appreciate its meanings for the critical theorists. As Adorno (1974) observes, "Measured by its concept, the individual has indeed become . . . null and void" (p. 113). The concept of the person as a relatively autonomous, self-contained, and distinctive universe is thereby said to reflect the sham and the illusion that is the bourgeois individual, not its reality.

The *concept* describes an entity who is the integrated center of certain powers: one who is aware, who feels, thinks, judges, and acts. In concept, as we have seen, the individual is adopted as the primary reality, the ontological base from which issues the remainder, including society and social relations. As Protagoras said, this entity becomes the measure of all things. The critical theorists argue, however, that the *reality* is quite different. The concept describes a fictitious character, the bourgeois individual, whose integrated wholeness, unique individuality, and status as a subject with actual powers to shape events has become null and void. They do not greet this demise with joy but with sorrow over the death of someone who might have been and with anger at the deceit that passes for normal everyday life.

Furthermore, the critical perspective adopts a view about the real nature of personhood in which such notions as "integrated wholeness," "dynamic universe," or "self-contained center" are invariably more false than true. Recall that in this view, there is an essential interpenetration of society and individual that warrants our approaching with skepticism any view that makes the individual a transcendent entity. We do not begin with two independent entities, individual and society, that are otherwise formed and defined apart from one another and that interact as though each were external to the other. Rather, society constitutes and inhabits the very core of whatever passes for personhood: each is interpenetrated by its other.

To speak of the end of the individual, therefore, does not refer to the end of the ideological bourgeois individual: that is, the end of some transcendent figure. It refers to the end of the possibility for people collectively to exercise control over the social forces that govern their lives. The ideology of the bourgeois individual fosters a belief in rational control and autonomy even as that control wanes and the key shaping forces operate behind the backs of those who should know but do not.

The complexity of the critical perspective and the arguments for its conclusions can be reduced to several major themes which I will briefly introduce. The result of this examination will be a perspective on the nature of personhood that is far removed from the autonomous bounded universe of ideology; it defines a new kind of personhood that, were it realized, would be party to a radical restructuring of the society within which all notions of personhood necessarily gain their standing.

Concepts Are Historically Formed

Both the concept and the actuality of persons does not transcend society or history but emerges invariably as an integral part of the history and the underlying structures and mechanisms of a given society. Basically, all things and entities, including ideas and concepts, are formed in and through relations that are rooted in social history (e.g., Horkheimer, 1941; also see the discussion in Chapter 6). Personhood is a relation embedded within the social totality in which it takes shape and is defined. As Ollman (1971) states this principle, "The conditions of its [the person's] existence are taken to be part of what it is" (p. 28). What a person is, therefore, cannot be grasped independently of the social and historical conditions that shape and define personhood.

This perspective not only introduces a sociohistorical dimension to the analysis of personhood but also challenges all notions that introduce a transcendental subject: a mind, consciousness, or subjectivity that subjects but is not subjected. This view challenges the notion of an autonomous, primary (i.e., unmediated) subject, either Cartesian or Kantian, who constructs a world but from beyond the reaches of that very world. It rejects a structuring first principle, such as transcendental subjectivity, that is not a part of and thus mediated by the very structure that it structures.

The Bourgeois Individual and Early Capitalism

Habermas (1975) provides a helpful account of the large-scale historical shifts in the underlying organizational principles of society that constituted different meanings and realities for personhood. He outlines four such principles: the primitive, the traditional, the liberal capitalist, and the advanced capitalist. Within the primitive social form, kinship played a dominant role in defining the nature and scope of personhood. People were not meaningfully defined apart from their family units.

In the traditional social form, the bureaucratic apparatus replaces the family unit: "This allows the transference of the production and distribution of social wealth from familial forms of organization to ownership of the means of production" (Habermas, 1975, p. 19). Fromm (1941) briefly describes this transition: the feudal household is shattered; individuals emerge from the shadows of their communal existence into the harsh glare of individual freedom of movement and choice. As Marcuse (1968) observed, the liberation that characterized this postmedieval period empowered people as individuals to shape their own destinies. Life seemed to be unmediated: individuals directly and immediately confronted the tasks of self-maintenance and survival without being the delegated representatives of some "higher social bodies." The individual "arose as a dynamic cell of economic activity" (Horkheiner & Adorno, 1972, p. 203), interested in securing as many economic benefits as possible.

From Liberal to Advanced Capitalism

The further development of the bourgeois individual awaited the liberal capitalist organizational principle. A group of corporate owners emerged, entrepreneurs with a generally wide latitude of autonomous functioning, and a class of workers emerged whose autonomy, while limited, was more substantial than in previous eras. A civil society developed with laws to protect the rights and freedoms of the individuals—this new character on history's stage.

Habermas suggests that the liberal form functioned according to the relatively anonymous market forces of supply and demand. There was a certain reasonableness to the concept that self-contained individual actors could function autonomously as little economic calculators, guided by the unseen hand of the marketplace. Success and failure where somewhat connected to the wisdom of choices made and the intensity of personal motivation and individual achievement. This unseen hand of the marketplace that characterized the liberal form was replaced in the advanced form by the longer arm of state intervention in market manipulation. Advanced capitalism developed along with the growing concentration of capital and the extension of corporations into international markets: that is, with the change from a local or even national economic system to an international marketplace and web of complex economic interdependencies.

Although the bourgeois ideas regarding freedom of individual choice and decision making remain, they become increasingly disjunctive with the objective realities of systemic functioning under the advanced organizational principle. Autonomous entrepreneurs no longer compete on the open market, seeking a fair exchange and following principles of supply and demand. Rather, state intervention creates and seeks to control conditions of supply and demand, scarcity and abundance. The state participates actively in establishing pricing policies and market options. The range of individual choice becomes restricted and narrowed; opportunities are channeled by national priorities that reflect the requirements of system maintenance, security, and enlargement.

Decision processes form around alternatives dictated by such imperatives as corporate expansion and the control of international markets. Rationality of choice becomes limited to choosing between alternatives already predetermined by socioeconomic forces of which one is only vaguely aware or which one is hardly able to affect (see Adorno, 1967). And yet, the ideology of autonomy and individuality remains carved deeply in the subjective consciousness of the culture.

Ideology, the Bourgeois Individual, and Societal Reproduction

Societies create both the characters they need to reproduce themselves and the ideologies that are necessary so that those characters will function to achieve societal reproduction. The bourgeois individual is such a character; the ideologies concerning individuality, autonomy, and freedom play an essential role in societal reproduction. As Fromm (1955) once observed, society today requires a person who feels free to move about, to act intelligently, and to make sensible choices dictated by personal interest and desire even while its productive system demands people whose movements and choices are sufficiently well known and programmable that they can be readily predicted and controlled.

Ideological concepts of personhood are not merely akin to a cloud concealing a sun which remains shining though hidden. Rather, ideology is an essential, constitutive element in the phenomenon's status itself. In this case, the underlying social structures and mechanisms could not persist without the essential functioning of this ideology of personhood. Thus the concept of the bourgeois individual is an illusion essential to the reproduction of the advanced capitalist social form in which it exists as a concept but to which its actuality is suspect.

Caplan and Nelson's (1973) review of psychology's understanding of black Americans, to which I previously alluded, is illustrative of what I mean. Their review discovered that over 80% of the psychological studies of black Americans attributed their problems to something about them rather than to their circumstances. This tendency to interpret social ills as psychologically derived creates a psychological subject who is given the full burden of responsibility for correcting her or his troubles. In this manner, underlying structures that systematically thwart a group's opportunities (e.g., structures of racism and sexism) are reproduced insofar as we view the troubles of people to be a problem of their will power, motivation, intellect, or personality dynamics.

The Cult of Psychology

The critical theorists describe the outcome of advanced capitalist social dynamics by pointing out that although the individual has become more myth than reality, the myth is used to define what is real. This is what is seen as so objectionable about most modern social science. As Adorno (1967) states it, "Psychology. . . . Ignoring the social process of production . . . makes a first principle out of a mediated product, the bourgeois individual" (pp. 78–79). Psychology extols the virtues of a lost character and thereby participates in the delusions, not the enlightenment of the era.

Adorno (also see Sarason, 1981) sees psychology as an American cult movement that not only emerged historically along with the emergence of the bourgeois individual but now plays its tune even more loudly as that social character rapidly moves into decline. He likens this to the situation in ancient Greece in which "the cult of the individual" reached its zenith at the very moment when individuality was in its decline (Adorno, 1974; Horkheimer & Adorno, 1972). The moments in which the individual is worshiped most strongly mark the very times of farthest remove from the actuality of that esteem. The intensely subjectivist doctrines of cognitivism in psychology (see Sampson, 1981a) and of psychology's humanistic thrust are thereby seen as ideological: "the cult of human subjectivity is not the negation of bourgeois society but its substance" (Jacoby, 1975, p. 103).

The Dialectics of Interpenetration

The critical perspective argues that the real subject of history requires people who can act collectively, with will and with consciousness, to shape the history that shapes them. By arguing that the concept and the actuality of personhood is thoroughly inhabited by the social, economic, and historical, the critical theorists have directed our attention to the inevitable interpenetration of society within the individual. The concept of personhood as an autonomous, bounded universe remains primarily an ideological cover story to conceal the truth: that history is being made behind the backs of those supposedly autonomous centers of action—that insofar as that illusory character occupies the limelight, the forces that shape human destiny will not enter the realm of rational human governance.

THE CRITICAL SYSTEMS ALTERNATIVE

Although much of psychology, in my view, has persisted in taking the bourgeois individual as its subject, providing an ideological slant to the discipline's understanding, an important alternative has existed, though somewhat in the background. I refer to this as critical systems theory. Wilden (1980; also see Churchman, 1979) introduced roughly six separate meanings for the concept of *system*; he also registered his disagreement with all of them, terming them pseudosystemic. His list ranged from highly mechanistic analyses to those that, while speaking in systems language, insisted on an additive formulation in which the ontological primacy remained within the parts and not the relations that constitute the whole system. It is clear from Wilden's account that a proper systems perspective grants primacy to relations and sees the parts to be mediated derivatives.

Because of the many uses of the term *system*, I have intentionally chosen to describe this alternative view of psychology's subject as *critical* systems theory. I hope that this will separate my view of an alternative epistemology from the views that "talk" systems but "mean" elements.

Critical systems theory introduces an alternative framework of knowledge, one that forces us seriously to question the status given to the notion of the individual subject as such. A helpful beginning point for an examination of this alternative epistemology appears in the 1949 paper by Dewey and Bentley.

The Transactionalism of Dewey and Bentley

Dewey and Bentley (1949) outline three developmental epochs in the history of human inquiry: "self-action," "inter-action," and "trans-action." They link self-actional inquiry to the Aristotlean notion of substances: "things which completely, inherently, and hence necessarily possess Being; that . . . continue eternally in action . . . under their own power" (Dewey & Bentley, 1949, pp. 122–123). They observe that self-actional notions survive even today in such notions as the " 'mind' as 'actor' . . . in charge of behavior" (p. 129); they liken this survival to a form of charlatanism (their word). To this, we might well add the Western conception of personhood as a kind of self-acting universe—another survival worthy of challenge.

In rejecting the quasi-animistic, self-actional frame, Galileo replaced it with an interactional formulation. Bodies in motion were not driven by some inner substance or essence, but were seen in terms of an interactional formulation. Newton further developed this interactional mode; the world was now to be viewed "as a process of 'simple forces between unalterable particles'" (1949, p. 123). With Einstein, the movement away from interaction and toward a transactional framework emerged. Dewey and Bentley introduce several key distinctions between interaction and transaction, two of which impress me as of particular importance.

1. Unlike interactional inquiry, in which it is possible to offer reasonably complete descriptions of the things that wil inter-act *before* their encounter, one can offer only very provisional descriptions of the elements implicated under the transactional mode. In other words, the presumption of the interactional model is that "facts" exist in independence from one another and that each can be described apart from its encounter with other so-called facts. The presumption of the trans-actional model, by contrast, is that one cannot adequately indicate a fact independently of its determination on the basis of its relation with other facts with which it engages in an encounter.

2. Given the presumptive adequacy of the descriptions of the elements *prior* to their encounter under the interactive model, the major task is primarily to examine what ensues following this encounter. By contrast, given the provisional understanding of elements prior to their encounter under the transactional mode, the main task is to examine the manner in which the

parts are reorganized in the encounter and thus to observe their freedom to be redetermined and to take on new attributes as the transaction unfolds.

Parts, Wholes, and Reasons Why. Clearly, the parts have priority within the interactional model while relations retain primacy within the transactional. On the one hand, one begins with parts and from them achieves an understanding of the whole (interaction); on the other, one begins with the transactions within the whole system in order to arrive at any adequate understanding of the nature of what appear as elements.

In order to highlight this distinction, let me quote a lengthy passage in which Dewey and Bentley reflect on why self-actional and interactional treatment seem so dominant in the human sciences:

> The organism . . . seems in everyday life and language to stand out strongly apart from the transactions in which it is engaged. This is superficial observation. One reason for it is that the organism is engaged in so many transactions. . . . A "business man" would not be called a business man at all if he never did any business; yet the very variety of his other transactions is what makes it easy to detach him and specialize him as a business man. Consider the great variety of his other transactions, and it becomes still easier to make "a man" out of him in the sense of an "essence" or "substance." . . . He comes thus . . . to be considered as if he could still be a man without being in *any* transaction. (p. 131)

The subject-as-such is abstracted as an entity with mind, consciousness, essence (or whatever); it is culled from the web of transactions and treated as though it had a definition, reality, and existence apart from that web. In its fundamental outlook, by contrast, the transactional epistemology rejects entity and substance over relation. Ontological priority is granted to relation; entity and substance occupy a mediated status. In this model, psychology's subject does not exist as an independent or self-contained entity with properties that can be defined apart from its location as a mediated element within the larger system of which it is a part.

Maruyama's Mindscapes

In an intriguing series of papers, Maruyama (1979, 1980) has developed what he terms a theory of *mindscapes*:

> a structure of reasoning, cognition, perception, conceptualization, design, planning, and decision making that may vary from one individual, profession, culture or social group to another. (1980, p. 591)

Maruyama outlines four mindscapes: independent-event, homogenisic, homeostatic, and morphogenetic. I interpret the first two as defining nonsystemic epistemologies, while the remaining two introduce two forms of systemic world view. Rather than taking up space to introduce the details of each—he offers several helpful tables summarising their key distinctions in his 1979 paper—let me briefly observe the nature of the differences in general terms.

Systemic and Nonsystemic Views. Basically, whereas nonsystemic epistemologies adopt a view of nonreciprocal causality, systemic epistemologies see events in terms of reciprocal causal loops. Maruyama argues that this distinction became possible in the Western world view only after some 2,500 years of domination by the nonreciprocal model. The challenge marks a revolution in understanding made possible, according to Maruyama, by the advent of error-correcting feedback systems (e.g., he cites the guided missile or the thermostat), which are based on a reciprocal, homeostatic model.

Maruyama sees this movement from nonreciprocal to reciprocal models to mark a radically new perspective for understanding biological, psychological, and social phenomena. In this regard, Maruyama and Bateson (1972) appear to have adopted very similar analyses of the revolutionary import of these epistemological transformations. Bateson, for example, suggests that the time period 1946 to 1947—in which cybernetics, communication, information, and systems theory all began to take off—marks "the biggest bite out of the fruit of the Tree of Knowledge that mankind has taken in the last 2000 years" (p. 476). For a timely and revealing proposal that suggests a far earlier coming of this alternative epistemology, contained in women's spirituality and hence suppressed by the world of *man*kind, see the edited collection of papers presented by Spretnak (1982). Long before missiles and thermostats, the critical system's alternative was alive and well but dishonored. Needless to say, both Maruyama and Bateson seem to be reflecting their male-dominated cultural bias by making the kinds of originary attributions that mark their works.

Nonreciprocal versus Reciprocal Models. A nonreciprocal model involves a linear sequence of cause and effect: for example, A's actions cause B's behavior. We see this in Dewey and Bentley's notion of inter-action: two entities, each of which has an existence independent of the other, meet, such that one's action causes the action of the other.

Reciprocal models build upon a nonlinear view of causality. In a self-correcting feedback system, for example, A's impact on B leads to B's reciprocal action back on A. In such a system, it is meaningful to say that B causes B's behavior: that is, the reciprocal loop joining A and B operates such that B's return of A's effects on B affects B's later performance. With homeostatic,

error-correcting (i.e., negative) feedback loops, a specific goal is maintained
by feedback from B to A that moderates A's actions on B around that targeted
goal. In a thermostat, for example, the register (A) responds to room temper-
ature and sends a signal to the furnace (B) to turn on or off. A's message affects B's behavior, which in turn feeds back to affect A's behavior: as the
room heats up, A tells B to shut off.

The so-called elements in homeostatic reciprocal networks of this sort
are meaningfully understood as such only within the transaction that joins
them into the system of which they are elements. One and the same "entity"
is both subject and object, both cause and effect. This challenges the simple
identity notions that characterize Aristotelean logic. Whether A, for example, is cause or effect depends on where in the system it is located, at what
moment in time, and from what point of view. This transactional point of
view forces us to reconsider the logic of identity as well as the root notions of
causality.

Homeostatic versus Morphogenetic Frames. The crux of the distinction that Maruyama draws between homeostatic and morphogenetic systems
reveals the further advances in the original systems conceptualization.
Homeostatic systems retain their basic structural relations as they function;
morphogenetic systems undergo changes in these structural relations.
Homeostasis involves negative feedback; morphogenesis involves positive
feedback. The former revolve around a set point; the latter grow and evolve
and are structurally transformed.

Maruyama illustrates this distinction by describing Japanese and European conceptions of architectural space. He sees the former as involving
multiple meanings and alternatives, while the latter stress "identity,"
"permanance," and "specialized function." In his view, European spaces and
rooms follow an Aristotelean identity principle: a given room serves a given
purpose and only that. Japanese spaces, by contrast, reflect the essence of a
morphogenetic epistemology or mindscape: "the same room may be a bedroom at night, a dining room at mealtime, and a living room for the rest of
the day" (1980, p. 598).

Systems versus Psychology's Abstracted Subject

It should be apparent that my intention has not been to summarize all
those who have contributed to the systems perspective. My aim, rather, is to
provide a sufficient context for this perspective to contribute further to ques-
tioning the traditional notions of personhood on which psychology has been
constructed. The systems approach forces us to take a very different look at

the nature of personhood and the epistemology on which that concept is built. The new epistemology warrants a new concept of personhood and thus a new subject for psychology's inquiry.

I see two major distinctions differentiating the systems subject from psychology's subject: The systems subject is (1) multicentered and multidimensional, not necessarily unified or integrated into a single identity as such, and (2) nonhierarchically and reciprocally related with other subjects and elements of the total field of which it is a part. A good sense of this twofold challenge emerges from briefly considering Bateson's (1972) analysis:

> The total self-corrective unit which processes information, or as I say, "thinks" and "acts" and "decides," is a *system* whose boundaries do not at all coincide with the boundaries either of the body or of what is popularly called the "self" or "consciousness." (p. 319)

Let me briefly summarize the distinctions captured by Bateson in the preceding passage and contained in the review of the challenge posed by critical systems theory.

1. The identity logic which insistently yields a single, coherently organized entity, the subject, meets with stiff resistance once we reconceptualize and refocus our inquiry in terms of the critical systems perspective. There is no entity with a bounded identity (as Bateson observes, no skin-enclosed thinking and acting machine) unless, in the name of demanding that there be a center, we abstract a hypothetical center from the wide variety of transactions in which the skin-bound organism is engaged. Only with this demand and this abstraction will we arrive at this illusory figure. The systems perspective recommends that we see relations, not elements; relations appear on many dimensions and appear without a center or identity as such. Relations permit what seems to be the selfsame entity to be both selfsame and other without any absolute essence that *is* its alone.

As Ogilvy (1979) observes, within a logic of identity, it is correct to maintain that an object cannot have two opposing properties at the same time: for example, something cannot be A and not-A at the same time. However, within a systemic perspective, "it is perfectly possible to be both generous and stingy, both loving and hating, both downcast and elated in quite the same respects at the same time" (p. 206).

The lesson is important for understanding psychology's subject. We have invested substantial time, money, and energy in techniques that assess properties that people possess. We define a person as *having* or as *being* of a certain type or as behaving in a particular manner. These traits and behaviors become things that constitute the person as such. We fail to consider that people are both A and not-A, and that this is contradictory only within an identity framework that demands a selfsame, integrated center.

I believe that what has occurred is precisely what Geertz observes so keenly in his analysis of the "depersonalized" quality of Balinese ritual. In this ritual, coherence and integrity are assured by the portrayal of roles that subdue the inevitable contradictoriness and multidimensionality making up the person. The rituals that mute individuality constitute the coherent center. Western culture also accomplishes an integration. In this case, however, that integration is fixed in the skin-bound person as entity rather than in culturally prescribed (and proscribed) rituals. To phrase this differently, we make the individual into our cultural ritual, whereas the Balinese restrict the ritual to a cast of recurring characters in a drama.

We demand that the individual be either-A or not-A, that his or her essence be one or the other, not both/and. Our center thus becomes a character who, while constructed in multidimensionality, is expected to become unified into a coherent identity or center. We look with some puzzlement at the Balinese, who seem to us to distort themselves in order to play their ritual roles. I believe that we might also look at the distortions we undergo in order to play ourselves. If they seem depersonalized from our nonsystemic point of view, we appear overly personalized from a systemic point of view.

2. The systems perspective emphasizes reciprocity rather than hierarchy, differences rather than oppositions in which one term has ascendancy over the other. In a reciprocal relation, neither term occupies a privileged position; both contribute to the fate they each experience. The register and the furnace play important parts in the drama of the thermostat; we fail to see this once we arrange them hierarchically, giving primacy to one or the other (also see Bateson, 1972).

Psychology's subject, as a "bounded universe," recommends hierarchy over difference. We speak of the priority of the ego over its other or of mind over body and thereby seek to accomplish priority within the skin-bound person. Where reciprocity reigns, hierarchy fades except as some necessary (i.e., ideological) societal illusion. The cultural demand for hierarchy fails to consider the reciprocal nets that join the elements into the whole. The challenge to hierarchy that flows from the systems analysis tests our requirements for that controlling center, that locus of mastery and control, that entity which knows.

PART FIVE

Psychology and Society

The intent of the preceding section was to introduce the three foundations on which pure psychology has been built and to suggest some alternative pathways to psychological analysis and understanding. The purpose of this part is to explore in more substantial detail what I consider to be the primary consequences of building a psychology on a foundation of positivist empiricism, truncated subjectivism, and abstracted individualism.

I believe that the themes to be examined in this section provide a partial but important answer to a nagging question: Why did psychology, given alternative pathways that it might have followed, pursue the three just discussed? Any complete answer to this question would require an examination of the society in which pure psychology has developed and been nurtured, including its economics and politics; only in this way would we appreciate the route the discipline followed and its resistance to alternatives. It is not my intent to undertake a full-scale social analysis. My more modest aims are, first, to explore the relationships between psychology and society (Chapter 10); second, to examine the rationale for a transformative relationship between psychology and society (Chapter 11); and, third, to bring this understanding to bear on the critique of pure psychology (Chapter 12).

THREE POSITIONS

There are three typical but, I believe, erroneous positions that have been adopted concerning the psychology–society relationship: the impotent, the pure, and the liberal.

The Impotent

I cannot testify to the seriousness with which the "impotent" position is adopted, but its basic thought is that psychology has little impact on human life and therefore one need not be much concerned about what forms it adopts or what it has to say about human life and behavior. I am not speaking about those who insist that psychology is a basic science; we will hear from them in my discussion of the purists. Rather, I am addressing myself to those who insistently believe that their field has little fundamental impact on people, that it makes very little practical difference. Besides leading one to wonder why these practitioners insist on continuing with their practice if it makes little difference, their position reflects a kind of psychological burnout. It is not well founded on any careful examination of the actual or potential role of psychology in society but seems more to reflect a personal quirk, disposition, or ongoing depression on the part of its proponents.

The Purists

The purists, on the other hand, at least have a well-reasoned but, I suggest, incorrect understanding of the relationship between psychology and society. These are the scientists who remain fully wedded to the positivist notion of science. In this view, because science is founded on the clarity offered by empirical observation, we have an objective—that is, neutral—basis for science. The underlying reasoning is that the terms of an observational language give us privileged access to the facts that exist independently of the persons who observe them; hence the facts uncovered by the proper methods are without bias; they are neutral.

It is obvious that for the purists at least two worlds exist; these run in parallel and are clearly disconnected. The one is the world of everyday practical reality in which decisions must be made, ends and goals chosen, interests and values taken into consideration. This is the world of "ought;" it is not the world within which the scientist *qua* scientist works.

The world of the proper scientist is a world of "is," not of "ought." The scientists' concerns are not with ends, goals, or values but with the sheer discovery of truth—that is, with what actually exists. And that truth, once discovered, can be used for good or for evil; in and of itself, however, it is neither. Perhaps the most recent clear statement of this purist position appeared in Joseph McGrath's (1980) review of the past decades of social-problem research reported in the *Journal of Social Issues*.

McGrath employs a military metaphor and speaks of psychology's armamentarium of techniques and approaches for social problem solving. He suggests that the real dilemma we face is not whether our understandings and techniques for intervention are effective—they are, he asserts—but rather whether they will be used for good or for evil. He does not believe that the approaches employed are in themselves good or evil; the material in our armory is fundamentally neutral and indifferent. Like bullets and bombs, the techniques can be used for good or for evil; this important determination of value, however, lies outside the realm of the properly scientific.

Critics of the purist perspective have argued in several different ways. Some (e.g., Keat & Urry, 1975) have suggested that there is no such thing as pure observation; that every time we observe something, that act itself is thoroughly infused with interpretation. And thus our particular standpoint necessarily intervenes to influence what we see. A variant of this position argues that even the terms employed to describe a phenomenon that we and others observe are derived from a given time and place and so necessarily involve some evaluative overtones: that is, the world of "is" and the world of "ought" cannot be as neatly separated as the purists would hope (see Bhaskar, 1979).

The Liberalists

In answer to these and other criticisms, some of the purists have adopted a third position on the psychology–society relationship, the one I have termed "the liberal." In one version, the position is that although issues of value do enter into decisions about what to study, they are not relevant to decisions involving the validation of the factual findings of our studies. This is represented by Reichenbach's (1938) distinction between the value-liable contexts of discovery and the value-free contexts of verification. Needless to say, the essence of this liberalism is its search for some middle ground. In this case, there is the frank admission that values do enter our work and thus that society and psychology are not two entirely separated realms; yet at the same time, where it *really* counts, values and science part their ways.

Another version of this liberalist resolution, recommended by persons such as Myrdal (1959) among others, argues that although psychology and society are intertwined, the goal of a value-free science can be approached as long as the investigators make their own value positions clear. In other words, once we can uncover our own biases, we can somehow extract them from the work we do and arrive at relatively value-free, hence objective statements about the nature of reality. Needless to say, if our biases are either unconscious or ideological and so unavailable to our awareness or to that of others of our time and place, we cannot even know of them in order to correct them (see Bhaskar, 1979, p. 72, on this point).

Recall Ricoeur's (1972) definition of ideology as *in principle* being unaware of itself as ideology. Husserl's (1965) critique of modern science contains a similar formulation. He argues that the neutrality of pure science is an illusion, disguising within itself the hidden and unexamined empirical *a priori* on which science is based. In other words, science itself is based on a given, prescientific empirical reality that remains unexamined by science.

Thus whatever particular characteristics and ends are given in the empirical *a priori* are carried into the science disguised under the illusion of value neutrality (also see Marcuse, 1978).

Needless to say, this introduces us to a fourth position on the psychology–society relationship, the position that we examine in detail in Chapter 10.

CHAPTER TEN

Psychology

Reproductive and Transformative

It is apparent from the manner in which I have presented the previous three points of view that I find comfort in none of them. I would like to recommend a different position on the entire issue of the psychology–society relationship. In this position, the issues of "ought" and "is" are inextricably and necessarily bound together; this casts a different light on the relation between what we do as psychological scientists and the society in which we live. The position that I recommend derives in great part from the important account developed by the realist philosopher Roy Bhaskar (1979). His ideas crystallize some of the complex issues confronting all social scientists concerning both the relation between the individual and society and the relation between science and society.

Bhaskar develops many of the insights that Marx presented in his own important and, at times, contradictory and confusing treatises. Certain aspects of Bhaskar's model also have compelling parallels with Freud's thought, especially in his metapsychological works. By way of preface, the model stands in opposition both to the positivist tradition that lies at the foundation of pure psychology and to the so-called hermeneutic countermovement that has been gaining significance within the human sciences. The model attempts both to reveal the nature of the science–society relationship and at the same time to provide a perspective that addresses itself to the problems involved in the three biases of pure psychology noted in Part 4.

OUTLINES OF THE MODEL

To oversimplify, the model has four key aspects: (1) underlying social structures and mechanisms; (2) the prevailing reality or everyday world in which we live and to which our phenomenal experience refers; (3) the practices, activities, and the social relations that characterize a particular society's everyday reality; and (4) the self-understandings, including the beliefs and ideas, that make the prevailing reality and its practices intelligible to the participants.

Several important points need to be made about this model. First, it informs us both about behaviors and ideas. In other words, it deals both with what people actually do (e.g., their practices and activities) and what they know, believe, and understand (e.g., their self-understandings).

Second, the model is holistic; it operates reciprocally and in a systemic manner. The behaviors and understandings that constitute the prevailing reality are generated by the underlying structures and mechanisms of the society; in turn, they act back upon those structures and mechanisms, either to reproduce or transform them. Giddens (1979) describes this systemic quality as a *duality of structure*: the structural properties of social sytems are both the *medium* for the practices that constitute the system and also the *outcome* of those very practices.

A third feature of the model suggests that social actors tend to function consciously in ways that unconsciously (without intent) reproduce certain underlying structures. In other words, the processes of social reproduction may involve the unintended yet necessary outcome of actors' consciously intended behavior. Giddens addresses himself to this point in speaking of the critical role that the unintended consequences of action have for societal reproduction and transformation. He observes how activities tend to "escape . . . from the scope of the purposes of the actor" (p. 59). This introduces us to a point shared with hermeneutic analysts who note the extent to which a text, for example, becomes independent of its author's intentions as it moves through historical time (e.g., Ricoeur, 1979).

For our purposes, the main lesson of this third point is the manner in which actions done intentionally, in the service of one set of reasons, may unintentionally reproduce the underlying social structures from which they emanated in the first place. It was a commonplace experience for many citizens in the United States during the mid-1970s energy crisis, for example, to discover that in their very act of driving their cars to work they were contributing to sustaining an inflated price for gasoline and the entire underlying world market system.

COMPARISONS AND CONTRASTS

Before we go further in examining this model and its broad implications for psychology, let me first build upon Bhaskar's discussion contrasting this view with several more familiar analyses. Three contrasting perspectives are noted: voluntarism, reificationism, and interactionism.

According to the voluntaristic approach, the social world is built up on the basis of the intentional acts of the individuals it comprises. Objects are defined in terms of the subject's point of view; actions proceed on the basis of the subject's intentions and definitions of the situation (see Chapters 8 and 9). Reification emphasizes the independence of social objects from people and stresses the coercive or constraining properties of the social world. Murray's (1938) term *press*, developed to describe characteristics of situations, aptly captures this sense of the demand quality of the social world.

The interactionist perspective appears to straddle the extremes and attempts to build upon the best of each. In sociological thought, it is represented by Berger and Luckman's (1966) analysis of person–society interaction: the society constitutes the person who constitutes the society.

In Bhaskar's view, the purely reificationist position is in error because human activity is still necessary for there to be a society. Thus social objects have the peculiar standing of requiring human activity in order to exist. The purely voluntaristic position is also in error, but *not* because of its correct identification of intentionality and purpose as essential to human activity. Rather, its error lies in depicting people as actually *creating* society and social objects. Society preexists the individual; it is incorrect to say that individuals create society. What they do is reproduce or transform society through their activities: "Society stands to individuals, then, as something that they never make, but that exists only in virtue of their activity" (Bhaskar, 1979, p. 42).

Bhaskar argues that interactionism fails on two counts: "it encourages, on the one hand, a voluntaristic idealism with respect to our understanding of social structure and, on the other, a mechanistic determinism with respect to our understanding of people" (p. 42). It is his contention that people and society are not dialectical moments of the same process but, instead, two rather different phenomena, neither reducible to the other yet each intimately dependent on the other.

Person–Society Relationship

Bhaskar suggests that the true relation between the individual and society is more on the order of sculptor to block than God to universe: the sculptor fashions objects from a material that already exists, using available tools. Thus,

Society is both the ever-present *condition* (material cause) and the continually reproduced *outcome* of human agency. And praxis is both work, that is conscious *production*, and (normally unconscious) *reproduction* of the conditions of production, that is, society. (pp. 43–44)

This returns us to Giddens's duality of structure, to which Bhaskar has added a duality of human *praxis* or activity.

The notion of duality may initially appear peculiar to psychologists and other social scientists who are not accustomed to thinking in such genuinely dialectical terms. The formulation, however, shares a certain affinity with Mead's (1934) understanding of the individual–society relationship. The basic idea of duality is that something is both medium for and outcome of something else. As a medium, for example, the underlying economic structure of a society is the ever-present condition (the social form) that gives expression to particular practices and self-understandings. This structure is also reproduced (or transformed) as a result of these practices and self-understandings and hence is an outcome both intended and unintended of their performance.

For Mead, the underlying social process is the medium through which the human mind and identity develop. In turn, the minds and selves that have arisen through this social process participate in reproducing that process; in this sense, therefore, the social process is an outcome of the functioning of mind and identity. A structure that emerges from social interaction (e.g., the "me") functions within the interactive process either to confirm that structure or to transform it. The latter involves other people in the interactive encounter; their responses complete the social process. In this, we can see how the interactive encounter is both the medium whereby the "me" emerges and an outcome of the responses of the interactants. The latters' responses reproduce or transform the process within which the "me" itself has arisen.

In light of our previous discussion centering around the Cartesian substance–essence–entity notion of traditional Western epistemology, the concept of duality introduces a clearly relational analysis. Mind is a social relation, not an entity (see Wilden, 1980, and Chapters 8 and 9). It arises within the social process and joins biological individuals (entities) to that process. Mind participates in the reproduction of the totality of which it is a part and through which it was constituted. People do indeed act in accordance with their understandings; however, those understandings are not properties of entities as such but rather of social relationships that are reproduced (or could be transformed) as the actions governed by those understandings are carried out.

Insofar as we insist on entity-based rather than relational analysis, we necessarily reduce the individual–society relationship to one extreme or the other: e.g., voluntarism or reificationism. Only when one takes a relational view can one grasp the medium-outcome quality of the individual–society connection.

The relational model of the individual–society connection is important to our examination of the psychology–society connection in that the latter stands in the same relationship as the former: the activities of psychology build upon a preexisting foundation even as those activities either reproduce or transform that foundation. The activities have the property of production in the sense noted—working on and with the ever-present material conditions and either reproducing or transforming them.

AN ILLUSTRATIVE EXAMPLE: CAPITALISM

Let us examine an illustrative case that permits us to work with this model. We begin with a kind of Marxian assumption that the underlying structures and mechanisms of relevance (i.e., the preexisting social forms) involve the advanced capitalist mode of production and of state intervention in the economic process (see Part 4). The next step in the model suggests that this underlying organizational principle generates a prevailing reality. In other words, the prevailing reality, the world of our everyday existence, is generated by the underlying forms of advanced capitalism: for example, the qualities of our daily work, our career choices and chances, the kinds of conflict we encounter, the ideas, beliefs, and self-understandings we have about our world and our life, and so forth.

As Bhaskar notes, as people carry out their daily activities, they reproduce (or could transform) the very social forms that underlie and generate those daily activities in the first place. For example, although people may not marry in order to reproduce the nuclear family, this is a consequence of their marrying. Likewise, even though the intention of working is not to reproduce the underlying social formation, this is what results from our work activities. Social practices and social relations help reproduce the structures that generate and govern those very practices.

Much this same point is made concerning those ideas and self-understanding that make people's activities and practices intelligible to them. People act on the basis of their understandings and conceptions about the meaning and the purpose of what they are doing. For example, both the activities of working and the reasons that are accepted for working—to make money, to be a useful member of society, to achieve salvation—help reproduce the underlying social form that has generated both the work and its accompanying rationale.

One of the more intriguing features of this model is the role it sees for ideas and self-understandings in social reproduction and, by implication, potentially in social transformation. The ideas and self-understandings generated by the underlying societal structure help reproduce that underlying structure. These self-understandings are *necessary* components of social reproduction; without them, the underlying system would erode.

Recall that although the structures preexist the individuals who work with them, they require individual activity in order to be either sustained or transformed. And this essential activity is guided by the conceptions that people have about what they are doing and why. Thus, without the conceptions to guide the activities, the underlying structures that have generated these conceptions and activities would not be reproduced. The very recursive quality of society thereby depends on human agency—that is, on the self-understandings that participate in societal reproduction.

PSYCHOLOGY AND THE HUMAN SCIENCES

The human sciences enter this model in one important manner: they are the contemporary vehicle that *organizes and develops* societal self-understandings. Needless to say, they are not alone in this endeavor, as the media and religion also have their hand in developing, organizing, and propagating societal self-understandings. However, the human sciences play an especially central role in that they provide the scientific seal of approval, with all that it connotes in our world today, to the kinds of self-understandings they develop: an added sense of truth, fact, objectivity, and hence *legitimacy*.

From the perspective of the model I have outlined, the social sciences are themselves an outgrowth of a particular underlying social formation (e.g., capitalism); in this view, they have an *internal* and *causal* relation to the very society and individuals they study. The relation is internal in that they emerge from the same fabric of underlying structures and mechanisms as do the other institutions of the society. The relation is causal in that the self-understandings they develop and organize are causally connected to these underlying structures and, in turn, causally participate in the reproduction of these very structures.

Basically, in this view the sciences that study people participate in constituting the very subject matter they study. We might say, therefore, that psychology organizes self-understandings that reproduce the preexisting structures generating these self-understandings. In this sense, therefore, psychology is causally linked to its society.

None of this, however, is invariable. The self-understandings that develop can also be employed in the service of societal transformation. When those understandings are distorted and provide the relatively unqustioned background justifications essential to societal reproduction, and when the social sciences uncritically reflect these understandings, a kind of vicious circle of reproduction rather than transformation results.

What I have thus far said is that psychology and the other human sciences are a key part of the process whereby the underlying social form is reproduced. They could become a key part of the process whereby the underlying social form is transformed. In either case, the relationship between the sciences of human life and society is bound up with matters of interest and value. They cannot be neutral, indifferent, and disinterested, for their understandings of human life will either contribute to societal reproduction or potentially contribute to societal transformation.

CHAPTER ELEVEN

A Transformative Rationale

The rationale for my recommending a transformative over a reproductive relationship between psychology and society emerges both from a consideration of the effects of the particular underlying organizational principle of contemporary society and the values embedded in the emancipatory interest previously considered: that people employ their self-reflective abilities to determine the conditions that determine them.

If a particular social form establishes the very conditions that dominate and exploit many, that give advantage to a few, and that conceal this real relationship so that people cannot act with will and consciousness to change these conditions, then a transformative perspective is called for. As Freire (1970) states it, the ontological vocation of humanity is to become a subject, one "who knows and acts" (p. 20); conditions that thwart this achievement therefore must be transformed, not reproduced.

The value that is to be affirmed speaks of the possibility of people collectively making their own history; social formations that constrict this possibility are disvalued. What is intended is the restoration of the human potential to be aware of the circumstances that shape people's lives so that they can become informed and active participants in this shaping.

The model presented in Chapter 10 argues that people's self-understandings are both generated by society's underlying structures and act to reproduce or transform the very structures that generate them in the first place. The value to be affirmed involves gaining a critical understanding of the structures that form people, so that they can participate in their own formation. This value is nothing new. Without tracing its complete history, it goes back to the Greek conceptions of reason and builds upon the human capability to reason self-reflectively.

And Survival

A related, but somewhat differently accented argument on behalf of a transformative relationship between the human sciences and society emerges from a consideration of Wilden's (1980) ecosystemic analysis.

Wilden agrees with the thesis suggested here and elsewhere concerning the exploitative nature of the contemporary social forms. He sees the distortions in human communication and in the understanding of the subject (the substance–entity–essence model), including especially the scientific discourse, to have been derived from this underlying social form and to play a role in its reproduction. This problem is that the long-term survival of the ecosystem, rather than any short-term gain, depends on breaking free from this distorting ideology which our sciences continue to affirm.

Building his case on several points developed by Bateson (1972), Wilden argues that we have misplaced the basic unit of survival by locating it within either the fittest individual or the fittest species. This misplacement is a derivative of the underlying social formation and its resultant ideologies. Because of it, we fail to assure the survival of the actual relational unit, the ecosystem of organism and environment. Basically, if in the name of its own survival an organism destroys its environment or its "other" (e.g., through exploitative human relationships), it lays the foundation for its self-destruction. Any organism that destroys what it takes to be opposite to itself (e.g., the environment, nature, others) destroys itself in the process. The unit of survival is not the organism in itself or nature in itself but the unity, the both/and (self and other; organism and environment), not the either/or.

The key to Wilden's argument on behalf of a transformative relationship thereby hinges on his analysis of long-term survival. Insofar as any perspective develops in which relationships of nonexploitative difference (e.g., between self and other) become relationships of exploitative opposition and domination (e.g., self vs. other), their transformation is essential to long-term ecosystemic survival.

The subject of history will not be a subject who can act with will or with consciousness insofar as that subject is defined and experienced as an entity apart from and in opposition to others or to nature. This describes our present conception of the subject: one who cannot act to shape history from outside history without destroying itself in the very process. Without a transformative move, this pessimistic scenario is precisely what Wilden envisions (see Chapter 9 for an additional discussion of this analysis).

DOMINATION

Domination is a concept often discussed within the context of critical analyses. It describes the antithesis of action undertaken with will and consciousness. With domination, one becomes an object and not a subject, even if one believes himself or herself to be a subject: this describes what Lacan (see Lemaire, 1977) and Wilden, using Lacan's terminology, refer to as an imaginary subject. Domination can be based on the use of brute force. On the other hand, it can also exist in a more deeply structured, psychological form: people internalize the kinds of self-understandings that permit some to set the terms for the behavior and life experiences of the many; in turn, the many fail to penetrate sufficiently into the workings of their lives to grasp or know how to act in terms of their real interests. This is the kind of domination that enters the deep structures by which human (including scientific) discourse takes place. It involves the very conception of the subject as entity that we have been and will continue to consider. At lesser levels, we can see other manifestations of this seemingly benign form of domination.

For example, suppose that you believe that it is not only fair for some to have more benefits than others but that it is fair because some work harder than others. Domination exists here in that if you fail to achieve as much as another, you believe that the reason is somehow connected with a personal failing in your motivation or character: that is, your essence is somehow damaged and so is undeserving.

Let us take as another example the relationships between men and women. Suppose you believe that there is a kind of natural necessity governing male–female relationships, where *natural* should be read as involving either a religious or a scientific-biological edict involving brain neurophysiology or hormones. On the basis of this self-understanding, you think that it is right and proper for males to have more access to societal positions of power and privilege than females.

Whether you are male or female matters little once you have internalized a belief system of this kind, which participates in reproducing the underlying social system of inequality in which some, who are seen as "naturally" deserving, dominate and exploit others. In this particular example, a difference between biological entities (males and females) is systematically confused with a distinction between persons (the sociocultural and socioeconomic males and females). Differences in deserving are then attributed to the sociocultural persons because of differences between biological entities. This process conceals the real bases of the distinctions, which are social and exploitative. In other words, an imaginary subject (in Lacan's and Wilden's sense of that term) is constituted as an entity with a presumed essence that warrants particular kinds of deserving. The social basis of this construction is repressed and appears as though it were a real distinction of a biological, hence natural, sort.

Let me not belabor the point. The idea that I am leading up to is that whenever a social system systematically benefits a few at the expense of many and yet does so with the apparent consent of all, we have an instance in which domination has seeped deeply into the consciousness of the culture, including all its structures and relationships. We are dealing with a case of ideology. In other words, the kinds of self-understandings that enter the deep structures of humanity and become elements essential to the reproduction of a dominating and exploitative human relationship are properly termed ideology.

IDEOLOGY

When we refer to something as ideological, we mean that the ideas and understandings that prevail within a group mask a true state of affairs. The very concept presupposes a model of the sort I have outlined—one in which the prevailing forms of reality can be analyzed within the context of certain underlying productive and political practices. The appearances of everyday reality conceal an underlying layer that fixes certain meanings over other possibilities (also see the discussion in Chapters 6 and 8).

In their analysis of language, Coward and Ellis (1977) take issue with a simplistic view of ideology as merely a false consciousness. They suggest that the image of a consciousness that is somehow false can give the impression of ideology as a kind of covering of clouds floating over an already existing and true set of meanings. By contrast, they argue that ideology describes the process by which societal meanings are constructed in the first place, including the construction of the very social subjects who employ those meanings in their everyday lives. Ideology fixes or limits the meanings that evolve within a society to certain possibilities rather than others; it frames or punctuates the continuities and open horizons of reality and, in so doing, constitutes the forms within which that reality is grasped by societal members (e.g., Watzlawick, Beavin, & Jackson, 1967; Wilden, 1980; plus the discussion in Chapter 8).

In basing their analysis of ideology on a model of language and communication, Coward and Ellis present ideology as a practice central to all social life. Without the fixing of meanings and of a subject for those meanings, no communication and hence no other social practices could occur. In this view, the role of ideology is to produce the very subject, the "I," who engages in the social processes of communication and who is thereby able to participate in the other practices and social relations that describe any social system.

A central element in this view of ideology is its argument that the human subject is not simply a bearer or carrier of ideological consciousness but rather is constituted as a subject *in and through* ideology. To phrase this differently, ideology is part of the deep structure within which human communication and human subjectivity are developed; it is part of the very fiber of the society and so seems natural, "the ways things are."

Ideology is not an entity in itself, a thing apart from the underlying productive structures and mechanisms of a society. The underlying structural forms develop (that is, punctuate, fix, or close the open possibilities of reality) the symbolic practices that characterize a society. Those practices, in turn, are essential elements in the ongoing maintenance and reproduction of the underlying organizational principle. The way that reality has been punctuated in symbolic practice is a key element in the reproduction of that reality.

The efforts on the part of the poststructuralist movement (see Chapters 8 and 9) and the parallel ecosystemic analysis proposed by Wilden attempt to get at the root of Western ideological thought: its fixing of a noncontradictory, homogeneous, consistent, and—to employ Marcuse's (1964) fine term—one-dimensional subject. This is the Cartesian entity who is at the center of the universe, the prime mover, the first cause, the originator. This subject is essential to the operation of the underlying structural principle of the civilization; the system could not properly function without it:

> Ideological practice is necessary to societies of whatever kind because the individual is not the centre of the social whole: the social process has no centre, no motivating force in the sense that Renaissance humanism saw man as the centre of the world, actively willing the events of his social organization. Instead, society is composed of multiple contradictions in relationships of overdetermination. It is necessary then, that the relationship of people to the structure is produced in a process of representation so that they can act within the structure. . . . In practical terms, this means that . . . the ideology of the free worker, freely selling his labour at its market value, is a representation which it is necessary to live in order to function within the capitalist system. (Coward & Ellis, 1977, p. 74)

Thus, the various efforts to *decenter* this subject can be seen to be part of a program designed to break up the ideological practices that support the domination and exploitation characterizing the civilization that has constructed this subject in ideology.

Testing for Ideology

There are two basic tests to put to something that is ideological. First, does it systematically distort reality? Second, is its understanding essential to reproduce the underlying structures that have constituted it?

According to the first test, we are dealing with something ideological when there is a discrepancy between the surface appearance of reality and its underlying form. The reduction of multidimensionality to unidimensionality is one such example (e.g., Ogilvy, 1979). In ideology, real relationships of domination are concealed as such by forms of consciousness that portray what *is* as though it *must* be or *ought* to be. If we follow Giddens's (1979) discussion, there are several aspects to such ideological thought.

1. Values and interests that give advantage to one segment of the population are represented as though these were the general interests of all societal members.
2. There is either a denial of or, in Giddens's terms, a *transmutation* of systemic contradictions. Tensions and crises that originate in the depths of the economic system, for example, are either denied as existing at that level or are transmuted and so become psychological problems. For example, urban unrest is attributed to the lack of impulse control among young men raised in households without strong father figures.
3. Ideological thinking appears whenever the present moment is reified and so made natural and inevitable. The previous examples, but especially the naturalization of male–female social differences, represent this third form of ideological distortion.

What all three forms share is the way in which they disguise real relationships and thus make them less available for critical scrutiny and change: the status quo is reproduced. It is as though the rules of the game were set so as to provide key advantage to one side; yet those rules cannot be changed. Whenever the game is played with those rules, one side will necessarily win and the other lose.

Ideology presents what now is as though it must be and ought to be. In doing this, ideology robs people of their will and consciousness in shaping the course of their history by leading them to believe that the circumstance they encounter here and now is somehow ordained to be that way. Ideology is invariably part and parcel of systems of domination. It describes the ideas and the self-understandings that, according to the second test, are essential for that system of domination to be reproduced. If people did not believe as they did, the system that requires those beliefs for its maintenance would begin to falter and crumble.

Successful ideologies so deeply penetrate the consciousness of a culture that people unquestioningly accept their premises without further thought. Such ideologies provide the kind of baseline givens that are never examined. For example, one begins the analysis with the given capitalist form of socioeconomic organization. The given is not examined and is not to be tampered with. The only solution for whatever difficulties are encountered is to deal with the products of the underlying system but never with the given system itself.

Bramel and Friend's (1981) critical analysis of the original Hawthorne studies illustrates this point. The original investigators adopted as a *given* that workers and management shared the same basic interests. Therefore, conflicts between them were not understood in terms of any fundamental contradiction between the two groups' basic concerns but rather were attributed to some deviant forms of individual behavior. Bramel and Friend note, for example, that one employee who seemed less open to the managerial directives was initially presumed to be "ill." Hostility between workers and management was assumed to be "irrational;" thus its elimination required developing management techniques that "cooled" workers' tempers and helped to integrate them into the existing structures. Never were those structures or the underlying socioeconomic system subjected to any critical examination.

People are typically unaware of the ideologies that govern their existence, at least as ideologies. We cannot expect them to be able to talk openly or easily about ideological themes. The world simply is as it appears to be. Perceptions are real and taken without doubt. But with ideology, something that is real is not necessarily true.

What Is Real / What Is True. Since ideologies are essential to societal reproduction, they stand in a very complex relationship to truth. As Adorno (1976) frequently observed, what is ideological is both false and yet true. It is false for the reasons just cited. Its truth, however, is revealed in its very essentiality to societal maintenance. That is, what people falsely believe—false in that the beliefs are not statements about an inevitable or immutable reality as such—is also a true statement of their circumstances.

For example, Adorno asks us what sense we would make of the data from an extensive public opinion survey showing that people no longer described themselves as workers. He first rejects the simple truth of this assertion, noting that simply because people no longer define themselves as workers does not mean that they are, in fact, no longer workers. Thus, if they occupy particular roles within the societal productive process, objectively they can be said to be workers. Their subjective belief that they are not represents the false side of ideology, their false consciousness. Our question here would inquire about the particular interests that were served by this ideological veil.

Yet, as Adorno also notes, insofar as people no longer believe themselves to be workers, this consciousness accurately reflects a constituent element of their social reality. In this sense, what is ideological is also true. As Adorno states it,

Appearance is always the appearance of reality. . . . If indeed nobody realizes any more that he is a worker, then that affects the composition of the concept "worker," even when the objective criterion of separation from the means of production remains fulfilled. (Adorno, 1976, p. 255)

One cannot grasp ideology merely by examining the shape of empirical reality; I will return to this point in the next chapter. Basically, we are dealing with a situation in which people accurately perceive what is fundamentally a distorted world view. Therefore, in matters involving ideology and false consciousness, it is not people's perceptions that are somehow at issue but rather the shape of the reality within which they live; this must be more closely and critically examined.

CHAPTER TWELVE

Pure Psychology and Societal Reproduction

We are now ready to reintroduce the three foundations of pure psychology in the context of societal reproduction and ideology. Let me first simply assert my conclusion and then develop the bases for it: the building blocks of positivist empiricism, truncated subjectivism, and abstracted individualism on which psychology's deep structure is based contribute to societal reproduction and are primarily ideological in their social function. Insofar as the existing socioeconomic and sociocultural system generates the necessary domination of many by a few, psychology's role is to help foster the very self-understandings that reproduce both the underlying system and its accompanying system of domination and unfreedom.

My task is to demonstrate how each of the three building blocks of pure psychology not only derives from a particular underlying social form (e.g., advanced capitalism) but also generates the very self-understandings that help sustain that form: how psychology helps develop and organize the kinds of self-understandings that legitimate people's fitting into the existing social system. In Part 6 of this work, I will endeavor to indicate how psychology's treatment of justice fits this model of pure psychology, thereby deflecting attention from the more profound issues of justice to questions whose answer does not penetrate sufficiently to challenge and undo existing injustices.

POSITIVIST EMPIRICISM

As noted in Chapter 7, the positivist–empiricist perspective leads us to begin and conclude our inquiry with the phenomenal world as given to our sense observations. The only check against what one observer sees are procedures designed to approach intersubjective validation. Basically, however, the prevailing empirical reality is taken as it is found; there is little probing beyond or behind that reality, no search for the underlying structures and mechanisms that have generated that prevailing form. What occurs thereby is that a historically generated social product—the prevailing reality—is adopted as the basic and fundamental reality. I am not disputing its reality but only its status as the only or the most fundamental stratum of reality.

By declining to probe beyond this sociohistorically produced reality into the structures and the mechanisms that have produced it, the immediate now is taken as though it were somehow eternal. The result is covertly to affirm existing social arrangements as though these were basic. The psychological science thereby builds upon an empirically real but potentially distorted base without, however, recognizing this possibility. The field develops and organizes self-understandings that can only fail to inform people about the distortions and contradictions shaping their lives. A pure psychology of this sort implicitly helps to legitimate domination, special interest, and privilege as though these were somehow natural or necessary.

Almost any reading of the major journals in the field will demonstrate what I mean. The research studies are reported as though they were gaining access to the basic nature of things as they essentially are, not the nature of things as they have become and might be modified. In my writings on androgyny (Sampson, 1977; also Chapter 5), to use this as one example, I pointed out that even if an investigator discovered that people who scored high on androgyny were more adaptable to a variety of situations as compared with sex-typed people, this did not tell us something fundamental about human psychology but rather something about the kind of characterological qualities that may bring success in today's world. To be androgynous is not intrinsically better than not to be; rather, it seems to embody a set of qualities that permit one to fit in better today. The real questions, however, pertain to the meaning of "fitting in better" today; these are questions about the potentially self-contained and narcissistic quality of such a character.

Once the concept appears and a measurement technique is developed to assess it, the normal science of the field proceeds to test it without examining its relationship to the underlying social system from which the concept emerged and to which it applies. Therefore, the kinds of question asked about androgyny, for example, focus on improving its measurement, checking out its validity in a variety of experimental situations, comparing it to alternative conceptions, and so on. Hardly any serious effort is devoted to examining the nature of the underlying social system within which such a concept develops or the broader societal implications of the androgynous ideal. As long as our inquiry is directed towards checking matters out in the prevailing world, we participate covertly in reproducing that world, never having probed its interior or the role that we play in a potentially ideological enterprise.

Psychology and Societal Contradictions

What is most likely to occur under the preceding conditions is the emergence of concepts that either "fit" the ongoing structures of the underlying societal reality or that reveal its internal contradictions, without, however, any recognition that this is the case. I believe that androgyny provides a useful illustration of both.

According to Habermas (1975), one of the contradictions of an advanced capitalistic social principle is its creation of a strong trend toward privatism: dedication to matters involving family, personal career, and consumption. Even as this *press* develops, there is also increasing public intervention into areas that were once held to be personal and private: for example, family law.

It would not be surprising to see psychological concepts that emphasized privatism, or what I have termed self-contained individualism, emerging in this context and describing so-called successful people. These concepts likewise emerged from earlier social forms in which independence and self-reliance were necessary virtues, given the demands of survival in a frontier society. Indeed, a dominant theme in much of our contemporary psychology is its stress on self-containment, self-reliance, independence, autonomy, assertiveness, and so forth as personal qualities that are essential to success and healthful adjustment.

Few if any of these concepts, however, are ever joined with the societal context in which they make sense; rather, they are presented as though they were absolutes of healthy human functioning. Their healthful qualities, however, pertain to a given social form in which they have emerged and in which they provide the kinds of self-understanding that are essential. For example, if people must go out on their own to sell their products, including their labor in the marketplace, then the greater their self-reliance and self-containment, the more likely they are to work successfully in this kind of framework.

Needless to say, if an underlying social form has certain inherent contradictions, then we might expect those contradictions to appear as well in the character and self-understandings of the people socialized into that society. I believe that the theme of self-containment or self-reliance is of precisely this sort and can readily be seen in terms of narcissism. The truly privatized individual might also be described as the narcissist, one whose social disease, so to speak, lies in being nonsocial.

Contradictions within an underlying framework participate in creating social characters who both reproduce the structure and who, while following its contradictory qualities, thwart that very reproduction. The success of self-containment is lost by the failures of narcissism: both, however, derive from the same underlying social structure and reveal aspects of its inherently contradictory nature. The system that creates self-containment as a virtue also creates the very kinds of social problems and traps that demand cooperation and interdependence of a high degree in order to be handled. The latter suffer from the excesses of narcissism and self-containment.

I hasten to observe that the advice one typically encounters from the presidential level through the halls of social science involves "changing people's character," never the underlying system that has produced the contradictions of character which prove so intractable to social problem solving. Nearly every social commentator has come to recognize how destructive narcissistic self-containment is to cooperative problem solving; therefore effort is directed toward cajoling, coercing, or retraining people into caring more for one another: witness the popularity of altruism research in psychology.

Some approaches argue that since people are basically (that is, genetically or naturally) selfish and narcissistic, there is little hope other than potentially nondemocratic means to curb their narcissism and solve social problems that demand cooperative efforts. Others believe that resocialization approaches might still work. What all such approaches share at their root, however, is ideological blindness to the underlying system, which creates the very contradictions that are now found to be so destructive.

By adopting the prevailing reality as its *given* and by not probing beyond to discover its qualities and contradictions, what psychology accomplishes is a reproduction of the historical moment. This failure to connect the social product to the underlying system that produces it fails to help people penetrate into the very conditions that are shaping them and their life experiences. This is a failure to provide the kinds of knowledge that would be essential if people were to become subjects to their lives and not objects.

My intent in all of this is not to pick on androgyny, the conceptual vehicle that led me into this discussion, or to hold it up as the worst case. My intent is simply to use this as one of several illustrations of the more general and more important point that I have been making about psychology's relation to society.

Another Illustrative Example: Locus of Control. Another instructive example comes from Rotter's (1966) effort to determine a personality type who attributed her or his fate to internal and self-controlled actions or to external processes beyond personal control. Rotter captured the Protestant ethic in this concept and in his implied affirmation of the internal ideal. The ethic argues that there is a correlation between hard work and social achievement: basically, that one is in control of her or his own destiny. It is an ethic of individual effort and has little if anything to say about external, structural impediments to achievement. The internally disposed individual follows this ethic; the externals, by contrast, believe that luck, chance, or even politics governs their fate and that individual effort may or may not pay off.

Of course, if you are female or belong to an ethnic minority in which hard work, personal motivation, and effort might be only minimal components of social achievement, are you manifesting a defect in your character when you adopt the external orientation or are you simply perceiving the reality of your circumstances accurately? The problem with formulations of the Rotter type is that they freeze the historical moment into a psychological character trait and then fail to see the connections between the resulting personalities they uncover and the real world within which such people live.

Later investigators (e.g., Gurin, Gurin, & Morrison, 1978) did address some of the ideological meanings of Rotter's thesis and provided a more sociohistorically meaningful understanding of what otherwise passes for a purely psychological variable. Gurin *et al.* report, for example, a distinction between people who believe themselves competent to exercise some control over their lives and yet are aware that the larger social system opens opportunities for some and closes doors for others: this reflects a kind of external ideological orientation. At least the recognition of this distinction, based on the Gurin's efforts to link personality with society, provides a more accurate and helpful portrait than Rotter's original analysis and understanding.

An interesting updated version of this same kind of thesis has been proposed by Bandura (1982), who explores the concept of self-efficacy as a fundamental mechanism of human agency. It is clear that Bandura has attempted to advance beyond the merely psychological by recognizing conditions in the real world that shape the experience of self-efficacy: that is, the perception that one can influence events. He even introduces a chart in which perceived self-efficacy constitutes one side and environmental responsiveness the other. This permits him to argue that people with different efficacy perceptions will react differently as a function of the openness of the environment to change-oriented actions. People may feel that things are futile because that is their characteristic manner of coping with life; or their sense of futility may derive from a nonresponsive environment.

Bandura's little diagram leads him to argue that one would have to remedy feelings of futility differently if they were a function of the person or the situation. Personal futility, deriving from a low sense of self-efficacy, requires techniques to help reempower the individual; environmentally based futility demands efforts designed to alter the unyielding situation. Although I believe Bandura's perspective to be an advance over Rotter's original formulation, there remain some nagging suspicions and doubts concerning its formulation. For example, the accent remains heavily on helping people feel themselves to be empowered (accomplished somewhat mechanistically and in terms of a social-learning model) through their *perceptions* of themselves and of their situation. Given the real possibilities that perceptions are too readily manipulated in the direction of creating the illusion of power without its actuality, one pauses to question any view that places so much emphasis on this subjective realm. For example, helping people vote in an election as a way of giving them a sense of personal efficacy to change circumstances will not work in reality if the issues on (or the candidates) which voting is permitted have previously been determined by nondemocratic practices. Voting thereby appears to be efficacious but basically changes very little in reality.

Concluding Comment. The general point remains, however, that the purely empiricist approach to knowledge that characterizes much of psychology today typically fails to examine the ongoing reality as a sociohistorical product and so leads us to view a changeable resultant as though it were somehow an eternal, timeless, and basic building block. This inadvertently gives a system-maintaining role to psychology.

Recall that one of the manifestations of an ideology is its transmutation of a social defect into a psychological or a characterological fault. The previous examples in one form or another manage to do this. In Rotter, for example, we see that the blame for failure is placed squarely on the individual, thus freeing the underlying social forms from any real involvement. Even Bandura's somewhat improved model moves too closely in this same direction, as he observes how collective action calls for individuals who are themselves high in self-efficacy (see Bandura, 1982, p. 143), thereby implying that only with properly motivated individuals can change occur. Although this may appear to be a reasonable position, it locates the source within the individual's psychology and could thereby tend to deflect our attention from the underlying structures that inhabit these individuals, routinely weakening efficacy.

Psychological crises thereby replace social crises and psychotherapy rather than societal transformation becomes the major vehicle for problem solving. We cannot hope to help people penetrate the underlying social formations that generate their reality when we adopt that reality as the dominant perspective for our analysis and forcefully eschew the legitimacy of probing further. It may well be that, contrary to the seemingly sensible appeals for more self-efficacious pulling together—as opposed to divisive factualism (e.g., Bandura)—the lesson we need to learn is that the reality which now prevails may be at the root of the problems, and not people's possibly accurate perceptions of that reality.

ABSTRACTED INDIVIDUALISM

We have seen that the individual is a product of an underlying social formation, although the individual as such cannot be reduced simply to that. We have also seen that one of the prime qualities of this contemporary social product is what can only be termed the illusion of independence and autonomy or of self-efficacy. Erik Fromm (1955) phrased it nicely several years ago (as we previously noted) in describing the marketing personality as comprising those who had to think of themselves as agents who were in control but whose actual choices were sufficiently predictable to fit neatly into the market demands.

In the previous discussion of self-reliance and autonomy, I did not develop the distinction that I am addressing here: namely, the difference between genuine and illusory autonomy. Fromm's point is that the underlying structure of capitalism calls for people who believe themselves to be free agents while they are actually governed by forces that press them this way and that, but behind their backs. This describes the kind of illusory autonomy that is essential to system reproduction. Genuine autonomy, in which people are cognizant of the forces that shape them and so can begin to act collectively to govern what governs them, is a very different matter.

We can extend Fromm's insights and this distinction by observing how psychology has most often adopted "the illusion" as its subject of analysis. The study of decision making offers one of the clearest examples of what I mean. Elaborate theories and research methodologies join with elaborate mathematical procedures to help us better understand the dynamics of individual choice and decision making. In the basic paradigm, the individual confronts several choices, and our task as psychologists is to predict which choice will be made. The emphasis is on grasping the elements within the individual's psyche that contribute to the decision route finally taken. One key element that we fail entirely to examine is how those decision choices were generated and how they present themselves to the individual in the first place. Arguing that the choices were put there by the experimenter does not address the fundamental issue involved in real decision contexts, although it does represent matters symbolically.

Note the important distinction between attending to the individual who is to choose between A and B versus attending to the social processes that have cast up the options of A or B in the first place. If we stress the former, we help to create the impression that what is really important in freedom of choice is a purely individual matter; thus it makes sense to probe the processes within the individual's mind that come into play as either A or B is chosen. We deflect attention away from an examination of why A and B are the options presented. These are the "givens."

However, what is given in the abstracted individualism of pure psychology is the very heart of the matter of freedom and autonomy. What is the meaning of autonomy if it involves only freely selecting between A and B but *not* actively being involved in the process by which A and B are presented as options? The processes involved in choosing between A and B are not the same as the complex sociohistorical processes that determine the options from which choices are to be made.

Let me use a simple and overworked example. Suppose we are interested in determining the TV channel that a person will watch on a given evening between eight and eleven o'clock. Suppose further that we develop some excellent procedures permitting us to predict, within reasonable bounds of accuracy, the programs that particular types of people will watch. Suppose even further that we now believe we have understood something central to individual freedom of choice and decision making in the area of viewer behavior. The problem, of course, is that we have neglected the highly complex and nonindividual processes that lead to the selections that appear on TV from which the individual is then "free to choose."

The emphasis on the individual chooser's psychology tends to mask the underlying social structures and processes that provide the particular alternatives from which people can freely choose. This psychology of abstracted individualism can all too readily serve the existing structures and social interests. It suggests a self-understanding of human choice in which we maintain that what is really important is to choose wisely and rationally between this rock and that hard place. We deflect attention away from understanding why the choices are only between rocks and hard places. We make it appear as though an individual could *in fact* act wisely, rationally, or autonomously when confronted with choices that have been cast up by a social process that disallows rationality and autonomy in any sense other than fitting one's behavior into the achievement of pregiven ends. We fail to inform people about the impossibility of being rational when the choices presented are themselves nonrational. And so our psychology supports the distortions and the contradictions of the underlying social formation and contributes little if at all to its potential transformation.

A Relational Reprise

Psychology's abstracted individualism helps to reproduce an underlying social form that requires the illusion of individual autonomy, self-efficacy, and freedom. Real individual autonomy and freedom, however, stand in a contradictory relationship to this underlying structure, and thus pure psychology participates in the deceptions of our era, not in uncovering or challenging them.

Let me be clear on this critical point regarding psychology's ideological function. I have contrasted the illusory autonomy of an illusory subject with the real autonomy of a real subject. It is important to recognize that the former represents the Cartesian tradition of substance–essence–entity that emerged with a particular social formation and became essential to its reproduction. It is this tradition that psychology continues to represent, as though this imaginary character were the real subject of the discipline.

That real subject which could become psychology's focus, however, cannot be the Cartesian entity, but rather would necessarily have to be of a more decentered sort: that is, a subject in relation—defined in and through that relation—not a transcendent entity, the imaginary atom of society. The decision-making example illustrates this difference: psychology focuses its inquiry on the atomistic entity, failing to understand the systemic constraints within which real choices are made and failing to provide informative insights about the consequences for the real rationality of human choice and agency.

The decentered subject in relation cannot become the master of history if by that we mean to employ the same framework of understanding that has persisted throughout the greater period of our civilization: that is, a god constituted in human form who has full and absolute control. The decentered subject in relation exists within a larger system, is constrained by that system, and yet has collective powers to affect the system—but only as a participant and not as its master. Psychology's most significant contribution to human history can lie in its own radical transformation: *from* analyzing the abstracted atomistic individual and thereby affirming the social form that requires this imaginary type *to* the understanding of the decentered subject in relation, whose mastery emerges from within and as a participant of the system of which it (the collective "it") is a part.

TRUNCATED SUBJECTIVISM

By this point, the reader can undoubtedly complete this section without further guidance. Let me simply reiterate the emerging theme that links this basis of pure psychology to the ideological support and reproduction of society. I previously suggested that psychology's understanding of the subject failed to grasp the dialectical connection between subject and object: psychology builds around the primacy of the subject. One of the most apparent problems with a truncated subjectivism of this sort is its vacuousness: that is, it is unable to gain either a critical understanding of the material bases of human consciousness or to act effectively to transform the material world itself. Basically, a subjectivist primacy traps us within the potential deceits of the mind.

There are two aspects to this quality of deceit. In the first, when the subjective is divorced from its material base, we have no foothold by which to generate a critique of the mind or of perception itself. Only when we can evaluate the prevailing phenomenology against the underlying material reality can we hope to gain a critical understanding of the potential phenomenal distortions involved. Recall Adorno's example. If we took an extensive public opinion survey and discovered that people reported themselves to be very happy with their lot in life, we might not accept this at face value. We require a model that permits us to examine the linkages between people's perceptions and understandings (e.g., their reports of happiness) and the underlying structures of the society in which they live and work. This might lead us to doubt the reports of happiness; yet psychology's truncated subjectivism fails to generate this kind of more critical analysis.

The second and related deceit of the mind is our capacity to act conceptually and rest satisfied without ever engaging in material action. If we believe that a mental transformation suffices, we are unlikely to be eager to work actively on any material transformation. Most cognitivist psychology is based on this notion; one of its unintended effects is to provide comfort and solace to the status quo by advocating mental gymnastics as the solution to all our difficulties (see Sampson, 1981a).

The theory of cognitive dissonance is one prime example (Festinger,

1957). Listen to its message. The mind is said to abhor dissonance and so tries to reduce it through mental gymnastics. Reality as such remains relatively untouched. Dissonance theory tells us, for example, that because we cannot change or take back what we have already done or been induced to do, the only recourse is to change our cognitions about our actions so as to produce inner harmony in the face of a dissonant reality. The "hero" in this story is the person who manages a self-change rather than a reality change. This person, for example, has just participated in a very boring task, lied to someone else by telling how enjoyable it was, and now finds satisfaction in overrating the boring task and seeing it as really fun and exciting (see Festinger & Carlsmith, 1959, for the actual study). The psychological fool is the person who declines to conceal an objective contradiction with a subjective fig leaf and persists in remaining dissonant rather than harmoniously submitting to the real-world contradiction by an internal transformation.

Dissonance theory thereby describes people for whom harmony is achieved by abandoning the hope of influencing material reality. To reduce cognitive strain, one changes things inside the head, not outside in the world. I would suppose that a *first* stage in a material transformation might require retaining the contradiction in awareness and not changing oneself into a harmonious adapter. When seen in this light, the psychological process of dissonance reduction involves denying the reality in which we live and work in exchange for the hollow pleasure that the absence of cognitive strain may bring. What is objectively boring is lost in the name of inner peace.

In what kind of social world—with what arrangements, institutions, and practices—does such a psychology make sense? Insofar as a psychological theory teaches us that we can solve material strain by mental manipulation, I believe that we have an instance of a theory in psychology that contributes to the reproduction of the existing social form by valuing its mental but never its material transformation. I am not arguing that dissonance is somehow an incorrect portrayal of today's consciousness. What I am saying, however, is that we need to see the manner in which dissonance and other truncated subjectivist theories in psychology are potentially ideological. A psychology that lives within the head and never probes beyond into the material reality as such is one that is geared to social reproduction and not social transformation.

CHOSEN PATHWAYS: A CONCLUDING COMMENT

My intent in this section has been to present a model of the psychology–society relationship that provides a central place in societal reproduction or transformation for those sciences that study human behavior. I have suggested that the founding theses of pure psychology contribute to societal reproduction and fail thereby to inform in ways that are essential to any societal transformation. The very kinds of self-understandings that members require in order to penetrate their circumstances sufficiently and thus to act with will and consciousness to transform them cannot be obtained through the practices of pure psychology. Rather, its messages help to maintain the existing social form—including the particular values, interests, and patterns of domination provided by its arrangements.

At this point it should be apparent that I do not view the varieties of work in psychology, including its tendencies toward momentary faddism in both topics of study and in methodologies, or any of the legion of other components of its normal practice, to be simply unrelated bits and pieces. More on the order of the psychoanalyst who seeks to uncover some of the unconscious roots and deep structures that join together seemingly disparate parts, the model employed in this analysis urges that we seek the connections between each part and the underlying structural whole.

Needless to say, I have not undertaken here, nor was it my intent to do so, any detailed examination of all the links between pure psychology and the underlying structural principle of an industrialized, capitalist social form. It would be my contention, however, that if such an enterprise were undertaken, substantial connections would emerge, further supporting the general framework I have outlined. In other words, what now may appear to be a puzzling array of faddish pursuits would begin to appear as a more or less understandable derivative of a given system of socioeconomic and sociocultural organization. I leave this fascinating and challenging task to others.

PART SIX

The Critique and Justice According to Psychology

My critical pen is not yet dry. Unfortunately, the role of the critic is often seen to provide only a negative world view, as though something affirmative could not emerge from the negative side of what surely is a dialectical process. My criticism is not quite yet of the variety that both Marcuse (1968) or Adorno (1973) recommend. Marcuse urges us to engage in the "great refusal," while Adorno avoids all affirmative statements lest they fall into the wrong hands. My critical bent still remains soft in comparison with their hard-line position. I offer it, therefore, in the hope that a positive impact on the nature of psychology's understanding of justice can emerge once the dimensions of the problem are developed.

My intent in Chapter 13 is to apply the insights of the previous critical analyses to psychology's study of justice motivation and behavior. My argument is that the prevalent model of justice work in psychology has adopted the very model of pure psychology that I have challenged. Given what I see to be the ideological implications of this model of pure psychology, I trace some of the possible ideology-serving consequences of the major views of justice developed in psychology. Chapter 14 introduces a concept, frame of address, as a way to reconceptualize justice motivation and behavior in less individualistic and more contextual ways. I present this as a modest proposal about the direction toward which I see a more helpful contribution to the study of justice might move. I claim this to be only a modest proposal in that I recognize its many limitations with respect to addressing the great issues of injustice that people face today. And yet, I believe that insofar as psychology's understanding of justice can become more interpersonal at its roots, it will have taken one step in the proper direction. The final chapter (Chapter 15) attempts to pull things together and offer a concluding note and commentary on where we have been and where we might go.

CHAPTER THIRTEEN

A Critique of the Psychology of Justice

Sufficient progress has been made in our understanding of the bases for a critical perspective to warrant a chapter that goes beyond the preliminary comments on the psychology of justice developed in the first part of this work. My intention in this chapter is twofold: to examine the ways in which pure psychology has dominated our understanding of justice and to probe the ideological consequences of this endeavor. My conclusion is clear: the psychological study of justice has uncritically adopted the empiricist, individualist, and subjectivist bases that characterize pure psychology; the work thereby has inadvertently functioned to legitimate the present configuration of society and, in deleting some of the important socioeconomic factors involved in issues of justice, has deflected our attention from effectively understanding and transforming conditions of injustice.

PURE PSYCHOLOGY AND THE STUDY OF JUSTICE

When psychologists confronted the question of justice, armed with their implicit framework for understanding human behavior, they tended to go about their business in the same manner as before. The psychological approach to justice was little different than the psychological approach to any other topic that happened to present itself. We might reason, along with Kuhn (1962), that this illustrates normal science following a discipline's dominant paradigm. Although psychology is supposedly preparadigmatic, there is sufficient agreement among those who are interested in the topic of justice to warrant our considering the three foundations previously noted as providing a substantial basis for paradigmatic agreement.

I am not simply casting stones without guilt. As even a cursory review of my own works on justice indicates, they too were carried out in the standard mold that dominates the discipline. It was only somewhat fortuitously that I encountered several disconcerting findings that led me away from conducting more empirical research and into a more proper avenue for the time, critical reflection on the entire model of study itself.

There are several aspects of psychology's endeavor to understand just-ice that clearly reveal the three founding perspectives that constitute psychology's heritage. Let me list and briefly examine several of the most important among these.

Truncated Subjectivism

Psychology's major approach involved defining justice in terms of the actor's phenomenology. Regardless of what kind of justice principle was theorized to exist—whether equity, equality, the just-world need, or whatever—it was defined entirely in terms of the actor's point of view. An allocation was just and fair, for example, if the actor said it was. This kind of truncated subjectivism yields an interesting but only partial picture of the operation of justice within society. It adopts the actor's framework as though it defined the topic of justice; it fails to grasp the extent to which the actor's framework may reflect an ideological or false consciousness.

The field, trapped by its simple phenomenological base, is unable to get beyond and probe the underlying material reality that might demand the very deceptions of awareness that psychology studies and defines as just and fair. We seem pleased to discover, for example, the prevalence of an equity formulation. We observe that when many people are asked to tell us whether a given allocation is fair or not, they do so according to the proportionality of investments and outcomes. And so we now take the actor's perspective as the fundament of reality and define justice in the very terms she or he has. We fail to consider several important matters: the extent to which the actor's definitions already reflect the outcome of a social process and the extent to which that process might require those conceptions among actors in order to be sustained. Whether or not this phenomenology reflects justice must be determined more critically by probing beneath and beyond the actor's phenomenology rather than being defined entirely in its terms.

Abstracted Individualism

For the most part, in the hands of psychology, justice was defined, studied, and understood entirely in individualistic terms, as though there were no larger context to be considered. For most, this meant examining justice from the point of view of a single actor engaged with a single other actor or from the point of view of an observer examining two other actors behaving in some kind of allocation or exchange. As part of this, it was only natural to assume that the locus of justice lay within the individual—in particular, within the individual's mental apparatus, which somehow required justice in order to function even as it needed glucose. Thus equity, for example, was seen to be a fundamental principle of human mental functioning. Admittedly, it was not genetically programmed, although in some references it almost seemed to be. But it was internalized very early and functioned to assure that justice would be done.

The tendency to individualize and to psychologize justice led the discipline to work upward from an individual psychological principle to society rather than to make any serious effort to reverse the process. Justice in society was presumably built upon the combined justice intentions of its individual actors. The problem with all purely psychological approaches is that, in being built on individual subjectivity they deny intersubjectivity. Furthermore, by making justice a psychological principle, they remove attention from the social forms that are reproduced when social actors internalize and act upon a given principle. That is, once we put ourselves inside the actor's head and search for mental functioning divorced from its social origins, we covertly accept the very conditions that require our critical scrutiny—that is, those social forms.

We spend our time probing the individual's mental apparatus, which we believe will provide the key to the mysteries of social justice. We fail to probe the underlying social process which interpenetrates that mental apparatus. The social process passes by unnoticed, part of the taken for granted background of our analysis. The forms that describe this background and the particular values and interests it represents enter as unexamined givens.

Uncritical Empiricism

I experience a kind of gnawing passivity in response to psychology's understanding of justice. The discipline seems comfortable in describing the way reality appears today; there are few if any concerns about connecting this portrait of today with action designed to transform or change its character. The theory of justice, in other words, is divorced from a workable theory about creating justice. Needless to say, the positivist–empiricist bent of the discipline inclines one toward just this kind of apparent passivity: describe the facts as you find them. Unfortunately, it is only an apparent passivity, for in the very act of merely describing the world as it is found, the discipline contributes to reproducing that very world. Hardly a passive endeavor.

The most active-sounding solution to social injustice offered by psychology is to rearrange the psychological ingredients. For example, if a given person feels that her or his relationship with another is unfair, then this person might do several things designed to improve this inequitable situation:

change investments, influence the other to change investments, seek better outcomes, psychologically leave the field, and so on.

None of these activities is designed to transform the circumstances that underlie and generate the injustice but only to manage the microcontext in a highly individualistic way. These activities tend not to penetrate the social forms that undoubtedly will continue to manufacture the injustices for which psychology's remedy must seem weak and impotent. These "change activities" seem poorly designed to further enlightenment; they work primarily within the framework of the existing system to make fine-tuning adjustments.

Postallocative Analyses

The overly individualized and overly psychologized approach to justice has led investigators to examine justice-related decisions comprising elements that have already been predetermined by earlier stages in the social allocation process. Thus justice is defined after an injustice has been committed. We have seen this point illustrated in the earlier discussion of decision making. The focus of psychology is not on how options have been cast forth among which choice is to be made but rather with what the decision is among the options that are presented. The social mechanisms that confront people with particular kinds of allocation are never examined in a theory of justice. What is examined is the behavior of people who are already constrained by what may be an unjust allocation and who are then asked to behave in a just and fair manner.

For example, a group of three nine-year-olds is given one candy bar to divide among themselves after they have worked together on a task. How will they make this division so as to be fair and just? If one of the youngsters has done more work than the others, will that child take the largest piece of the candy bar? Will they divide it equally, or perhaps find some other solution? Will children make different allocations at different ages? My concern in asking these questions is not to uncover the answer in the form presented; thus my concern is not with reviewing the growing body of studies informing us about what will happen under these precise circumstances (see Damon, 1977, for some of this work). Rather, my point is that however the children decide to divide this candy bar, we will have only learned about how justice and fairness can be attained in a situation that—in this case, by experimental intervention—is already unjust. The only option not made available to the children is to demand three candy bars so that each can have one or to demand some other kind of arrangement.

This small example is only illustrative of the much larger and I believe more significant point. Insofar as the psychological investigator is content to examine how people make seemingly rational choices in allocating the scarce resources presented to them by an underlying allocation process that is itself unjust, we in psychology will contribute more to mystifying the understanding of justice than helping probe its real operations. Statistical analyses of income data inform us, for example, that the top 20% of the population of the United States gets approximately 40% of the national wealth while the lower 20% receives only 5% (Sampson, 1976, p. 450). When we now inquire of people about their small-scale allocational behavior within this large-scale context, which systematically allocates more to a few and less to many, what is our contribution to understanding justice?

We enter a business establishment and ask the workers whether they believe they are being paid justly for the work they do *in comparison* to other people doing much the same work. We discover that they feel it is just as long as their investment-to-outcome ratio parallels that of comparison others. We do not inquire about the allocational process that gives them so little in comparison with their supervisors, the business managers and the owners. We do not tamper with this element of the allocational scheme, which, I submit, is highly informative about justice. Rather, we wile away our time reproducing the same illusions that describe many of the workers: namely, your circumstance is just as long as your investments and outcomes are roughly parallel to those of your comparison group. Basically, we place the very limits around our psychological inquiry that the social form places around its populace. We fail to probe the system producing the possible injustices by accepting its terms as our givens.

Even the concept *comparison person* reveals a quietistic acceptance of both the class system and the local or national system on the part of the very disciplines that purport to be studying justice. Why shouldn't the plant worker compare herself with David Rockefeller and feel that a basic injustice exists? Any psychologist who would argue that the latter's investments are greater and that he therefore deserves more than the former will not only have failed to understand how money is transported across family lines but will also help contribute to maintaining the very social formation that is founded on this principle.

And what happens when the worker understands that "Women compose one-half of the world's population, receive one-tenth of the world's income, and perform two-thirds of the world's working hours" (Oxfam, 1982, p. 1)? What happens to our understanding of justice when we restrict it to local and even national comparisons but fail to adopt a worldwide perspective? Is this not a further instance of complicity in maintaining an underlying social principle that feeds off a narrow conception of justice in a world in which injustice is more the norm?

Psychology studies justice in postallocational contexts. It tends to miss the crucial concerns about justice by restricting itself to the uncritical examination of narrow ranges of behavior after the fact. What new insights can we hope to offer about justice when we foreclose our examination of the roots in favor of the surface?

A Socioeconomically Restricted Understanding

With few exceptions (e.g., Lerner), the very terms by which psychology has examined justice derive from and reflect a given socioeconomic system. Insofar as those terms are employed uncritically, the study of justice manages primarily to reproduce the very society that generates those terms in the first place. The Marxist critique of political economy focused on the concept of exchange value. The liberal capitalist social form was one in which the value of a given item was determined by its ability to be exchanged for another item. Labor gained its value as a function of its worth in a marketplace of exchange.

As this social form increased its worldwide domination, concepts within economics became central to other facets of human life. The value of another person, for example, was no longer something intrinsic to that person but was gauged in terms of its worth in an exchange. Many psychologists studying justice simply appropriated this concept of exchange value in their understanding of how allocations between people proceeded.

As several economic historians have observed (e.g., Polanyi, Arensberg, & Pearson, 1957), the price-making market that characterizes capitalism is not the only possible form of marketplace exchange, nor is it the only form that has existed throughout human history, nor, for that matter, is it a more advanced form as compared with other exchange systems. What is unique about the capitalist marketplace is its price-making character: that is, the marketplace is not merely a place in which goods are exchanged but also the context within which the value of the goods to be exchanged is established, initially in terms of a supply-and-demand principle.

As Polanyi and his associates note, exchanges between individuals and collectivities need not involve prices at all; other ways to establish equivalents among the items to be exchanged can be and have been historically noted. Exchanges may be based on nonprice principles—on nonacquisitive and noneconomic motivations—and may serve functions that help integrate the society along traditional lines based on kinship, friendship, or ritual practice.

In describing the exchanges in an Indian village, for example, Neale (1957) comments on the problems the British had imposing their market forms on the forms they observed:

Instead of finding landlords and tenants operating through a system of prices, bargaining and contracts, the British found a maze of caste and custom regulating interfamily relationships. Where the British expected to find an owner they found a profusion of overlapping claims. (p. 221)

Neale continues by noting how the atomistically individualistic conception— held by ourselves (and the British)—that property belongs to the individual and can be given or sold by that individual fails adequately to describe this village's system of exchange or its conception of property.

A similar point has been made by Parkin (1972) based on his study of the redistributive palm wine economy of the Giriama of Kenya, contrasted with the capitalist forms that appeared when the Giriama changed from wine to copra. Property rights were communal and traditional under the wine economy, but they became private and *exchangeable* as such—that is, in our sense of that term—with the accumulation of personal wealth that the trade in copra permitted.

Neale's review of exchanges in the Indian village adds further to this picture. He comments that their system of redistribution of the goods that are produced does not follow any simple formula we would readily grasp, in which "equality of treatment, fair shares, or payment for value" (p. 223) is a dominant feature. Let me quote freely from some of his conclusions:

The matter [of exchange] is certainly intricate . . . it is not possible to express it in any formula shorter than several pages in length. . . . There was scant regard for economic rationality in the distribution. Some rough approximation to work rendered is indicated in the carpenters' and the blacksmiths' shares based upon number and size of ploughs . . . but this cannot be said of basing the washermans' and barbers' shares on the same criteria. (pp. 225–226)

This brief excursion into economic history is intended to convey the notion that the marketplace form of exchange, which we take for granted as part of our own system, is not the only way by which exchanges between people can take place or the only system by which equivalencies of the goods exchanged can be established. Goods and services can be exchanged in a wide variety of forms, governed by a wide variety of practices, serving a wide variety of collective purposes and motivations. Needless to say, even judgment as to what items legitimately enter into exchanges varies as a function of different marketplace conceptions.

When psychologists adopt the terms and the concepts of the price-making market form as the basis of exchanges that produce psychological justice, they simply take the present moment and freeze it into the eternal forever. They psychologize a moment of socioeconomic history by assuming that the terms of one marketplace mechanism are the fundamental structures of human psychology. In other words, as this brief history lesson reveals, exchanges can take place between people in a society without ever involving issues of investment, outcome, proportionality, and so forth—the terms by which our price-making market system functions and by which its exchanges are carried out.

In the psychological study of justice, few have introduced this kind of possibility. In one sense, Lerner's (1975, 1981) efforts to define relationships in terms of "identity," "unit," and "nonunit" approximates this recognition of different forms of allocation and justice as a function of the differing systems whereby people are bonded to one another. My contention is that the forms of interpersonal bonding derive from particular underlying socioeconomic structures and mechanisms and so vary culturally and historically. By contrast, Lerner appears to stress individual learning histories. Thus, he heads in the direction of sustaining a critical awareness of "contextual demands" yet remains wedded to the excessively individualistic thesis typical of most psychological understanding: what he takes to be individual decisions, I presume to be socially governed options.

Alienation in Exchange.   As noted in Chapter 4, one of the key qualities of exchange value is that all items of potential value are reduced to one scale—the price they can bring in the price-making marketplace. In the hands of many psychological investigators, the items entering into the consideration of who deserves more in an allocational decision turn on this concept of exchange value. Everything is judged as an exchangeable commodity. Human qualities are relevant only for what they can bring in exchange.

Ollman (1971) has observed that the exchange-value concept carries one of the principal themes of human alienation. We seem to have psychologists studying justice who have adopted the essential qualities of human alienation as the terms for their analysis of normal, harmony-producing activity! It is not surprising that this should happen. Psychology is so thoroughly embedded in its society that it is unable to see, let alone critically evaluate, its own embeddedness. It is almost "natural" that psychology would adopt the alienating forms of society as though these were the life-affirming forms of social justice.

In their study of justice, many psychologists, paradoxically but understandably, have employed a formulation that is more useful in helping us to understand alienation than justice. Insofar as they claim that people feel happy and comfortable with the allocational choices that are made in terms of an exchange-value principle, we have furthered our understanding not of the way that justice operates but of the way that the ideology necessary to the legitimation of a given social formation operates.

Psychology and Societal Lag

In Chapter 9, I used Habermas's analysis to describe the change in the underlying social form of the Western world from liberal to advanced capitalism. The former described a situation in which individuals retained a semblance of freedom to enter into market exchanges; the latter describes a situation in which state intervention seeks to control prices, resources, allocation, and so on. In the latter, there is less of a fit between the free-marketplace model and the realities of economic functioning.

Insofar as many of psychology's theories of justice derive from the earlier, marketplace form, there is a lag between these analyses and the realities of the economic system. In other words, the prevalent theories of justice behavior in psychology have been derived almost entirely from the liberal marketplace form: people enter into a market system of free exchange and the outcomes are just insofar as the natural law of this marketplace is followed. The concept that justice involves a proportionality of investments and outcomes is based on this underlying social form.

However, insofar as the underlying social principle has changed, the very form on which the psychology of justice has been based lags behind the reality. Under advanced capitalism, the state has replaced the market system as the governing mechanism. People do not simply enter into free exchanges governed by the unseen hand of the free market's supply and demand; they now enter into exchanges in which the state has intervened often to secure advantage for some at the necessary disadvantage of others, including others worldwide: that is, in order to sustain competitive advantage for the United States, intervention is required that can create disadvantages for other nations.

Habermas (1975) has observed how this transformation from the relative anonymity of market forces to the obvious political interventions that describe modern capitalism has created a legitimation crisis: extensive justifications must be developed to rationalize the kinds of governing interventions that develop. I will shortly examine this important theme. What I would like to comment on at this point, however, is the meaning of the apparent *lag* in psychology's conception of justice. The point that I am developing is that psychology's analysis of justice is based on a social form that is rapidly fading into the historical past. Psychology continues to speak as though justice between individuals who could enter freely into exchanges with one another were actually obtainable; yet such individuals and such possibilities are rapidly decreasing.

There may remain some few sectors of life in which relatively free-market principles continue to have a degree of application, but, overall, the main thrust of the underlying social form is toward state involvement in governing and hence in legitimating the nature of the entire exchange process. The unseen hand is now seen; new questions, challenges, and issues have emerged, and psychology describes a world and a view of justice that lags behind the times.

This lag may reflect a parallel lag in people's awareness of the changing conditions of their social existence. If so, then psychology is studying a nostalgic phenomenology on its way out. Of course, perhaps we are dealing with a case of ideology: the state mechanism is concealed under the guise of a continuing, so-called free-enterprise system. In this scenario, psychology's analysis of justice plays a role in a cover-up. Its understanding of justice in terms of a marketplace exchange deals with a principle that is out of sync with the reality of the world today; under these conditions, psychology would be participating primarily in the masking of those real-world factors (also see Skillen, 1977).

JUSTICE IDEOLOGY AND SOCIAL LEGITIMATION

The study of justice is not of the same sort as the study of many other content areas that have long fascinated psychologists. Although there is no overwhelming agreement with this assertion, it is a point recognized among many scholars and has proved to be central to the lifelong works of Lerner and his associates. Justice takes us to the roots of the social order, in particular to the matter of its legitimacy. Questions of justice and fairness are not simply minor complaints within an individual's psyche; those psychic cries of "unfair!" reveal the fault lines of a given social form.

All social forms, no matter how governed, must deal with questions of legitimacy and hence matters involving justice. Since people operate in terms of their understandings of their circumstances and opportunities, legitimacy involves the acceptability to social actors of the ways things are in their society. If we adopt a version of Habermas's analysis (1973, 1975; also see McCarthy, 1978), legitimacy requires that the various claims of different segments of the society can in principle be justified by a process of rational consensus. Habermas refers to this discursive redemption of validity claims as the *ideal speech situation*.

Ideal Speech Situation.   Habermas sought to ground the truth claims of both matters of empirical *fact* and matters of social *value* in a discourse process rather than in pure observation as such. Thus, in matters involving justice and legitimacy, the claims to truth must be justified in terms of a systematic discourse. This involves the ideal speech situation: a discourse process in which people can examine the very context of interaction in which they are involved and arrive at what he defines as an unforced consensus concerning the validity of the truth claims that have been made.

In the ideal situation, four conditions are to be met: (1) discourse proceeds without external force or threat of force; (2) discourse proceeds without the internal constraints of either neurotic or ideological distortions; (3) discourse proceeds with all parties having an equal opportunity to initiate or to continue with the interactions; and (4) parties in the discourse have the same chance to call into question all aspects of the very process in which they are involved.

The essential point in Habermas's account is that all matters of truth, including those central to the issues of justice and the legitimacy of social arrangements, must eventually be redeemable through a critical dialogue. This dialogue must be free from any constraints that would produce a *de facto* consensus rather than a rationally motivated one. This describes the ideal speech situation, a "form of interaction that is free from all distorting influences" (McCarthy, 1978, p. 308). This ideal provides the framework or the "critical standard against which every actually achieved consensus can be measured" (McCarthy, 1978, p. 309).

Explaining the Inequitable Distribution of the Social Product

My contention is that the study of justice gets to the very heart of the legitimacy of the social order. The manner by which the social product is distributed opens to question the legitimacy of the underlying social form itself. We can thereby anticipate that whenever the social product is distributed in a manner that potentially raises questions of justice and fairness and when that allocative form is an essential element of the underlying social principle itself, we will discover extensive social mechanisms at work creating and maintaining legitimacy.

As McCarthy's review of Habermas's study of legitimacy under capitalism comments, its basic dilemma involves distributing the social product inequitably yet legitimately. The private appropriation of public wealth under the advanced capitalist form must be legitimated; citizens must reliably agree to be loyal and accepting of a state system that does not distribute the products of their society in either equal or equitable ways.

Habermas argues that under advanced capitalism, questions of legitimacy have reached a crisis point. Liberal capitalism legitimated itself in terms of a submission to market forces and the inherent justice of the nature of such forces. Advanced capitalism however, requires state intervention to govern and steer production and distribution. The state, and not the unseen and presumptively just market forces, thereby is the critical element in creating the social product and in its distribution throughout the society.

Legitimation ideologies that manage potential discontent with the existing framework emerge as elements essential to reproducing the social order, including its built-in injustices. Employing Habermas's notion of the ideal speech situation, we can say that the validity claims of the existing order cannot be redeemed discursively, for to do so would unmask the domination and advantage that exists. In this case, legitimacy requires suppressing the kinds of dialogue that Habermas describes as ideal.

Under the circumstances described, we would expect to discover a connection between the understanding and analysis of justice and the ideologies requisite to legitimating the social order. The theories that organize and develop the societal self-understandings of fairness and justice can thereby be critically examined for their ideological components. They need to be critically examined for the role they play in legitimating the existing social formation and in managing its ever-present crises.

If we accept Habermas's argument, advanced capitalism is especially prone to legitimation crises, given the essential role of the state and political forces in social production and distribution and given the loss of traditional mechanisms of legitimation. Such crises especially develop when state intervention is necessary to rationalize and administratively manage all spheres of life, invading even once-private domains: new areas of human life enter the political arena where they too must be legitimated.

Quite simply, once the state intervenes to govern the market forces, its administrative machinery is soon required to manage the other spheres of human life that flow from the marketplace and that require a certain kind of citizenry so that the market can function. To paraphrase both Habermas and McCarthy, intervention extends beyond the purely economic sphere and enters the sociocultural sphere as well. Legitimation crises thereby do not merely involve the allocation of material benefits but appear as well in every sphere of human endeavor. Thus, matters of material production and allocation must be legitimated so that the underlying social form can be reproduced; however, potential crises also develop around the "reproduction of reliable structures of intersubjectivity" (McCarthy, 1978, p. 359). It is in this latter arena that the ideological contributions of the human sciences to social reproduction are most apparent.

The separation of the public world (work) from the private world (home) that evolved in the 16th and 17th centuries, and the establishment of different mechanisms to govern the operation of each sphere, was not only the product of the enlarging hand of industrialization and of capitalism but also the medium for their significant expansion. Habermas's description of the contemporary forms of this historical movement indicates the reentry of the state into spheres of the private and thus a new merger between the public and the private. In this latter case, the rationalized and administered world of the public is swamping the world of the private without, however, the validity claims that characterized traditional society. Therefore, serious and new questions of legitimacy are developing as the political process intrudes upon matters of home, family, leisure, and so on.

Psychology's Contributions

Legitimation crises, as I have noted, are crises that are central to questions of justice within a society. What, then, is psychology's contribution to this important matter? Stated more directly, do psychology's analyses of justice contribute to the public discourse requisite to examining the legitimacy claims that now exist? Or do psychology's analyses of justice manage to further the ideology of human self-understanding that is required in order to maintain the existing enterprise?

By now, my position in this matter should be evident. It is my position that psychology's studies of justice fail to address the question of legitimation, even as they serve its cause, because they are founded on a framework that systematically deletes society and history from that very framework. Therefore, what psychology primarily accomplishes is to join in the reproduction of the reliable structures of intersubjectivity requisite to reproduce the underlying principle of the society. Although the field does not engage in this practice with self-consciousness, it cannot do anything other, given its

basic framework for study. Psychology cannot contribute to a public discourse (the ideal speech situation) around questions of either justice or legitimacy because it has thus far failed to engage in its own discourse about its
own sociohistorical siting.

A FURTHER NOTE ON CONTRADICTIONS AND THE PSYCHOLOGY OF JUSTICE

One final point remains to be discussed again in this present context.
The point involves the relationship between the psychology of justice and
the underlying societal contradictions.

Habermas defines something as involving a "fundamental contradiction" when the same underlying organizational principle confronts people
with "claims and intentions that are, in the long run, incompatible"
(Habermas, 1975, p. 27). Giddens (1979) somewhat more formalistically defines a social contradiction "as an *opposition or disjunction of structural
principles* of social systems, where those principles operate in *terms of each
other* but at the same time *contravene one another*" (p. 141).

For both, a system is contradictory to the extent that it simultaneously
produces element A and element B and the latter thwarts the functioning of
the former. Needless to say, if such contradictions are fundamental to a
given social form, that form contains in its very operation the seeds of its own
destruction. This was Marx's point about capitalism: its internal contradictions produce the problems that lead to its eventual failure.

Recall that Habermas argues, first, that one of the basic contradictions
uncovered in the contemporary socioeconomic form involves its allocation of
the social product in ways that give substantial advantage to some and, second, that this is the very condition that produces a legitimation crisis; that is,
people begin to challenge the legitimacy of this unequal distribution of the
public wealth. Insofar as the human sciences help explain why an unequal
distribution is proper because it reflects a fundamental aspect of human psychology, then the existing system of allocation has been scientifically affirmed as though it were an essential element of human nature and not an
element of contemporary social dynamics.

For example, the various psychological disguises in which the work
ethic has been packaged help justify why some deserve more and others less.
Or, as noted, the use of an uncritical social comparison theory helps to legitimate differentials in allocation—for example, defining justice in terms of
class-linked comparison groups in which it is deemed right and proper for
managers and owners to get more and workers less. There are additional ele-

ments of this same basic contradiction to which psychology has addressed itself.

Privatism and Formal Democracy

One manner whereby societal contradictions can be handled and the state's intervention on behalf of private accumulation legitimated, according to Habermas, is to engage in a system of what he terms *formal democracy* rather than *substantive democracy*. The latter is one in which citizens can actually engage in a discourse about their circumstances; this ideal situation can bring to light the contradictions and the legitimating mechanisms that mask their real situation. In a formal democracy, by contrast, key decisions are made without actual, will-forming citizen participation. In order for this latter process to be successful, citizens must grant their society a diffuse mass loyalty while declining serious political participation. This is what Habermas terms *privatism:*

Civil privatism here denotes an interest in the steering and maintenance . . . performances of the administrative system but little participation in the legitimating process. . . . Civil privatism thus corresponds to the structures of a depoliticized public realm. Familial-vocational privatism complements civil privatism. It consists in a family orientation with developed interests in consumption and leisure on the one hand, and in a career orientation suitable to status competition on the other. (1975, p. 75)

Habermas's discussion of privatism and my earlier discussion of self-contained individualism (Chapter 9) can now be seen to be different sides of the same coin. The difference between my analysis and his is primarily one of focus and emphasis. My concern is to demonstrate that psychology fostered a self-contained ideal in its theories. Habermas's intention is to suggest how privatism helps to legitimate advanced capitalism by turning people to self-focused concerns and to formal but not substantive democracy.

From my perspective, the self-contained ideal contravenes successful social problem solving, in which cooperation and interdependence are necessary. From Habermas's perspective, privatism constitutes a problem of legitimation. The very creation of private spheres and private concerns contradicts the state's needs to administer all facets of social life.

In both my view and Habermas's, a contradiction in the social form emerges and sets into motion elements that are potentially self-disruptive. My concern is with psychology's role in all of this. I have suggested that psychology enters in a peculiarly sensitive way to detect this social contradiction yet not truly to recognize it as such. Psychology's self-contained ideal has a contradictory relation to the successful management of the social upheavals and dislocations that are produced along with this privatistic ideal. Psychology, however, has neglected to observe this contradiction or in some cases has even sought to argue that there is no real contradiction in the first place.

As long as psychology persists in its refusal or inability to gain access to the sociohistorical dimension of its theories, concepts, and modes of understanding, it will continue to occupy a troublesome position with respect to understanding human behavior. It will both detect and yet be blind to societal contradictions; it will help to develop an image of the modern ideal without awareness of the contradictory nature of this ideal.

CONCLUDING OBSERVATION

In an earlier discussion, I observed that although capitalism is the underlying social form that has received the greatest scrutiny by the critical theorists and also occupies a substantial portion of my own concerns, this is not the only underlying socioeconomic system with fundamental problems that need to be unearthed. The deceptions that pass by, typically *noticed* in more obviously regulated and totalitarian systems, are barely ideological in the sense of being part of the deep structures of both the person and the society. By pointing out the "gun," one is hardly unmasking a system that regulates its citizens' obedience through brute force and blatant intimidation. Legitimacy by force is clearly neither legitimate nor infused with an ideological underpinning that requires much disclosure to become visible.

What is so intriguing about the Western world view and its contemporary capitalist socioeconomic formulations, by contrast, is the apparent legitimacy of its fundamental structure of inequality. Without the obvious use of brute force or blatant intimidation, citizens more or less routinely agree to permit unequal allocations of the society's products to take place, even if they receive substantially less and others substantially more. To be sure, challenges are frequently raised, serious questions asked, strains revealed, and occasional remedies proposed; yet the underlying system appears to function with reasonable citizen acceptance.

Whereas some viewpoints might have let this apparently agreeable arrangement pass by unnoticed, other perspectives, ranging from the clearly political one of the critical theorists to the less directly politically motivated analyses of systems' theories (to cite but two examples), have found in this very acceptance a more profound cause for concern. That concern has increasingly focused on the deep psychological structures that must be implicated for legitimacy to be experienced when, at least to these and other ob-servers' eyes, it is not truly warranted by objective conditions: for example, the disproportionate concentration of wealth in a few; the racist, sexist, and ageist bias in access to societal benefits; and so on. This turn to psychology forces all of us within the field to take a second and, I believe, necessarily critical look at what we are doing and for whom.

In this chapter, I have taken a position, one which this entire work inev-itably recommends, that the very forms by which we conduct our analyses lead us more towards reproducing and legitimating the existing social order than toward seriously challenging its legitimacy. If, indeed, deep psycholog-ical structures are at issue in affirming a social form—even one that appears comparatively more humane than others—then those whose works address these deep structures must be held especially responsible for the nature of their contributions. If we claim *something* to be just while that something participates in systematically granting substantial benefit to some over oth-ers, I submit, we are contributing to accepting and legitimating what we need not accept or legitimate. Too much of the psychology of justice motiva-tion and behavior has been of precisely this sort.

CHAPTER FOURTEEN

The Frame of Address
A Modest Proposal

Every critic faces a risk once she or he steps out of that role and into a more affirmative position. Yet, it seems at this point that I must accept that risk and introduce one of my own efforts designed to move psychology from its purist roots down an alternative path. In this chapter I introduce the concept *frame of address*, which I believe offers a small but helpful step in the right direction.

Let me first briefly review what I mean when I speak of psychology's moving in the right direction. Based on the critique offered in the preceding chapters, it is clear that the central problem with psychology today is its relatively noncontextual, nonhistorical, and overly individualistic framework. The field requires concepts that transcend these biases. In particular, alternative conceptual frameworks in psychology should ground themselves in the social world by viewing as interpersonal those processes that have traditionally been understood as intrapersonal. In this manner, psychology can begin its journey of understanding from a social and historical base rather than attempting to reconstruct society and social interactions at the end and from individual elements.

There are historical precedents for psychology's adopting the more contextual turn that I am suggesting. George Herbert Mead (1934), Lev Vygotsky (1978), C. Wright Mills (1975), and Harry Stack Sullivan (1953, 1954) are four analysts who stand somewhat apart from the dominant paradigm of contemporary psychological understanding. Although others also come to mind (e.g., Barker, 1965, 1968), I intend to focus here primarily on the preceding four. Each offers a distinctly interpersonal view of what are usually assumed to be basic intrapsychological processes. For Mead and Vygotsky, mind and self are interpersonal emergents of social interaction. For Mills, motivation is not an intrapsychic trigger to action but a public ac-

Parts of this chapter first appeared in E. E. Sampson, "Social Change and the Contexts of Justice Motivation," in M. J. Lerner and S. C. Lerner (Eds.), *The Justice Motive in Social Behavior*. New York: Plenum Press, 1981.

counting practice or reason for action. For Sullivan, personality is a property of the interpersonal field and not a thing residing within the individual's psyche. In the hands of these theorists, psychology's most cherished intrapsychic qualities are given an alternate conceptualization.

And Justice?

I hasten to observe that several important theorists of justice have likewise referred to their works as "interpersonal," especially Lerner (1975, 1981) and recently Mikula (1982). However, Lerner's attempts for the most part involve understanding justice in terms of cognitive principles, and those principles remain locked securely within the psyche of the individual. Although interpersonal schemata or templates for processing experiences and determining justice do develop and involve, as we have previously seen, perceptions of others as same (identity relations), similar (unit relations), or different (nonunit relations), these remain very much individual accomplishments residing within the person as such. Indeed, Lerner and Meindl (1981) go so far as to suggest that

given a reasonably stable environment involving clear contingencies between various acts and outcomes, the developing human organism with its cognitive potential and experiential demands would generate a psychology of entitlement-deserving without the necessary presence of other people. (p. 216)

Mikula (1982) argues that his own most recent understanding of justice lies within an interpersonal rather than an individualistic frame; he freely admits, however, the difficulty of accomplishing this and that he might be "overstretching" himself (his word) by employing the very term *interpersonal*. His model, which shares important similarities with the notion of address frame that I develop in this chapter, reverses the history of my own "discovery" of justice (see Chapter 3) by viewing justice within a "control motivation" analysis. I discovered justice to be important once I abandoned the mastery framework that had guided by original works; Mikula concludes that justice must be understood within a control–mastery framework.

Mikula suggests that justice enters less on its own feet (as Lerner insists) than as a device for justifying allocative decisions and negotiating a settlement of competing claims. Somewhat akin to Lerner, he argues that in growing up people learn that the notion of justice legitimates and regulates actions in exchange and allocational situations. When a situation is experienced as "just," the participants can feel more secure about their ability to control future outcomes:

In other words, for an individual who strives to have control over his outcomes, it becomes important to be able to believe that his actions are just. He can then count upon the (long-term) satisfaction of his hedonistic motives. (Mikula, 1982, p. 6)

From this, Mikula reasons that "the primary issue in concerns for justice is to be able to *justify* one's actions, decisions and claims . . . in the eyes of others as well as for oneself" (p. 7). As we will see, by this turn, Mikula lines himself up with Mills: what was an intrapsychic motive now becomes part of an interpersonal justification process.

Justification is said to be the central core of justice. This describes an interpersonal process in which the participants evaluate the specific qualities of the situation and negotiate a settlement of the various competing claims. In other words, there is no simple or set formula for considering justice; an interpersonal process is essential. I will have more to say about Mikula's perspective later in this chapter; for the moment, however, his analysis offers a movement in the direction of a more interpersonal rather than purely intrapsychic basis for justice.

Before proceeding with the introduction of the concept of address frame, let us set the several other elements of the background we need by reviewing the four major theorists who I believe represent the essentials of an interpersonal approach to what have heretofore been primarily intrapsychic concepts.

THE CONTEXTUALIZATION OF MIND

Mead's joining of mind, self, and society is no accident; it represents his view that society and social interaction form the field from which both thinking and identity emerge and to which both continually refer. There can be no thinking apart from a society (i.e., others) to whom such thinking is addressed; there is no self apart from others to whom that self refers.

To think is to engage in an inner conversation of gestures in which another is being addressed. People address themselves in thought to an audience whose perspective they adopt and from whose standpoint they view themselves. To hear ourselves, we adopt what we assume to be another's attitude as though that other had addressed us.

In saying that thinking is an inner conversation, Mead intends cognition to be akin to a dialogue in which we and some other are involved:

In responding to ourselves we are . . . taking the attitude of another than the self that is directly acting, and into this reaction there naturally flows the memory images of the responses of those about us, the memory images of those responses of others which were in answer to like actions. Thus the child can think about his conduct as good or bad only as he reacts to his own acts in the remembered words of his parents. (p. 180)

Later, the parental audience expands to include other people as well as what Mead terms *the generalized other* of the community: an abstracted audience based on the many others with whom people have interacted and from whose perspective they view (that is, address) themselves. Because we live in many different social environments and address many others, we thereby have many different minds and many different selves.

What is critical for our present concern is to observe that Mead's view of cognition gives it a distinctly interpersonal meaning. In the very act of thinking, including abstract thinking, there is an audience that is being addressed and whose standpoint provides the thinker with the terms for understanding. Mead notes that even the abstruse thinker fills "out the bare spokesman of abstract thought . . . in seeking his audience" (p. 180). We will shortly return to this formulation of cognition.

Vygotsky

Mead has not been alone in offering an interpersonal theory of mind and human thought. L. S. Vygotsky, a major figure in Russian psychology, independently offered a view of thinking that further develops the central thesis captured by Mead: interpersonal formulations precede and lay the foundations for the development of intrapersonal structures of the human mind.

A helpful way to understand Vygotsky's position is to work through one of the examples he introduces in his discussion of the process of *internalization:* "the internal reconstruction of an external operation" (1978, p. 56). Vygotsky describes a little child who is reaching for a toy beyond his grasp. His fingers extend outward and wiggle as he tries to grasp the toy. His mother enters and comes to the child's aid; she views the child's extended hand and wiggling fingers as meaning that he wants a particular toy. For the mother, the child's uncoordinated and hesitant grasping means "pointing":

The child's unsuccessful attempt engenders a reaction not from the object . . . but *from another person*. Consequently, the primary meaning of that unsuccessful grasping movement is established by others. (p. 56)

In time, the child transforms the vague movements of grasping into the more refined gesture of pointing.

> It becomes a true gesture only after it objectively manifests all the functions of pointing for others and is understood by others as a gesture. Its meaning and functions are created at first by an objective situation and then by people who surround the child. (p. 56)

As he outlines the process by which mind, as an internal representational system, comes into being, Vygotsky repeatedly emphasizes the point that we have seen in Mead:

> *An interpersonal process is transformed into an intrapersonal one.* Every function in the child's cultural development appears twice: first, on the social level, and later, on the individual level; first, *between* people (*interpsychological*), and then *inside* the child (*intrapsychological*). This applies equally to voluntary attention, to logical memory, and to the formation of concepts. All the higher functions originate as actual relations between human individuals. (p. 57)

By linking the human mind to the social and cultural world of interpersonal relations, Vygotsky, like Mead, provides us with a view of human thinking that necessarily is situated and subjected to variations as a function of changing cultural and historical factors. Thought does not rise above or transcend its sociohistorical locus; it is invariably interpenetrated by it.

A Critique

Although I do not intend to pursue the point in detail at this time, it is important to note a problem with both of these conceptions that appears as well in my address-frame concept. In each case, the analysis is successful insofar as mind is contextualized and related to a social process; the analysis fails, as Giddens (1979) and others have noted, insofar as it does not develop any differentiated understanding of social organization. Mead's best offer in this regard is to speak about significant others—the small, intimate primary group and the generalized other, or the community and society. Unlike an analysis in which society becomes a highly complex, differentiated, and major feature of the system, Mead and Vygotsky give us only a general sense of the social context for mind.

At this stage in the attempt to move psychology from an intrapsychic to an interpersonal formulation, I am not bothered by this absence of a more fully developed theory of social organization. I believe that once the first step can be taken, so that psychology gains an interpersonal grasp of its basic concepts, the next step is more likely to occur. To envision all mental processes within a social context—rather than persisting with theories in which the context derives from mental processes that seem firm and relatively independent from it—is the essential step at this time.

MOTIVATION AS ACCOUNTING PRACTICES

In an important work, C. Wright Mills (1975; also Gerth & Mills, 1953) introduced a view of human motivation that removed motives from the individual as such and gave them a more social and interpersonal direction. For Mills, motives are not conditions existing prior to action and serving as the springboards to action.

Motives may be considered as typical vocabularies having ascertainable functions in delimited societal situations. . . . Motives are accepted justifications for present, future, or past programs or acts. (pp. 162, 164)

Motives enter as reasons or *public accounting practices* that provide adequate grounds for action that has already been undertaken or that the individual intends to take.

Perhaps the best sense of Mills's analysis comes from examining one of his own examples:

Individualistic, sexual, hedonistic and pecuniary vocabularies of motives are apparently now dominant in many sectors of twentiety-century urban America. Under such an ethos, verbalizations of alternative conduct in these terms is least likely to be challenged among dominant groups. In this milieu, individuals are skeptical of Rockefeller's avowed religious motives for his business conduct because such motives are not *now* terms of the vocabulary conventionally and predominantly accompanying situations of business enterprise. A medieval monk writes that he gave food to a poor but pretty woman because it is "for the glory of God and the eternal salvation of his soul." Why do we tend to question him and impute sexual motives? Because sex is an influential and widespread motive in our society and time. (pp. 166–167)

This passage describes the public and interpersonal quality of the concept of motive. Insofar as sexual and economic reasons serve today as adequate grounds for behavior, they and not religious fervor serve as integral parts of our motive vocabularies. It is not a matter of our behavior's being mechanically triggered by sexual or economic drives, as the dominant psychological paradigm suggests. Rather, these have become socially acceptable formulations that render our behavior intelligible to others and to ourselves. What we take to be motives must be evaluated within a given sociohistorical context and its understanding of acceptable grounds for human action.

On Reasons

I have concentrated my attention here on Mills. His work, however, is but one part of a much larger movement within both philosophy and sociology that emphasizes the role of accounts (i.e., reason and motive statements) in human behavior (see Keat & Urry, 1975). The focus is upon the ways that intelligibility emerges in social interaction by means of interpretative schemes that the actor and the observer both employ as resources in governing their behavior. Giddens's phrasing of accountability captures this sense of its role in human behavior:

I take "accountability" to mean that the accounts that actors are able to offer of their conduct draw upon the same stocks of knowledge as are drawn upon in the very production and reproduction of their action. (1979, p. 57)

In other words, accounts, motives, and reasons emerge from within a sociohistorical context and provide the stock of knowledge at hand upon which actors draw both to produce their particular action and to make it intelligible to themselves and to others.

This formulation views reasons and accounts as playing a causative role in behavior; yet, reasons need not be conscious. Unconscious reasons exist and serve what Bhaskar (1979) refers to as the *real reasons* (i.e., causally efficacious) for human action:

The logical possibility of error about, misdescriptions and misrecognition of one's own state of awareness, and hence inter alia of one's reasons, is a condition of any reflexive intelligence. . . . If such a reasoning process occurs or has occurred, it figures in an explanation of the action in virtue of its causal efficacy, *not* in virtue of its validity. Just as real reasons may be false, real reasoning processes may be invalid. (pp. 117, 139)

My intent in briefly noting these theories of "accounting" is primarily to emphasize the point derived from Mills's thesis. Even if our focus is on the individual actor's motives for behaving, our analyses necessarily demand that we employ a theory of motivation that is at once sociological and historical. Our psychology, in other words, cannot be an autonomous science; its limits are established by the particular society and history in which it is embedded.

The implications of this view for the justice motive is clear. Justice motivation is to be understood in terms of the vocabularies of justice or justice accounting practices that characterize a given society at a given point in its history (e.g., Mikula, 1982). Therefore, we should speak of justice reasons: public accounting practices or grounds for explaining past acts as "fair" and formulating future, intended acts which will be recognizable as "fair" or "just." The intrapsychic quality of the motive is removed and an interpersonal base and meaning are installed in its place. I will have more to say on this point later.

INTERPERSONALIZING PERSONALITY

Harry Stack Sullivan's definition of personality conveys an interpersonal rather than an individualistic-intrapsychic emphasis: *"personality is the relatively enduring pattern of recurrent interpersonal situations which characterize a human life"* (1953, pp. 110–111).

In a manner reminiscent of both Mead and Vygotsky, Sullivan sees the individual as a portion of an interpersonal field and not an entirely separate entity. Therefore, processes that we usually assume take place *within* the individual occur within the interpersonal field, *between* individuals. Sullivan's view of the self system (1953, 1954) also parallels Mead: both see the self as an emergent of social interaction. And, for Sullivan as for Mead and Vygotsky, language plays an important part in the process by which personality emerges and is sustained.

Because of his psychiatric focus, Sullivan was especially concerned with distortions in self-system and personality. As fitting his interpersonal theory, Sullivan saw mental disorders to involve problems of interpersonal life and association. Indeed, Sullivan's concept of parataxic distortions gives a rather Meadian flavor to the entire issue of transference. The parataxically distorting perceiver is addressing an audience in thought and action that includes "the *other* people in the room" in addition to those who are actually present:

The great complexity of the psychiatric interview is brought about by the interviewee's substituting for the psychiatrist a person or persons strikingly different in most significant respects from the psychiatrist. The interviewee addresses his behavior toward this fictitious person who is temporarily in the ascendance over the reality of the psychiatrist, and he interprets the psychiatrist's remarks and behavior on the basis of this same fictitious person. . . . Such phenomena are the very basis of the really astonishing misunderstandings and misconceptions which characterize all human relations. (1954, p. 26)

What may appear to be a crazy pattern of perception and experience is seen to be an address to someone not actually present. It is interpersonal, however, in that it involves addressing another and viewing the self from that other's perspective.

THE ADDRESS FRAME

This brief overview of the key ideas of Mead, Vygotsky, Mills, and Sullivan introduces the outlines of a more contextual approach for psychology. Thinking, motivation, and personality are conceptualized as interpersonal processes and not as intrapsychic events. Using these several ideas as its basis, I would like to introduce the concept *address frame* as an important formulation for psychological inquiry. I will then apply this concept to the analysis of justice.

I define an address frame as the standpoint which people assume or adopt in imaginatively completing the responses to their own gestures. An address frame therefore is the *whom* that people address in their external or internal conversation of gestures, the *other* whose responses render people's own gestures meaningful. For example, Jane adopts what she imaginatively construes to be Sandra's response to her own (that is, Jane's) gesture and thereby addresses herself as she would be addressed by Sandra. She sees and hears herself as an object from Sandra's standpoint.

Address frames fulfill Mead's basic formulation of thought and meaning and are likewise consistent with Vygotsky's interpersonal view of mind. Mead speaks of a three-phase process involving (1) P's gesture, (2) the completed social act that it indicates, and (3) O's response to the gesture. The first or initial phase of the social act involves a gesture that P makes or intends to make. This gesture is said to indicate some resultant or later phase of the social act which the gesture has initiated. Finally, there is the adjustive response of the other person (the reply) to the gesture and what it has indicated.

By adopting O's standpoint (i.e., taking O's role), P can imaginatively complete O's response to the gesture. In this way, the response called out in P is similar to the response called out in O, because by adopting O's standpoint, P can imaginatively construe O's response to the gesture. I refer to this as an address frame in that thinking involves another whose standpoint is taken (addressed) in order to render the gestures meaningful.

We formulate our thoughts within the context of an address frame involving the implied response of another to our gestures. The very act of thinking requires the imposition of some other whose responses we enact, if only in our imagination. This is what Mead meant when he noted that even those who engage in abstract thought refer the elements of their thinking to some audience whose implied response renders their thoughts intelligible. It is what Vygotsky meant in viewing human thought as having interpersonal origins. This is what Mills meant in arguing that motive vocabularies are socially accepted grounds for explaining and justifying action: in other words, the motive term locates an action within an address frame given in terms of the particular social group within which such frames operate. Likewise it is what Sullivan meant by his conception of personality as an interpersonal process.

Mead's three-phase process of social interaction can be conducted *externally,* in which case thinking is addressed to those actually present; it can also be conducted *internally,* in which case there is an implicit conversation of gestures in which the other is addressed imaginatively. This process (gesture/resultant/response) permits people to indicate to themselves what they indicate to others; they can call out within themselves, in response to their own gestures, the response which they assume will be called out in others.

For example, as I make the preliminary gesture of raising my arm with my fist tightly clenched, you, seeing this gesture, can project my intent as being harmful and so withdraw in a defensive posture as your adjustive response. In that I can imaginatively complete your response (withdrawal) to my gesture, I can thereby render the meaning of the gesture to be menacing rather than playful. I can put myself in your shoes and view myself making gestures and eliciting a response. In this manner, I can see myself as an object reflected through your perspective. I can also think about the meaning of my behavior as a function of the particular others whose responses to my gestures I assume.

To say that thinking occurs within a particular address frame, therefore, is to note—along with Mead, Vygotsky, Mills, and Sullivan—that this major and fundamental psychological process refers to an audience whose framework we adopt in conversing with ourselves and in grounding our action. Mind is an interpersonal process; it is located in society, between people in their acts of communication (see Bateson, 1972; Wilden, 1980; or the discussion in Part 4).

While there are many implications that flow from this formulation, for our present purposes the most important involves the way in which context (i.e., sociohistorical setting) has been brought directly into our understanding of psychological processes. The point is not simply that others are involved in the emergence of thinking, motivation, and personality but that these seemingly individualistic and transcendent concepts are in fact parts of a larger, ongoing social process.

Literal Versus Indexical Meaning

Because the existing formulations of pure psychology delete context in their search for fundamental universals of psychological behavior, they inappropriately treat *meaning* in a *literal* rather than an *indexical* manner (e.g., Wilson, 1970). To be literal is to assume that the meaning of a gesture has a transcontextual, objective quality. To treat a gesture as indexical, on the other hand, is to note, as Garfinkel (1967) suggested, that gestures "do not have a sense that remains identical through the changing occasions of their use" (p. 40).

Both Gergen (1978) and Harre (1977) make this same point. Gergen notes, for example, how "The pointing of a finger . . . may signify aggression . . . may be used to indicate an altruistic giving of information, a positive or negative attitude, egocentrism, or high achievement" (p. 1351). Recall Vygotsky's example of pointing in which the meaning is engendered in the child through the interpersonal process of interacting with the mother. Insofar as the child continues to address its acts as though it were addressing its mother, it will evoke a similar meaning for the gesture.

Harre (1977) describes a handshake, noting that

I may not know what you are doing when you take hold of my hand. I might be very puzzled as to what the gesture means, not knowing in which structured sequence of actions it occurs. It might be part of a betting ritual, or an opening move in a karate encounter, or parts of various other action sequences. (pp. 284–285)

Intelligibility therefore emerges only contextually (i.e., indexically) and does not have a literal, transcontextual quality (recall the discussion of metaphor in Part 4).

The concept of address frame requires that meaning be established in terms of the particular other whose standpoint is assumed; thought and meaning are thereby situated within a social context. The meaning or sense of a gesture is not rendered independently of the social process within which it emerges and to which it refers. Although the meaning of a given gesture may appear to achieve a transcontextual objectivity, this appears only insofar as members of a common culture have learned to adopt similar address frames in locating their gestures: for example, addressing the abstracted, generalized other.

JUSTICE MOTIVATION AS ADDRESS FRAME

There are several implications that follow once we conceptualize what heretofore has been an intrapsychic motive force or need (e.g., justice motivation) as an interpersonally based address frame. I will consider four ideas: (1) the meaning of justice as address frame, (2) the role of sociohistorical factors, (3) the negotiated quality of justice, and (4) the changing intelligibility of the justice address frame.

The Meaning of Justice Motivation as Address Frame

Our first task is to specify what justice motivation means within the context of an address frame. An address frame grounds action in the social process; it makes peoples' acts intelligible to others and to themselves. In this view, justice becomes part of a conversation taking place between people. Justice motivation is removed from inside the mind to become an interpersonal process because, in the view of address-frame theory, mind itself is interpersonal: the process of thinking involves addressing oneself within the frame or standpoint of others. By locating justice within social interaction, we are better equipped to understand how specific situational and general sociohistorical events influence the ways in which justice functions in guiding social behavior.

In address-frame terms, justice is a way in which people's actions become intelligible and are evaluated by themselves and others; it does not refer to an internal state of need. Intelligibility requires locating an intended or completed act within a particular address frame and seeing the act from the standpoint of others with whom people are interacting or who represent their social community. For example, if Bill adopts the address frame of his social group—he views his intended acts from their standpoint—then he and they can judge his acts to be warranted ways to constitute justice and fairness. This is what most of us routinely do.

If we say that it is just to allocate resources equitably by giving more to those with the greatest inputs, we employ an address frame that constitutes this meaning. In this view, there is nothing intrinsically, objectively, or literally fair about such an act. The sense of fairness emerges by virtue of its evoking a response from certain others that indicates this meaning. By addressing ourselves to those others, we can adopt their standpoint and view our intended act of equitable allocation to be one that will mean "just and fair."

Some Relevant Research. It should be apparent that when different frames are addressed, different meanings for the same act will emerge. To act equitably when addressing certain audiences, therefore, would not render the act as just and fair; perhaps it would appear to be exploitative, competitive, or status seeking. It is in light of this and because actors address themselves to others in guiding their actions that just meanings emerge as part of the social process.

A study on the naive psychology of motives reported by Maki, Thorngate, and McClintock (1979) is relevant to consider in this context. They had subjects make predictions about the motivations of what were actually preprogrammed game players. Their data indicated that motives of individualism and competition were more readily understood than motives of altruism and cooperation. Further,

To the extent that an actor repeatedly behaves in an atypical fashion (i.e., displays a preference for negative over positive outcomes to self) . . . observers . . . have difficulty identifying the actor's choice rules. (p. 211)

These findings support a view of motives as socially situated ways people employ to render actions intelligible. It was difficult for subjects to comprehend a selfless player in a competitive game. It is in cognizance of this social siting of motives and because thinking involves adopting an address frame that people are able to gear their actions into intelligible forms.

Although the authors did not explore the intelligibility that did emerge when actors were selfless and altruistic, we can speculate on several possibilities. If your acts lose points for you and give them to me, you are not addressing me as an opponent. Your overgenerosity might mean that you find me "needy" or possibly even "weak" or "incompetent." In this view, our acts communicate the qualities we assume that our audience has. Members of that audience fit the meaning of our behavior into a framework that is also informative to them about the kind of people we think them to be.

It is important to keep in mind that the meanings of the justice address frame do not simply emerge within this laboratory microcontext of social interaction but, rather, that microcontext serves as the vehicle for the meanings prevalent in the larger society. That people more readily understand competitive actions than altruistic ones in a game context speaks to us of the underlying social formation that generates and governs the meanings of particular actions, even as those actions, when carried out, participate in reproducing that underlying structure.

A second study (Morgan & Sawyer, 1979) noted that for one nonfriend or stranger to permit another to receive a greater allocation in an exchange would be to communicate an admission of inferior status for the former. This led the authors to suggest that in order to avoid this admission in the absence of good evidence to support it, a person would behave competitively in order to restore equality.

Their formulation is consistent with the address-frame concept. Actors address themselves to a nonfriend other; from that standpoint, they would appear to be of inferior status unless they behaved competitively. They do not seek equality in order to convey a meaning of solidarity; this might occur were they addressing themselves to a friend. Rather, given that they are addressing themselves to a nonfriend, they seek equality in order to create the meaning of noninferior standing.

Research reported by Clark and Mills (1979) further affirms the usefulness of the address-frame approach in the psychology of justice. They distinguish between exchange relationships (as in business dealings) and communal relationships (as in families and in friendships). They find that attraction between people varies as a function of whether an act is addressed within the proper frame (this is my interpretation of their findings).

To frame an act within an exchange relationship, for example, when people believe that communal bonds exist, is to invite lesser attraction than to frame the same act within its more proper (i.e., expected) address frame. Specifically, they report that when two people are in a communal relationship (e.g., they expect to be in a friendship rather than in a more impersonal, businesslike relationship) and one asks for a favor in return for a favor given, attraction is reduced. In their view, "treating a communal relationship in terms of exchange compromises the relationship" (p. 23).

The authors comment on the implications of this finding for the applicability of equity theory to liking relationships. Their findings indicate that to treat a liking relationship as though it were a business exchange, by insisting on equity as the defining rule of justice, is to challenge the communal nature of the relationship. These data further affirm the point I have been making: the context within which an action occurs defines the meaning of that action—in this case, the sense of justice that occurs. To repeat, because people engage an address frame in thinking and formulating both their intended and their completed actions, they introduce contextual factors (i.e., the standpoint of the other) and are thereby able to develop their ongoing course of action in light of the knowledge about its meaning to those with whom they are interacting.

From the perspective of justice as address frame, we can see how addressing oneself to another as business partner when that other expects to be taken as a friend can lead the act to be defined as inappropriate. In light of this, people typically address their acts in ways that take the other's standpoint into consideration. In order to do this, they think in terms of what their acts would appear to be from the other's point of view: for example, what meaning would my request for a return favor have when the other and I are friends?

Self-Presentational Theory and the Address Frame. Psychology, especially social psychology, has recently rediscovered the concept of "self" that once flourished as a central feature of the discipline (e.g., see Baumeister, 1982). This rediscovery introduces several compelling parallels with my own notion of address frame, as does the rethinking of justice as justification by Mikula (1982) to which I referred earlier. One consequence of this rediscovery and refocusing is that it has permitted an interpersonal reinterpretation of what were understood as essentially intrapsychic processes. Baumeister, for example, suggests how altruism, justice allocation, reactance, dissonance, aggression, attributions, and so forth are better understood as interpersonal processes driven by a self-presentational "motive" than as attributes of the "psyche."

The argument that Baumeister develops has a certain kinship both to my scheme and to Mikula's. He suggests that people are basically concerned about their self-presentation and self-image for two reasons: (1) in order to obtain rewards from others who control those rewards by presenting oneself as deserving such rewards and (2) in order to sustain an ideal self concept. I interpret the latter as emphasizing the importance of self-esteem and people's desires to present themselves to others in ways that will enhance or sustain a level of self-esteem.

Assuming this to be an important motive source, it then becomes possible to interpret what appear to be intrapsychic processes (e.g., reducing the tension of cognitive dissonance) as an effort on the part of people to appear self-consistent so as to protect or to repair their reputation and sense of self-esteem. With respect to issues of justice, Baumeister cites several investigations (also cited by Mikula) that warrant a reinterpretation in terms of self-esteem.

For example, if one's allocative behavior changes as a function of whether it is publicly observable or concealed from public scrutiny, a case could be made for the implication of self-esteem as a central feature of justice decisions. Several investigators (e.g., Kidder, Bellettirie, & Cohn, 1977; Reis & Gruzen, 1976; also see Mikula, 1982) have suggested that whether allocations were made equitably or equally varied as a function of the potential for audience discovery: that is, people took more for themselves when they thought it could be accomplished in complete privacy. Needless to say, this suggests the rather overwhelming role of others in the determination of one's self-esteem. One could also expect people to be less selfish in the service of their self-judgments even without an observing audience present; but perhaps the nature of the situation, the subjects used, or the times in which we live produced this audience-based assessment.

Both the analyses of Baumeister and Mikula reflect the growing awareness among psychologists of a need for a more interpersonal base to their understanding of human behavior. Justice motivation as address frame, as a principle of interpersonal justification, or as reflecting a concern with self-esteem has the clear effect of putting us directly into the social world. To be sure, there remains a confusion about how interpersonal matters have become, in that a "natural motive" is imputed to the individual; but there is a potential openness to sociocultural and sociohistorical factors that is missing in the typical psychological account.

The Role of Sociohistorical Factors

The concept of address frame, like the approaches suggested by Mikula and by Baumeister, permits sociohistorical factors to play a central role in our understanding of human social behavior. In their everyday activities, people address themselves to significant others as figures embedded within particular sociohistorical contexts. By rooting thought, motivation, and personality in society and in history, we have a basis for expecting that what we presently discover about human psychology (e.g., justice motivation) is not inevitable or even necessarily a universal view; rather, it represents a formulation thoroughly embedded in the contemporary social context.

The Negotiated Quality of Justice

The conceptualization of justice motivation in terms of an address frame also suggests that issues of justice have a kind of negotiated quality. This is clearly central in Mikula's formulation as well. Because people do not invariably address the same others in their thinking, they may fail to sustain a shared conception of social reality: all social interaction has this potentially negotiated quality about it.

Imagine a student who wants to take an exam one day late because of an important family affair on the exam day and a professor who claims that it would be unfair to give this one student special privilege. Both parties try to ground their behavior in terms of a justice analysis, each attempting to get the other to accept his formulation.

When we treat justice intrapersonally as a fundamental psychological force that operates in a similar manner in all people, we tend to overemphasize consensus over conflict and negotiation. However, if we view justice motivation in terms of a concept such as address frame, we introduce the process of people interacting together and attempting to negotiate some agreement or compromise over what will be accepted as just and fair.

The negotiated quality of justice motivation is especially relevant in the context of social change. It seems reasonable to suggest that changing social forms introduce competing formulations of social reality. Justice thereby does not involve simply fitting human behavior into a known and pregiven formula; it involves a complex process whereby people address their views to those with competing views and attempt to accomplish some reasonable, joint formulation of social reality.

Negotiation, however, is rarely simply a matter of equal partners, especially when we move from the laboratory into the larger social field. Negotiations over meanings involve power and domination. Once we view justice motivation in address-frame terms, we can better see how advantages to some and domination to others are sustained through the institutionalization of the power of the former to impose their meanings over the latter. To return to our student and professor, although both parties may attempt to ground their claims in terms of a justice analysis, the negotiation is typically one-sided: the professor's claims usually are victorious, even if the professor yields to this student's particular request. That is, the professor and student agree that although justice involves treating everyone equally, this exception is permissible because "the professor is a nice person."

I do not wish to convey the illusion that, simply because the address-frame concept gives a negotiated quality to human behavior, there is a continual, self-conscious action of this sort going on. Far from it. No social form could be reliably sustained were it dependent on its members renegotiating a contract and redefining its terms anew in each and every encounter. Those in positions of power with substantial advantages have a vested interest in sustaining their positions and their advantage and so in institutionalizing and routinizing (often through language and symbolic practices) what might otherwise be self-consciously renegotiated anew each time.

In other words, justice involves a definite dimension of power as part of its *core* understanding. The address-frame concept, in that it provides a sense of *process* to the entire concern with justice, at least alerts us to this dimension. More static or purely psychological approaches to justice, by contrast, lead us to delete what turns out to be a central element of power and its legitimation. They provide us with a more mechanical view, seen most clearly in formulations of the equity type, in which participants seem merely to be filling out the terms of an equation by plugging in the details of their particular situation (e.g., their specific investments and outcomes).

When the dimension of power is lost from our view, then power is sustained covertly; that power, however, is the power of those already in positions of advantage to sustain their advantage by making a sociohistorical product appear to be somehow normal or natural.

The Changing Intelligibility of the Justice Address Frame

Even to know when a situation involves justice requires something akin to a concept such as that of the address frame. I am not aware of work to date that has examined this matter. The standard research model has the investigator *implicitly* adopt an ongoing sociohistorical framework, which already assumes when justice is or is not involved and what its terms and meanings are. People's responses to these predefined situations are then studied. The determination of when an issue involves justice or fairness and when some other matter is involved is itself an issue of substantial importance. By ignoring this point, however, one carries on the existing framework as part of the "seen but unnoticed background." Mikula has raised a parallel point on this issue.

Basically, what happens in the usual psychological study involves the psychologist in a process that assumes the very matters that need to be questioned. In order to design a study of justice, for example, the psychologist who is already fully immersed in the existing society simply assumes the institutions and the arrangements of that society as background and then develops a "justice problem" based on that now unnoticed background. The study thereby reaches conclusions about justice without ever examining the ways in which particular situations get to be defined as justice-implicated in the first place *or* looking at what this teaches us about the underlying system of legitimation and power within the society.

One critic of Rawls's otherwise provocative analysis of justice makes this very point (see Skillen, 1977). Skillen claims that in his theory of justice, Rawls simply assumes the bourgeois capitalist form and departs from here. Skillen is especially keen to note Rawls's insistence that justice be defined in terms of political liberties, while socioeconomic standing is relegated to a secondary place (i.e., as involving something other than justice).

Since the basic good of self respect *should* depend, he claims, on status as citizens, not on position in the economy, a just society may well be one with great inequality in its economic organisation, just as long as this inequality leaves the "worst off" better off than they would be under other systems—a claim made for capitalism by its major proponents from Adam Smith to Milton Friedman. (Skillen, p. 17)

Let me repeat the point I have been making throughout: at minimum, the address-frame approach alerts us to an analysis that systematically *introduces* the otherwise assumed and concealed sociohistorical context. That context is a key part of the very notion of address frame; it is part of the to-be-noticed foreground. What results, therefore, is less likely to carry along unscathed the very set of background assumptions that need to be examined if psychology is to understand justice and its position within society and to contribute to self-reflective and critical intervention in the social process rather than helping to perpetuate machinelike societal reproduction.

I have not presented the concept of address frame as the final answer to the host of problems I have introduced in this work. Rather, I have introduced it as one vehicle for bringing a theoretical base into our formulations that includes the very elements that are systematically excluded by pure psychology. Indeed, recognizing the audience factor in human behavior might well lead the discipline to recognize the audience factor in its own productions as well. This latter move would surely open to disciplinary self-reflection psychology's role in societal reproduction and hence in possible societal transformation.

ADDRESS FRAME, JUSTICE, AND THE IDEAL SPEECH SITUATION

The address-frame concept that I have introduced in the examination of justice reveals important parallels with Habermas's dialogic model of reason as contained in his concept of the ideal speech situation (Chapter 13). The dialogic model—whether captured by the notion of an address frame, the view of justice as a justification practice, or the discursive redemption of truth claims within an ideal speech situation—presents a contrasting formulation to the typical, monologic views of Western philosophy and pure psychology.

As McCarthy observes in discussing Habermas, ethical principles such as justice, for example, cannot be obtained through the solitary, monologic reflection of the Kantian individual but, rather, are both discovered and formed by partners in dialogue. Thereby justice as an ideal to be achieved cannot emerge from the solitary moral consciousness reflecting on universal principles of fairness. Instead, it demands a morally engaged community of partners involved in a dialogue of the sort characterized by Habermas as the ideal speech situation. This distinction, central to the address-frame concept, is a significant advance over the typical monological formulations. Goodness, fairness, justice, and so on demand the engagement of actors in dialogue, where the dialogue is of the sort that ideally permits the testing of the validity claims that are proposed.

The kind of dialogue that Habermas describes as ideal permits the participants to evaluate the validity of competing claims as long as the dialogue is free from systematic distortions derived either from personal or ideological sources. While a monologue can occur in isolation from society and others (even though it necessarily employs societal terms), a dialogue demands both society and others for its realization. Ideal dialogue demands social structures and formations geared to the reproduction of the conditions of the ideal rather than to the suppression of its tenets. Justice cannot be achieved within the minds of individual thinkers each reflecting on the good life; it requires social conditions constitutive of the good life so that the dialogue itself can take place. The address frame concept cannot mean anything it if merely describes some purely subjective process.

The vacuous discussion of justice within a context that denies its realization speaks more of power and domination, and thus of distortion, than of dialogue designed to achieve the very ideal that is requisite to validating its claims to universality. As long as the framework within which competing claims can be discursively tested forbids this very testing, the kind of justice ideals that emerge will reflect more the interests of one societal segment than interests that have the potential of true universality.

What I have been suggesting in briefly reviewing the connections between a concern with justice, its formulation in terms of an address frame or related concept, and Habermas's communication-based ethics is the way in which a genuine understanding of justice obtains only when one introduces a dialogic rather than a monologic dimension. The latter, however, has been most typical of psychology as well as philosophy and so has missed some of the elements central to any understanding of justice in society.

The address-frame concept compels us to understand justice as part of a system of communication rather than in terms of abstract principles removed from human dialogue. Equity formulations, especially when refined in terms of some advanced cognitive calculus, for example, represent one far end of the extremely solitary monologue that passes for an analysis of justice. Somehow, each isolated calculator following some rules of mathematical summation and weighting will arrive at a solution that assures justice for all. Nowhere is there a dialogue with others. Nowhere is there room for testing the justice claims that each puts forth. Nowhere is there justice.

A CRITIQUE OF MODEST PROPOSALS

I introduced the concept of address frame as a modest proposal that at least lay in the general direction of change that I envisioned as necessary for psychology. I also observed its parallels both with several earlier theoretical models (e.g., Mead, Vygotsky, Mills, & Sullivan) and with some emerging developments that have sought to interpersonalize what have heretofore been essentially intrapsychic processes (e.g., Baumeister and Mikula, among others). My judgment is that something akin to the address-frame model succeeds insofar as it forces us to become systematically sensitive to the social dimensions of our analyses. In my view, however, it is not successful, if it fails to keep us cognizant of the ways in which that social dimension interpenetrates whatever we take to be the psychology of the individual.

If we see the social dimension in our work and yet insist, for example, that people are somehow fundamentally (i.e., intrinsically) concerned with self-esteem, hedonistic satisfaction, or environmental outcome control and mastery, we fail: that is, we plant a "natural" motive within the individual even as we attempt to bridge toward the underlying social and historical world. In doing this, we take one step forward and two in reverse. At the very moment we touch the sociohistorical we take it all back by imputing some fundamental motive, drive, or cognitive interest to the individual, thus denying what we have almost achieved.

I have no doubt that matters of self-esteem and outcome control are central features of the contemporary world. I do have doubts about their being an intrinsic part of human nature, at least in the way we understand and use them. Clearly, my worry is that once again the potential to move into the interpersonal arena will fail as we retranslate everything back again into individualistic essence–nature. The fundament we assume is given by our contemporary world and thus is not quite as fundamental or as inherent as we imagine.

I believe that my own notion of address frame can suffer this same fate and thus fail to move us beyond the base of pure psychology. Although the address-frame concept does not impute any fundamental motive or drive—it merely describes the process by which the social interpenetrates the individual—its very affinity with notions of self-esteem and mastery too easily permit it to be cast in the old molds. I see the address-frame notion as describing a process and not a vessel filled with content. The latter emerges within the particular society, with its underlying structures and mechanisms. The process is what moves us in what I believe to be the correct direction for psychology.

JUSTICE AS PROCESS

The dilemma, of course, is that a process does not provide a formula or an equation. Insofar as we search for justice as the realization of some absolute principle, as some intrinsic property of human cognitive structure, or as completing a formal equation, I believe we will continue to run into the kinds of problem about which this book has been written. The appeal to viewing justice as a process, akin perhaps to the ideal speech situation, is that it addresses itself to the ways by which legitimacy can be achieved in human affairs. It emphasizes justice not as a state of being but as a process whereby people collectively determine, without the domination of either ideological or physical force, the legitimacy of the various claims that are put forth. Needless to say, this view at present remains too abstract and incomplete and thus is by no means satisfying. Yet, justice as process at least is consistent with the kind of critical and reflective stance that I have addressed throughout this work.

There is a kinship between this process-oriented approach and some more recent concerns with the concept of *procedural justice* (e.g., Lerner & Whitehead, 1980; Leventhal, Karuza, & Fry, 1980; Mikula, 1982). There are also key points of difference. For the most part, those who have been concerned with procedures whereby justice is accomplished differentiate these rules from the actual outcomes. Thus, presumably just rules can produce an unjust outcome, or a just outcome can be achieved even if the procedures employed are unjust.

I must assume that in order to arrange matters in this dualistic manner, it is possible to speak of a condition of "justice in itself" apart from the process involved in its achievement. This forces us to understand a thing or state of justice that is somehow independent of the dialogic process producing it and continues to evaluate its viability and legitimacy for the parties involved. In other words, this duality returns us again to a monologic or individualistic perspective, the very position from which I believe we must move if we are ever to understand the dynamics of justice.

We separate process from outcome where I believe we must establish their unity. Basically, a decision reached without a process that encourages the kinds of critical self-reflection characterized by Habermas's ideal speech situation cannot be just, legitimate, or fair. A near analogue emerges from the psychoanalytic encounter in which a correct interpretation that is *given* is not a correct interpretation if it bypasses the process whereby understandings become self-understandings, rationally achieved.

CHAPTER FIFTEEN

Concluding Comments

There are two tasks to be accomplished in this final chapter: (1) briefly to summarize the main theme and message of this entire work and (2) to speculate on the likelihood of psychology's adopting a new approach for its study, given its relationship to society today.

BY WAY OF SUMMARY

I was neither born a student of justice nor was my formal education geared to its study. As in so many things, I entered the world of justice research by the back door. My intention was to examine the correspondence between the psychological principle of cognitive consistency and the sociological variable of status congruence. Admittedly, my intent was to reduce a social-structural variable to a basic psychological principle of mental functioning. As part of the series of investigations I undertook to examine this connection, I not only stumbled into the world of justice but also came to question and finally challenge the very basis of my own and others' work in psychology.

In my personal dialectic, the opening attempt to reduce a feature of social structure to the internal movements of the human mind led to a formulation that envisioned an intricate connection between the underlying social structure and the emergent psychological structure. I was not seeking to reduce sociology to psychology. Some might argue that I have only come part way thus far, by reducing psychology to sociology. I prefer to see the position I have been advancing in this work to be of neither sort. Rather, in order for there to be a meaningful psychology, there must be a corresponding structural analysis, even as that analysis demands an agent with a psychological interior for it to be meaningfully conducted. Neither can be reduced entirely to the other, yet neither is independent of the other. I suppose one might say that I arrived again at a social psychology as the basis for the human sciences.

In the course of this movement away from simplistic and mechanical reductions and more thoroughly into the heart of justice, my understandings became necessarily politicized. I say "necessarily" because it is virtually impossible to disentangle matters of power from other issues in our contemporary society. Those who seek systematically to study and understand human social life will invariably encounter some issue involving politics, power, domination, and control. I believe this was a very significant and critical realization. It cast my own work and the work of others in my field into a very different light; it required me to reexamine the field itself.

In a society and world in which questions of power and politics intrude into nearly every social activity, one cannot be neutral and disinterested. It became apparent that the claim of neutrality served primarily to cover covert advocacy on behalf of the order of power and advantage as now constituted. In no area of study was this more evident than in the concern with justice.

The issue of justice cuts to the core of the legitimacy of any social system. It not only raises questions of who gets what but demands answers to the question *why*. Psychology's answers to these questions were reminiscent of my own efforts to reduce the complexities of social life to individual mental functioning. In addition, however, psychology's answers impressed me for what they failed to observe. Any approach to the study of justice that presupposes what needs to be seriously examined at the inception—namely, the existing framework of society—serves the vested interests that are reproduced by that failure to examine. As I probed further into the psychology of justice, it became increasingly apparent that many of the very questions that needed to be asked were not being asked—that the existing framework of our own society was taken as the implicit given and matters of justice and fairness were studied within those limits.

I assumed that psychology was neither self-consciously deceptive nor self-consciously acting as the servant of the vested interests of established power and privilege. Therefore, I tried to understand what there was about the deep structure of psychology that disposed those who employed it in their practice inadvertently to reproduce the existing societal framework rather than to provide any serious enlightenment about its operation. Thus, I turned more directly to the critical study of pure psychology itself.

It is in the deep structure of the discipline that I believe I uncovered the roots of its conserving social role. It appeared to me that as long as psychology was founded on empiricism, individualism, and subjectivism, it could not probe sufficiently into itself to be anything other than socially reproductive.

Psychology's empiricist approach to knowledge limited it to the appearances of the present rather than the underlying structures and mechanisms that mediated this present. Psychology's discoveries therefore were both true and factual and yet liable to distortion and falsification.

Psychology's romance with abstracted individualism and its reduction of everything to the operation of either the individual's mental operations or behavior showed that the underlying social forms would remain relatively unanalyzed. The coherence and operation of societal structures as such is ignored by treating these as mere derivatives of individual activity. When these structures are not observed, they are covertly carried along in the discipline's understanding.

Psychology's subjectivist foundation, combined with its individualism, places the examination of social structure well beyond our view. Our attention is deflected away from the core to the periphery. This can only help sustain the relations of domination that feed off the core and rest easy as long as people tackle only the periphery.

Questionable Science and Suspect Values

The implication of my critique of pure psychology is clear, though it needs restatement. On two counts—questionable science and suspect values—psychology can be said to suffer. Its science as now constituted fails to provide us with a complete and accurate understanding of the subject matter—human life and behavior—that is purports to examine. A psychology that is not truly a *social* psychology, recognizing both the irreducibility of the psychological to the sociological or the sociological to the psychological because of the essential interpenetration of each by the other, cannot provide us with a genuine understanding of human life. We fail to achieve the science that we might by continuing to employ a foundation that does not permit its realization.

The values of pure psychology are also suspect. Although social systems are imperfect, their move toward perfection cannot be advanced as long as the potential movers (i.e., the human subjects) are systematically kept in the dark and unable to comprehend the wanted directions for change. When psychology's contributions organize and develop societal self-understandings that manage to conceal more than they reveal, that carry the present arrangements forward relatively unscathed because they cannot be publicly examined, I believe its contributions need to be challenged: all the more so when psychology's covert advocacy is conducted under the aura of scientific value neutrality. As I have repeatedly indicated, I do not believe psychology's role is self-conscious and intentional: the field itself is not yet sufficiently a self-reflective subject to carry that label and accusation. I believe that psychology's role *can* be involved in helping restore the subject to human history, but only after it restores a semblance of the subject to itself.

HOW LIKELY THE CHANGE?

The ways of doing social science do not arise from some mystical soil but from the same underlying structures that mediate other features of the society. Any changes in psychology will both emerge from and help constitute a differently structured society. Furthermore, changes that might occur are less likely to be in response to nagging and unanswered questions intrinsic to the science itself than to extrascientific matters. I believe this assertion to be even more true of the social than the natural sciences.

Structure, Activity, and Knowledge

The social sciences are an intimate part of the mainstream of their society. Their concepts and assumptive framework are mediated by the same underlying structures and mechanisms as the self-understandings of the society they study. Their knowledge could provide an intervention in the society of a different sort than the technical and mechanical interventions of the natural sciences. When we understand a law of nature, we understand something that is more universal, invariant, and independent of this knowledge than the laws we generate about society and human subjects. The latter are not only time- and place-dependent but also vary as a function of the knowledge people have about their operation. In principle there is a greater choice to obey or disobey a law of social nature than a law of physical nature. Furthermore, the physical laws pertain to structures that exist regardless of whether human activity engages their use, whereas social laws refer to structures that exist only in and through the active engagement of human subjects.

This latter point has been made by several authors, but the previously considered treatments by Bhaskar and Giddens are most cogent. Both observe that the underlying structural properties of a social system are not independent of the activity of human agents. To sharpen our understanding of this distinction between social structures and the structures of the physical world, Giddens suggests the following example. He observes first that we can meaningfully speak of the anatomical structure of the human organism apart from the living activity of that organism: in other words, after a person has died, we can still study the anatomical structure of the body. In this sense, structures are independent of the activity of human agents.

By contrast, social structures *"cease to be when they cease to function"* (Giddens, p. 61). In other words, social structures exist only by virtue of the activity of people; their activity reproduces the structure. Recall that Giddens refers to this as "a duality of structure." Structures generate human activity and thus are the medium for social practices, yet they exist only in and through that activity and thus are also the outcome of social practices.

This peculiar feature of human social and psychological life suggests that knowledge about the operation of structures can influence and transform them even as it typically and routinely reproduces the structures. What we know, therefore, is always a potential intervention in our society. Thus, what psychology helps us learn could intervene to alter the structures of society.

The sciences, including the social sciences, provide one of the important avenues still remaining to participate in societal transformation. The values of the scientific enterprise—open exploration, open discussion, a search for truth—permit this possibility. I have suggested that the present forms and deep structures of the social sciences work in opposition to this end of social transformation; this state of affairs, however, need not mean that an alternate science would be unable to contribute to hastening what in its present form is unlikely.

END

I believe that there is a profound crisis in our civilization today. Although it is not new, its scope is widening and its intensity deepening; the risks to humanity and to nature are greater than ever before. The moments of pause and rest grow shorter. The anguish is more intense, the joys and happiness more shallow. There are neither simple answers nor real experts who will guide us, for those we call experts are trained only to lead us further down the wrong path. The expertise required is of a moral sort, not the technical and instrumental type that passes for expertise today. Real human needs are not met by building technically advanced structures; people are needed who can evaluate whether or not that is the way we should invest our time, energy, and resources. In these matters, under the right circumstances, everyone can be an expert.

Will the social sciences and psychology enter on the side of the people who need to penetrate further into the world that seems to confront them as an alien enterprise? Or, will psychology enter on the side of that murky, alien enterprise? Paulo Freire (1970) speaks of the ontological vocation of humanity: learning to be a "Subject"—one who, with knowledge, will, and consciousness, is an active agent who works to shape the world and create human history. Up to this point in our history, psychology's contribution has not substantially facilitated that vocation.

The study of justice within the hands of psychological investigators stands as stark testimony to the truth of this assertion. If psychologists can pursue this ontological vocation, I believe they too can enter as Subjects with the possibility of participating in humanity's vocational mission.

A change in how we conduct our work as psychologists, in this case, is not some idle matter of purely intellectual concern. I am not describing the universe through the eyes of a Ptolemy versus a Copernicus or a Newton versus an Einstein. I am describing the world of human history—of joy and suffering. The true subjects of history are among us, waiting to be what they might be. What will be the role of psychology and the other human sciences in supporting, encouraging, and motivating this movement?

Psychology is not responsible for drudgery, pain, and suffering. By failing to address itself to humanity in forms that permit transformation, however, psychology continues to support what is harmful and unfreeing.

POSTSCRIPT

It seems that endings are almost as troublesome as beginnings. Both are written at the conclusion, after some time has passed, passion subsided, and traditional academic scholarship ascended. As I reflect back on what I have completed, I am struck by two issues: first, I have not gone far enough; second, I have gone a bit too far. Let me briefly address each in turn.

Although the direction of my concern is clear, have I taken us far enough along this route? I have a tendency to sweep out the dirt and then permit some of it to reenter. My real message, if it dared to rear its head for public display, is quite simple: the world we now live in and the ways we go about understanding ourselves in it share a profound disdain for human life and well-being. Even as our structures for conquering nature have turned about and now enslave and threaten us, we have adopted approaches for understanding human life that accomplish this same end. What is needed thereby is not more talk, more writing, or more contemplation but a clean sweep, a radical change, a dramatic turning over of what is basically an unnecessary and destructive way of being. It would be irresponsible to stand for anything else.

Needless to say, if I forcefully pressed that theme in this book, I would lose some of those who may be tempted to listen and even entertain the doubts and suspicions to which I have alluded, albeit somewhat cryptically. And so I pulled back a bit and did not go forward as far as I might have had I followed my temperament a bit more and my ego's fearful pride a bit less.

On the other hand, I have clearly gone too far, stretching beyond the very boundaries of rigor that demand p-values and proper methodologies before concluding that something is fundamentally evil, good, or neither. My colleagues who take comfort and experience conviction only when all the returns are in and thoroughly digested will believe that this work has simply gone much too far. They will be thoroughly unconvinced by its various assertions, modes of reasoning and style of argumentation, its occasional references to known and approved literature and personnel, and its frequent references to persons unknown or—if known—of, to them, somewhat dubious credentials. Thus, it is irresponsible to adopt the standpoint I have presented.

The most dreadful fate of all, of course, is one that I have probably achieved: to stand somewhere between these two judgments. How horrible! When the bridge is down and the populace is rushing headlong toward it in the dark and fog hoping to escape the torrent surging behind, I stand squarely in the middle shouting that (1) I think the bridge may be out and it would be irresponsible for me not to say so, but (2) I've heard several highly placed people suggest that one should wait before reaching that kind of conclusion lest one provide inappropriately premature information and thereby behave irresponsibly.

Well, the bridge is out.

References

Ackerman, N. W. *Treating the troubled family*. New York: Basic Books, 1966.

Adams, J. S. Inequity in social exchange. In L. Berkowtiz (Ed.), *Advances in experimental social psychology* (Vol. 2). New York: Academic Press, 1965.

Adams, S. Status congruence as a variable in small group performance. *Social Forces*, 1953, *32*, 16–22.

Adorno, T. W. Sociology and psychology. *New Left Review*, 1967, *46*, 63–80.

Adorno, T. W. *Negative dialectics*. New York: Seabury, 1973.

Adorno, T. W. *Minima moralia*. London: NLB, 1974.

Adorno, T. W., Albert, H., Dahrendorf, R., Habermas, J., Pilot, H., & Popper, K. R. *The positivist dispute in German sociology*. New York: Harper & Row, 1976.

Allport, G. W. The historical background of modern social psychology. In G. Lindzey & E. Aronson (Eds.), *The handbook of social psychology* (Vol. 1; 2nd ed.). Reading, Mass: Addison-Wesley, 1968.

Aronson, R. The individualist social theory of Jean-Paul Sartre. In New Left Review (Ed.), *Western Marxism: A critical reader*. London: Allen & Unwin, 1977.

Averill, J. R. Personal control over aversive stimuli and its relationship to stress. *Psychological Bulletin*, 1973, *80*, 286–303.

Bales, R. F. Adaptive and integrative changes as sources of strain in social systems. In A. P. Hare, E. F. Borgatta, & R. F. Bales (Eds.), *Small groups: Studies in social interaction*. New York: Knopf, 1955.

Bales, R. F. Task roles and social roles in problem-solving groups. In E. E. Maccoby, T. M. Newcomb, & E. L. Hartley (Eds.), *Readings in social psychology*. New York: Holt, 1958.

Baltes, P. B., & Nesselroade, J. R. Cultural change and adolescent personality development. *Developmental Psychology*, 1972, *7*, 244–256.

Bandura, A. Self-efficacy mechanism in human agency. *American Psychologist*, 1982, *37*, 122–147.

Bar-Hillel, Y. Indexical expressions. *Mind*, 1954, *63*, 359–379.

Barker, R. G. Explorations in ecological psychology. *American Psychologist*, 1965, *20*, 1–14.

Barker, R. G. *Ecological psychology: Concepts and methods for studying the environment of human behavior*. Stanford, Calif: Stanford University Press, 1968.

Bateson, G. *Steps to an ecology of mind*. New York: Chandler, 1972.

Baumeister, R. F. A self-presentational view of social phenomena. *Psychological Bulletin*, 1982, *91*, 3–36.

Benoit-Smullyan, E. Status, status types and status interrelationships. *American Sociological Review*, 1944, *9*, 151–161.

Berg, N. E., & Mussen, P. The origins and development of concepts of justice. *Journal of Social Issues*, 1975, *31*, 183–201.

Berger, P. L., & Luckman, T. *The social construction of reality*. Garden City, N.Y.: Doubleday, 1966.

Berkowitz, L., & Friedman, P. Some social class differences in helping behavior. *Journal of Personality and Social Psychology*, 1967, *5*, 217–225.

Bertalanffy, L. *General systems theory*. New York: Braziller, 1968.

Bhaskar, R. *The possibility of naturalism*. Atlantic Highlands, N.J.: Humanities Press, 1979.

Bramel, D., & Friend, R. Hawthorne, the myth of the docile worker and class bias in psychology. *American Psychologist*, 1981, *36*, 867–878.

Brandon, A. C. The relevance of expectation as an underlying factor in status incongruence. *Sociometry*, 1965, *28*, 272–288.

Buck-Morss, S. Socio-economic bias in Piaget's theory and its implications for cross-culture studies. *Human Development*, 1975, *18*, 35–49.

Buck-Morss, S. *The origin of negative dialectics*. New York: Free Press, 1977.

Buss, A. R. *A dialectical psychology*. New York: Irvington, 1979.

Caplan, N., & Nelson, S. D. On being useful: The nature and consequences of psychological research on social problems. *American Psychologist*, 1973, *28*, 199–211.

Carey, A. The Hawthorne studies: A radical criticism. *American Sociological Review*, 1967, *32*, 403–416.

Carey, A. The Lysenko syndrome in western social science. *Australian Psychologist*, 1977, *12*, 27–38.

Carlson, R. Understanding women: Implications for personality theory and research. *Journal of Social Issues*, 1972, *28*, 17–32.

Cartwright, D. Contemporary social psychology in historical perspective. *Social Psychology Quarterly*, 1979, *42*, 83–93.

Churchman, C. W. *The systems approach and its enemies*. New York: Basic Books, 1979.

Clark, M. S., & Mills, J. Interpersonal attraction in exchange and communal relationships. *Journal of Personality and Social Psychology*, 1979, *37*, 12–24.

Cole, R. E. *Work, mobility and participation*. Berkeley, Calif: University of California Press, 1979.

Colletti, L. *Marxism and Hegel*. London: Verso, 1979.

Coward, R., & Ellis, J. *Language and materialism*. London: Routledge & Kegan Paul, 1977.

Cronbach, L. J. Beyond the two disciplines of scientific psychology. *American Psychologist*, 1975, *30*, 116–127.

Damon, W. *The social world of the child*. San Francisco: Jossey-Bass, 1977.

Derrida, J. *Of grammatology*. Baltimore: Johns Hopkins University Press, 1974.

Derrida, J. *Writing and difference*. Chicago: University of Chicago Press, 1978.

Derrida, J. *Dissemination*. Chicago: University of Chicago Press, 1981.

Deutsch, M. Equity, equality and need: What determines which value will be used as the basis of distributive justice? *Journal of Social Issues*, 1975, *31*, 137–149.

Dewey, J., & Bentley, A. F. *Knowing and the known*. Boston: Beacon Press, 1949.

Edney, J. J. The commons problem: Alternative perspectives. *American Psychologist*, 1980, *35*, 131–150.

Edney, J. J. Paradoxes on the commons: Scarcity and the problem of equality. *Journal of Community Psychology*, 1981, *9*, 3–34.

Exline, R. V., & Ziller, R. C. Status congruency and interpersonal conflict in decision-making groups. *Human Relations*, 1959, *12*, 147–162.

Farkas, A. J., & Anderson, N. H. Multidimensional input in equity theory. *Journal of Personality and Social Psychology*, 1979, *37*, 879–896.

Festinger, L. *A theory of cognitive dissonance*. Evanston, Ill: Row, Peterson, 1957.

Festinger, L., & Carlsmith, J. M. Cognitive consequences of forced compliance. *Journal of Abnormal and Social Psychology*, 1959, *58*, 203–210.

Franke, R. N., & Kaul, J. D. The Hawthorne experiments: First statistical interpretation. *American Sociological Review*, 1978, *43*, 623–643.

Frankl, V. E. *Man's search for meaning*. Boston: Beacon Press, 1959.

Freire, P. *Pedagogy of the oppressed*. New York: Continuum, 1970.

Fromm, E. *Escape from freedom*. New York: Holt, 1941.

Fromm, E. *The sane society*. New York: Rinehart, 1955.

Fromm, E. *The heart of man*. New York: Harper & Row, 1964.

Gadamer, H-G. *Truth and method*. London: Sheed & Ward, 1975.

Gadamer, H-G. *Philosophical hermeneutics*. Berkeley, Calif.: University of California Press, 1976.

Gadlin, H., & Rubin, S. H. Interactionism: A nonresolution of the person–situation controversy. In A. Buss (Ed.), *Psychology in social context*. New York: Irvington, 1979.

Garfinkel, H. *Ethnomethodology*. Englewood Cliffs, N.J.: Prentice-Hall, 1967.

Geertz, C. *The interpretation of cultures*. New York: Basic Books, 1973.

Geertz, C. From the native's point of view: On the nature of anthropological understanding. In P. Rabinow & W. M. Sullivan (Eds.), *Interpretative social science*. Berkeley, Calif.: University of California Press, 1979.

Gergen, K. J. Social psychology as history. *Journal of Personality and Social Psychology*, 1973, *26*, 309–320.

Gergen, K. J. Toward generative theory. *Journal of Personality and Social Psychology*, 1978, *36*, 1344–1360.

Gerth, H., & Mills, C. W. *Character and social structure*. New York: Harcourt Brace Jovanovich, 1953.

Giddens, A. *Central problems in social theory*. Berkeley, Calif.: University of California Press, 1979.

Gilligan, C. In a different voice: Women's conceptions of self and of morality. *Harvard Educational Review*, 1977, *47*, 481–517.

Ginsburg, G. P. *Epilogue: A conception of situated action*. Unpublished manuscript, University of Nevada, undated.

Giorgi, A. Phenomenology and the foundations of psychology. In W. J. Arnold (Ed.), *Nebraska symposium on motivation*. Lincoln: University of Nebraska Press, 1976.

Goffman, E. *The presentation of self in everyday life*. Garden City, N.Y.: Anchor/Doubleday, 1959.

Gurin, P., Gurin, G., & Morrison, B. M. Personal and ideological aspects of internal and external control. *Social Psychology*, 1978, *41*, 275–296.

Haan, N. Two moralities in action contexts: Relationships to thought, ego regulation and development. *Journal of Personality and Social Psychology*, 1978, *36*, 286–305.

Habermas, J. *Toward a rational society*. Boston: Beacon Press, 1970.

Habermas, J. *Knowledge and human interests*. Boston: Beacon Press, 1971.

Habermas, J. *Theory and practice*. Boston: Beacon Press, 1973.

Habermas, J. *Legitimation crisis*. Boston: Beacon Press, 1975.

Handel, G. *The psychosocial interior of the family*. Chicago: Aldine, 1967.

Hardin, G. The tragedy of the commons. *Science*, 1968, *162*, 1243–1248.

Harre, R. *The principles of scientific thinking*. London: Macmillan, 1970.

Harre, R. The ethogenic approach: Theory and practice. In L. Berkowitz (Ed.), *Advances in experimental social psychology* (Vol. 10). New York: Academic Press, 1977.

Harre, R., & Madden, E.H. *Causal powers: A theory of natural necessity*. Oxford, England: Blackwell, 1975.

Harre, R., & Secord, P. F. *The explanation of social behavior*. Oxford, England: Blackwell, 1972.

Harris, R. J. Handling negative inputs: On the plausible equity formulae. *Journal of Experimental Social Psychology*, 1976, *12*, 194–209.

Heider, R. *The psychology of interpersonal relations*. New York: Wiley, 1958.

Hendrick, C. Social psychology as history and as traditional science: An appraisal. *Personality and Social Psychology Bulletin*, 1976, *2*, 392–403.

Homans, G. C. *Social behavior: Its elementary forms*. New York: Harcourt, Brace & World, 1961.

Horkheimer, M. Notes on Institute activities. *Studies in Philosophy and Social Science*, 1941, *9*, 121–123.

Horkheimer, M. *Critical theory*. New York: Seabury, 1972.

Horkheimer, M. *Eclipse of reason*. New York: Seabury, 1974.

Horkheimer, M., & Adorno, T. W. *Dialectic of enlightenment*. New York: Seabury, 1972.

Husserl, E. *Phenomenology and the crisis of philosophy*. New York: Harper & Row, 1965.

Jacoby, R. *Social amnesia*. Boston: Beacon Press, 1975.

Jay, M. *The dialectical imagination*. Boston: Little, Brown, 1973.

Kantor, D., & Lehr, W. *Inside the family*. New York: Harper & Row, 1975.

Keat, R., & Urry, J. *Social theory as science*. London: Routledge & Kegan Paul, 1975.

Kidder, L., Bellettirie, G., & Cohn, E. Secret ambitions and public performances: The effects of anonymity on reward allocations made by men and women. *Journal of Experimental Social Psychology*, 1977, *13*, 70–80.

Kidder, L. H., Fagan, M. A., & Cohn, E. S. Giving and receiving: Social justice in close relationships. In M. J. Lerner & S. C. Lerner (Eds.), *The justice motive in social behavior*. New York: Plenum Press, 1981.

Kohlberg, L. The child as a moral philosopher. *Psychology Today*, September 1968.

Kohlberg, L. Stage and sequence: The cognitive-developmental approach to socialization. In D. A. Goslin (Ed.), *Handbook of socialization theory and research*. Chicago: Rand McNally, 1969.

Kuhn, T. S. *The structure of scientific revolutions*. Chicago: University of Chicago Press, 1962.

Kurzweil, E. *The age of structuralism*. New York: Columbia University Press, 1980.

Lakoff, G., & Johnson, M. *Metaphors we live by*. Chicago: University of Chicago Press, 1980.

Lasch, C. *The culture of narcissism: American life in an age of diminishing expectations*. New York: Norton, 1978.

Lefcourt, H. J. *Locus of control: Current trends in theory and research*. Hillsdale, N.J.: Erlbaum, 1976.

Lemaire, A. *Jacques Lacan*. London: Routledge & Kegan Paul, 1977.

Lenski, G. Status crystallization: A nonvertical dimension of social status. *American Sociological Review*, 1954, *19*, 405–413.

Lenski, G. Social participation and status crystallization. *American Sociological Review*, 1956, *21*, 458–464.

Lenski, G. Status inconsistency and the vote: A four nations test. *American Sociological Review*, 1967, *32*, 298–301.

Lerner, M. J. The justice motive in social behavior: Introduction. *Journal of Social Issues*, 1975, *31*, 1–19.

Lerner, M. J. The justice motive in human relations: Some thoughts on what we know and need to know about justice. In M. J. Lerner & S. C. Lerner (Eds.), *The justice motive in social behavior*. New York: Plenum Press, 1981.

Lerner, M. J., & Lerner, S. C. *The justice motive in social behavior*. New York: Plenum Press, 1981.

Lerner, M. J., & Meindl, J. R. Justice and altruism. In J. P. Rushton & R. M. Sorrentino (Eds.), *Altruism and helping behavior*. Hillsdale, N.J.: Erlbaum, 1981.

Lerner, M. J., & Miller, D. T. Just world research and the attribution process: Looking back and ahead. *Psychological Bulletin*, 1978, *85*, 1030–1051.

Lerner, M. J., & Whitehead, L. A. Procedural justice viewed in the context of justice motive theory. In G. Mikula (Ed.), *Justice and social interaction*. Bern: Hans Huber, 1980.

Leventhal, G. S., Karuza, J., & Fry, W. R. Beyond fairness: A theory of allocation preference. In G. Mikula (Ed.), *Justice and social interaction*. Bern: Hans Huber, 1980.

Lévi-Strauss, C. *Tristes tropiques*. New York: Atheneum, 1968.(a)

Lévi-Strauss, C. *The raw and the cooked*. New York: Harper & Row, 1968.(b)

Lukacs, G. *History and class consciousness*. Cambridge, Mass: MIT Press, 1971.

Maki, J. E., Thorngate, W. B., & McClintock, C. G. Prediction and perception of social motives. *Journal of Personality and Social Psychology*, 1979, *37*, 203–220.

Marcuse, H. *Reason and revolution*. Boston: Beacon Press, 1960.

Marcuse, H. *One dimensional man*. Boston: Beacon Press, 1964.

Marcuse, H. *Eros and civilization*. Boston: Beacon Press, 1966.

Marcuse, H. *Negations: Essays in critical theory*. Boston: Beacon Press, 1968.

Marcuse, H. On science and phenomenology. In A. Arato & E. Gebhardt (Eds.), *The essential Frankfurt School reader*. New York: Urizen Books, 1978.

Maruyama, M. Transepistemological understanding: Wisdom beyond theories. In R. Hinshaw (Ed.), *Currents in anthropology*. The Hague: Mouton, 1979.

Maruyama, A. Mindscapes and science theories. *Current Anthropology*, 1980, *21*, 589–600.

Marx, K. *Capital* (Vols. 1–3). London: Lawrence & Wishart, 1961–1965.

Mayhew, B. H. Structuralism versus individualism: Part I, Shadowboxing in the dark. *Social Forces*, 1980, *59*, 335–375.

Mayhew, B. H. Structuralism versus individualism: Part II, Ideological and other obfuscations. *Social Forces*, 1981, *59*, 627–648.

McCarthy, T. A. *The critical theory of Jurgen Habermas*. Cambridge, Mass.: MIT Press, 1978.

McGrath, J. E. Social science, social action and the Journal of Social Issues. *Journal of Social Issues*, 1980, *36*, 109–124.

Mead, G. H. *The social psychology of George Herbert Mead* (A. Strauss, Ed.). Chicago: University of Chicago Press, 1934.

Mikula, G. Justice and fairness in interpersonal relations: Thoughts and suggestions. In H. Tajfel (Ed.), *The social dimension: European developments in social psychology*. Cambridge, England: Cambridge University Press, 1982. (Quotes from unpublished manuscript version)

Miller, D. R., & Swanson, G. E. *The changing American parent*. New York: Wiley, 1958.

Miller, J. G. Living systems: Basic concepts; structure and process; cross-level hypotheses. *Behavioral Science*, 1965, *10*, 193–237; 337–411.

Mills, C. W. Situated actions and the vocabularies of motive. In D. Brissett & C. Edgley (Eds.), *Life as theater*. Chicago: Aldine, 1975.

Mishler, E. G. Meaning in context: Is there any other kind? *Harvard Educational Review*, 1979, *49*, 1–19.

Morgan, W. R., & Sawyer, J. Equality, equity and procedural justice in social exchange. *Social Psychology Quarterly*, 1979, *42*, 71–75.

Muir, D., & Weinstein, E. The social debt: An investigation of lower-class and middle-class norms of social obligation. *American Sociological Review*, 1962, *27*, 532–539.

Murray, H. A. *Explorations in personality*. New York: Oxford University Press, 1938.

Myrdal, G. *Value in social theory*. London: Routledge & Kegan Paul, 1959.

Nader, L. Forums for justice: A cross cultural perspective. *Journal of Social Issues*, 1975, *31*, 151–170.

Neale, W. C. Reciprocity and redistribution in the Indian village. In K. Polanyi, C. M. Arensberg, & H. W. Pearson (Eds.), *Trade and market in the early empires*. Chicago: Regnery, 1957.

Newcomb, T. M. An approach to the study of communicative acts. *Psychological Review*, 1953, *60*, 393–404.

Ogilvy, J. *Many dimensional man*. New York: Harper & Row, 1979.

Ollman, B. *Alienation*. London: Cambridge University Press, 1971.

Oxfam America. Letter dated March 15, 1982.

Parkin, D. J. *Palms, wine and witnesses*. San Francisco: Chandler, 1972.

Parsons, T. *Essays in sociological theory, pure and applied*. Glencoe, Ill.: Free Press, 1949.

Pepitone, A. Lessons from the history of social psychology. *American Psychologist*, 1981, *36*, 972–985.

Pepper, S. *World hypotheses*. Berkeley, Calif.: University of California Press, 1961.

Platt, J. Social traps. *American Psychologist*, 1973, *28*, 641–651.

Polanyi, K., Arensberg, C. M., & Pearson, H. W. (Eds.). *Trade and market in the early empires*. Chicago: Regnery, 1957.

Rabinow, P., & Sullivan, W. M. *Interpretative social science*. Berkeley, Calif.: University of California Press, 1979.

Reichenbach, H. *Experience and prediction*. Chicago: University of Chicago Press, 1938.

Reis, H., & Gruzen, J. On mediating equity, equality and self-interest: The role of self-presentation in social exchange. *Journal of Experimental Social Psychology*, 1976, *12*, 487–503.

Ricoeur, P. *Freud and philosophy*. New Haven: Yale University Press, 1970.

Ricoeur, P. Ethics and culture: Habermas and Gadamer in dialogue. *Philosophy Today*, 1972, *17*, 153–165.

Ricoeur, P. Psychoanalysis and the movement of contemporary culture. In P. Rabinow & W. M. Sullivan (Eds.). *Interpretative social science*. Berkeley, Calif.: University of California Press, 1979.

Riegel, K. F. From traits and equilibrium toward developmental dialectics. In W. J. Arnold (Ed.), *Nebrasks symposium on motivation*. Lincoln: University of Nebraska Press, 1976.

Riegel, K. F. *Foundations of dialectical psychology*. New York: Academic Press, 1979.

Riesman, D. *The lonely crowd*. New Haven: Yale University Press, 1950.

Riger, S., & Galligan, P. Women in management: An exploration of competing paradigms. *American Psychologist*, 1980, *35*, 902–910.

Robinson, R. V., & Bell, W. Equality, success and social justice in England and the United States. *American Sociological Review*, 1978, *43*, 125–143.

Roethlisberger, F. J., & Dickson, W. J. *Management and the worker*. New York: Wiley, 1939.

Rothbaum, F., Weisz, J. R., & Snyder, S. S. Changing the world and changing the self: A two-process model of perceived control. *Journal of Personality and Social Psychology*, 1982, *42*, 5–37.

Rotter, J. B. Generalized expectancies for internal versus external control of reinforcement. *Psychological Monographs*, 1966, *80*, 1–28.

Rubin, Z., & Peplau, L. A. Who beleives in a just world? *Journal of Social Issues*, 1975, *31*, 65–89.

Sampson, E. E. Status congruence and cognitive consistency. *Sociometry*, 1963, *26*, 146–162.

Sampson, E. E. Studies of status congruence. In L. Berkowitz (Ed.), *Advances in experimental social psychology*. New York: Academic Press, 1969.

Sampson, E. E. On justice as equality. *Journal of Social Issues*, 1975, *31*, 45–64.

Sampson, E. E. *Social psychology and contemporary society* (2nd ed.). New York: Wiley, 1976.

Sampson, E. E. Psychology and the American ideal. *Journal of Personality and Social Psychology*, 1977, *35*, 767–782.

Sampson, E. E. Scientific paradigms and social values: Wanted—a scientific revolution. *Journal of Personality and Social Psychology*, 1978, *38*, 1332–1343.

Sampson, E. E. Justice and social character. In G. Mikula (Ed.), *Justice and social interaction*. Bern: Hans Huber, 1980.

Sampson, E. E. Cognitive psychology as ideology. *American Psychologist*, 1981, *36*, 730–743.(a)

Sampson, E. E. Social change and the contexts of justice motivation. In M. J. Lerner & S. C. Lerner (Eds.), *The justice motive in social behavior*. New York: Plenum Press, 1981.(b)

Sarason, S. B. An asocial psychology and a misdirected clinical psychology. *American Psychologist*, 1981, *36*, 826–836.

Sarbin, T. R. Contextualism: A world view for modern psychology. In A. W. Landfield (Eds.), *Nebraska symposium on motivation*. Lincoln: University of Nebraska Press, 1977.

Saussure, F. de. *Course in general linguistics*. New York: McGraw-Hill, 1959.

Schlenker, B. R. Social psychology and science. *Journal of Personality and Social Psychology*, 1974, *29*, 1–15.

Schroyer, T. *The critique of domination*. New York: Braziller, 1973.

Seligman, M. E. P. *Helplessness: On depression, development and death*. San Francisco: Freeman, 1975.

Skillen, A. *Ruling illusions*. Hassocks, Sussex, England: Harvester Press, 1977.

Smith, M. B. Perspectives on selfhood. *American Psychologist*, 1978, *33*, 1053–1063.

Sperry, R. W. A modified concept of consciousness. *Psychological Review*, 1969, *76*, 532–546.

Sperry, R. W. Bridging science and values: A unifying view of mind and brain. *American Psychologist*, 1977, *321*, 237–245.

Spretnak, C. *The politics of women's spirituality*. Garden City, N.Y.: Anchor/Doubleday, 1982.

Stouffer, S. A., Suchman, E. A., De Vinney, L. C., Star, S. A., & Williams, R. M., Jr. *The American soldier* (Vol. 1): *Adjustment during army life*. Princteon, N.J.: Princeton University Press, 1949.

Stouffer, S. A., Lumsdaine, A. A., Lumsdaine, M. H., Williams, R. M., Jr., Smith, M. B., Janis, I. L., Star, S. A., & Cottrell, L. S., Jr. *The American soldier* (Vol. 2): *Combat and its aftermath*. Princeton, N.J.: Princeton University Press, 1949.

Sullivan, H. S. *The interpersonal theory of psychiatry*. New York: Norton, 1953.

Sullivan, H. S. *The psychiatric interview*. New York: Norton, 1954.

Tajfel, H. Cited in G. Mikula, (Ed.), *Justice and fairness in interpersonal relationships*. Unpublished manuscript, 1982. (Also in H. Tajfel, (Ed.), *The social dimension: European developments in social psychology*. Cambridge, England: Cambridge University Press, 1982.)

Toffler, A. *The third wave*. New York: Morrow, 1980.

Turkle, S. *Psychoanalytic politics*. Cambridge, Mass.: MIT Press, 1978.

Vygotsky, L. S. *Mind in society*. Cambridge, Mass.: Harvard University Press, 1978.

Wake, D. Quoted A. C. Roard, A new synthesis in evolution leads scientists to ask when and how life began. *Chronicle of Higher Education*, March 23, 1981.

Walster, E., Berscheid, E., & Walster, G. W. New directions in equity research. *Journal of Personality and Social Psychology*, 1973, *25*, 151–176.

Walster, E., & Walster, G. W. Equity and social justice. *Journal of Social Issues*, 1975, *31*, 21–43.

Walster, E., Walster, G. W., & Berscheid, E. *Equity: Theory and research*. Boston: Allyn & Bacon, 1978.

Watzlawick, P., Beavin, J. H., & Jackson, D. D. *Pragmatics of human communication*. New York: Norton, 1967.

Weber, M. Class, status and party. In H. H. Gerth & C. W. Mills (Eds.), *From Max Weber: Essays in sociology*. New York: Oxford University Press, 1946.

Weiss, J., Sampson, H., Caston, J., & Silberschatz, G. *Research on the psychoanalytic process I & II: A comparison of two theories about analytic neutrality*. Unpublished manuscript, 1977.

Wellmer, A. *Critical theory of society*. New York: Seabury, 1971.

Wicker, A. W. *An introduction to ecological psychology*. Monterey, Calif.: Brooks/Cole, 1979.

Wilden, A. *System and structure* (2nd ed.). London: Tavistock, 1980.

Wilson, T. P. Conceptions of interaction and forms of sociological explanation. *American Sociological Review*, 1970, 35, 697–710.

Winch, P. *The idea of a social science and its relation to philosophy*. London: Routledge & Kegan Paul, 1958.

Winter, G. *Liberating creation*. New York: Crossroad, 1981.

Woodruff, D. S., & Birren, J. E. Age changes and cohort differences in personality. *Developmental Psychology*, 1972, 6, 252–259.

Index

Walster, E., Hobbesian understanding of
humanity, 5
Workplace
comparative justice in, 149–150
and development of justice theory, 9–11

Workplace (*cont.*)
reality versus fiction, 10–11
role of in justice studies, 6, 7
socioeconomic role of, 9